C. STEPHEN EVANS AND PAUL MARTENS

*General Editors*

The KIERKEGAARD AS A CHRISTIAN THINKER series seeks to promote and enrich an understanding of Søren Kierkegaard as a Christian thinker who, despite his many critiques of Christendom, self-consciously worked within the Christian tradition and in the service of Christianity. Volumes in the series may approach Kierkegaard's relationship to Christianity historically or topically, philosophically or theologically. Some will attempt to illuminate Kierkegaard's thought by examining his works through the lens of Christian faith; others will use Kierkegaard's Christian insights to address contemporary problems and competing non-Christian perspectives.

That Søren Kierkegaard profoundly influenced nineteenth- and twentieth-century theology and philosophy is not in doubt. The direction, extent, and value of his influence, however, have always been hotly contested. For example, in the early decades of the twentieth century, German theologians Karl Barth, Dietrich Bonhoeffer, and Emil Brunner all acknowledged deep debts to Kierkegaard, debts that would echo through the theological debates of the entire century. In spite of this, by the middle of the twentieth century, Kierkegaard was also hailed (or cursed) as a father of existentialism and nihilism because of his appropriation by Heidegger, Sartre, and others. At the same time, however, he was beginning to become the reveille for a return to true Christianity in North America through the translating efforts of Walter Lowrie and David Swenson. At the beginning of the twenty-first century, Kierkegaard's legacy is once again being seriously and rigorously debated.

While acknowledging and affirming the postmodern appreciation of elements of Kierkegaard's thought (such as irony, indirect communication, and pseudonymity), this series aims to engage Kierkegaard as a Christian thinker who self-consciously worked as a Christian in the service of Christianity. And, as the current discussion crosses the traditional boundaries of philosophy and theology, this series will necessarily do the same. What these volumes all share, however, is the task of articulating Kierkegaard's continuities with, challenges to, and resources for Christianity today. It is our hope that, in this way, this series will deepen and enrich the manifold contemporary debates concerning Kierkegaard and his legacy.

## KIERKEGAARD AS A CHRISTIAN THINKER

*Eros and Self-Emptying: The Intersections of Augustine and Kierkegaard*
Lee C. Barrett

*Kierkegaard and the Paradox of Religious Diversity*
George B. Connell

*Kierkegaard's Concept of Faith*
Merold Westphal

# KIERKEGAARD AND SPIRITUALITY

*Accountability as the Meaning of Human Existence*

C. Stephen Evans

WILLIAM B. EERDMANS PUBLISHING COMPANY

GRAND RAPIDS, MICHIGAN

Wm. B. Eerdmans Publishing Co.
4035 Park East Court SE, Grand Rapids, Michigan 49546
www.eerdmans.com

Published 2019
Printed in the United States of America

25  24  23  22  21  20  19        1  2  3  4  5  6  7

ISBN 978-0-8028-7286-9

Names: Evans, C. Stephen, author.
Title: Kierkegaard and spirituality : accountability as the meaning of human
   existence / C. Stephen Evans.
Description: Grand Rapids : Eerdmans Publishing Co., 2019. | Series:
   Kierkegaard as a Christian thinker | Includes bibliographical references
   and index.
Identifiers: LCCN 2019017687 | ISBN 9780802872869 (pbk. : alk. paper)
Subjects: LCSH: Kierkegaard, Søren, 1813–1855. |
   Spirituality—Christianity.
Classification: LCC BX4827.K5 E93 2019 | DDC 230/.044092—dc23
LC record available at https://lccn.loc.gov/2019017687

# Contents

# *Preface*

This book is an attempt to provide an understanding of Kierkegaard as a spiritual writer, a thinker who has much to offer someone who is interested in what it means to live as a spiritual person and to develop genuine spirituality. I have spent much of the last fifty years studying and writing about Kierkegaard. I have always believed that the center of Kierkegaard's work is his deep Christian faith. However, most of my work on Kierkegaard to this point has centered on Kierkegaard's contributions to Christian philosophy and theology. In this book, I have tried to give an account of what it means to *live* spiritually, looking at two different forms of spirituality: a generic human spirituality and a spirituality that is distinctively Christian. Kierkegaard has much to offer on both counts.

I try to show that spirituality is for Kierkegaard something that is grounded in our very nature as human beings. There is a sense in which human beings are always spiritual beings. Some of this spirituality is not recognized as such, and much of it is what we might call inauthentic or counterfeit spirituality. However, there are rich possibilities to live spiritually even outside of Christian faith. Kierkegaard clearly respects and appreciates this kind of spirituality, which I call Socratic spirituality in this book. Nonetheless, Christian faith offers the deepest and most profound possibilities for spiritual life as Kierkegaard sees it.

The heart of genuine spirituality, according to Kierkegaard, lies in seeing human existence as a *task* that is assigned by God to every individual. This is true for both Socratic spirituality and Christian spirituality; the upshot is that the spiritual life is relational. We live spiritually when we live *before God*, or *coram Deo*, as older theologians said. For Kierkegaard, therefore, spirituality requires a quality that I call "accountability," the virtue that is present when a person is grateful for the task God assigns, and understands that being accountable to God is a *gift*. The task is grounded in the debt we owe to God. However, the nature of the debt, and the nature of the task, is profoundly altered when God is known through Christ, God incarnate in human form, a God known not through philosophical reflection but in history.

Along the way, I deal with the worry some have raised that Kierkegaardian spirituality ultimately is incompatible with our humanness. I argue that this is not the case. Although Kierkegaardian spirituality makes strenuous demands on us, it is still a form of Christian humanism, although I admit that there are themes in Kierkegaard's final "attack on Christendom" that cannot be defended. Hence, my view, though a defense of Kierkegaardian spirituality, is not completely uncritical. Besides criticizing some of the newspaper and magazine articles Kierkegaard wrote in 1854–55, I raise some worries at times for other elements in Kierkegaard's view of spiritual life.

This book had its origin in a fellowship I held at the Biola Center for Christian Thought in the spring semester of 2013. The theme for the center that year was spirituality and its relation to human psychology. During that year, I wrote an article, "Living 'Before God': A Kierkegaardian View of Spirituality."[1] This article was the seed of this book. The Biola Center for Christian Thought was supported during that period by a grant from the John Templeton Foundation, and I am deeply grateful for this fellowship that made possible the ideas that eventually led to this book.

I am also deeply grateful to the Templeton Religion Trust (TRT), which awarded an "inception grant" for the school year 2017–18 to an interdisciplinary group of seven scholars, headed by myself, to think more deeply about accountability, understood as a virtue. This grant provided time for me to complete this book, which is therefore the firstfruits of this research project on accountability. The team has since been awarded a three-year grant from TRT to study accountability as a virtue, working from the perspectives of philosophy, theology, psychology, psychiatry, and sociology. I am deeply grateful to the Templeton Religion Trust for this support.

Although this may sound odd, I would also like to express my gratitude and my love for Kierkegaard. After fifty years of reading him and working on him, I find him as rich and profound as ever, and I know that much of

---

1. This article was published in Thomas A. Crisp, Gregg A. Ten Elshof, and Steve L. Porter, eds., *Psychology and Spiritual Formation in Dialogue* (Downers Grove, IL: InterVarsity, 2019), 77–103.

what is of value in my own work I owe to him. Kierkegaard himself says that, although he is a disciple of Jesus, Socrates was nonetheless his teacher. I should say that, although I too want to be a disciple of Jesus, Kierkegaard himself has been my teacher, even though I have learned a great deal from other philosophers past and present.

All references to Kierkegaard's writings in this book are given in parentheses, using a system of abbreviations (sigla) and page numbers. Almost all the references are taken from the Princeton University Press edition, *Kierkegaard's Writings*, edited by Howard V. Hong and Edna H. Hong, who also did the vast majority of the translations. References to *Fear and Trembling* are an exception, taken from the Cambridge University Press translation of Sylvia Walsh, which I coedited with Sylvia. However, I have on some occasions, while keeping the Hong page references, provided my own translations, based on the first edition of Kierkegaard's *Samlede Værker* (Copenhagen: Gyldendals, 1901–7). The pagination for this edition is provided by the Hongs in the margins of their edition, so any reader who wants to consult the original Danish can do so.

I also want to thank four Baylor graduate students who helped me with this project. David Skowronski, who was my research assistant for the spring semester of 2018, helped me finish several scholarly projects, including making great progress on this book. Derek McAllister, who was my research assistant for the summer of 2018, read through the whole manuscript. Derek converted footnotes to parenthetical references, looked up many references both in Kierkegaard and other writers, and offered many excellent suggestions about the book. John Rosenbaum provided generous and invaluable technical help with the computer files, helping me convert them to a readable form under great time pressure. Finally, I must thank Harrison Lee for preparing a high-quality index, which is a difficult task.

Finally, I simply cannot finish a book without expressing how grateful I am to Jan Evans, whose love and faithful companionship has made the whole of my life, including my life as a scholar, so satisfying. It is a great gift that we share an interest in Kierkegaard, and she is always present as my favorite conversation partner.

C. STEPHEN EVANS

# Sigla

CA             *The Concept of Anxiety*. Kierkegaard's Writings 8. Trans. Reidar Thomte, in collaboration with Albert B. Anderson. Princeton: Princeton University Press, 1980. (*Begrebet Angest*, by Vigilius Haufniensis, ed. S. Kierkegaard, 1844.)

CD             *Christian Discourses* and *The Crisis and a Crisis in the Life of an Actress*. Kierkegaard's Writings 17. Trans. Howard V. Hong and Edna H. Hong. Princeton: Princeton University Press, 1997. (*Christelige Taler*, by S. Kierkegaard, 1848, and *Krisen og en Krise i en Skuespillerindes Liv*, by Inter et Inter., *Fædrelandet* 188–91 [24–27 July 1848].)

CUP 1 and CUP 2    *Concluding Unscientific Postscript*. Two volumes. Kierkegaard's Writings 12:1–2. Trans. Howard V. Hong and Edna H. Hong. Princeton: Princeton University Press, 1992. (*Afsluttende uvidenskabelig Efterskrift*, by Johannes Climacus, ed. S. Kierkegaard, 1846.)

DCF            *Discourses at the Communion on Fridays*, including part 4 of *Christian Discourses*, *Three Discourses at the Communion on Fridays*, First Christian Exposition from No. 3 in *Practice in Christianity*, and *Two Discourses at the Communion on Fridays*. Trans. Sylvia Walsh. Indiana Series in the Philosophy of Religion. Bloomington: Indiana University Press, 2011. (*Christelige Taler*, by S. Kierkegaard, 1848; *Tre Taler ved Altergangen om Fredagen*, by S. Kierkegaard, 1849; *Indøvelse i Christendom*, by Anti-Climacus, ed. S. Kierkegaard, 1850; *To Taler ved Altergangen om Fredagen*, by S. Kierkegaard, 1851.)

EO 1 and EO 2     *Either/Or*. Two volumes. Kierkegaard's Writings 3 and 4. Trans. Howard V. Hong and Edna H. Hong. Princeton: Princeton University Press, 1987. (*Enten/Eller* 1–2, ed. Victor Eremita, 1843.)

EUD     *Eighteen Upbuilding Discourses*. Kierkegaard's Writings 5. Trans. Howard V. Hong and Edna H. Hong. Princeton: Princeton University Press, 1990. (*Atten opbyggelige taler*, by S. Kierkegaard, 1843–45.)

FSE     *For Self-Examination*. In *For Self-Examination* and *Judge for Yourself!* Kierkegaard's Writings 21. Trans. Howard V. Hong and Edna H. Hong. Princeton: Princeton University Press, 1990. (*Til Selvprøvelse*, by S. Kierkegaard, 1851, and *Dømmer Selv!* by S. Kierkegaard, 1852.)

FT     *Fear and Trembling*. Ed. C. Stephen Evans and Sylvia Walsh. Cambridge: Cambridge University Press, 2006. (*Frygt og Bæven*, by Johannes de Silentio, ed. S. Kierkegaard, 1843.)

JY     *Judge for Yourself!* In *For Self-Examination* and *Judge for Yourself!* Kierkegaard's Writings 21. Trans. Howard V. Hong and Edna H. Hong. Princeton: Princeton University Press, 1990. (*Til Selvprøvelse*, by S. Kierkegaard, 1851, and *Dømmer Selv!* by S. Kierkegaard, 1852.)

KJN     *Kierkegaard's Journals and Notebooks*, vols. 1–11, ed. Niels Jørgen Cappelørn, Alastair Hannay, David Kangas, Bruce H. Kirmmse, George Pattison, Vanessa Rumble, and K. Brian Söderquist. Princeton: Princeton University Press, 2007–.

NA     Newspaper Articles, 1854–55. In *"The Moment" and Late Writings*, including Newspaper Articles, 1854–55, and *The Changelessness of God*. Kierkegaard's Writings 23. Trans. Howard V. Hong and Edna H. Hong. Princeton: Princeton University Press, 1998. (*Øieblikket*, by S. Kierkegaard, 1855; *Guds Uforanderlighed*, by S. Kierkegaard, 1855.)

PC     *Practice in Christianity*. Kierkegaard's Writings 20. Trans. Howard V. Hong and Edna H. Hong. Princeton: Princeton University Press, 1991. (*Indøvelse i Christendom*, by Anti-Climacus, ed. S. Kierkegaard, 1850.)

PF     *Philosophical Fragments*. Kierkegaard's Writings 7. Trans. Howard V. Hong and Edna H. Hong. Princeton: Princeton University Press, 1985. (*Philosophiske Smuler*, by Johannes Climacus, ed. S. Kierkegaard, 1844.)

PV     *The Point of View*, including *On My Work as an Author*, *The*

# Sigla

*Point of View for My Work as an Author*, and *Armed Neutrality*. Kierkegaard's Writings 22. Trans. Howard V. Hong and Edna H. Hong. Princeton: Princeton University Press, 1998. (*Om min Forfatter-Virksomhed*, by S. Kierkegaard, 1851; *Synspunktet for min Forfatter-Virksomhed*, by S. Kierkegaard, posthumously publ. 1859; *Den bevæbnede Neutralitet*, by S. Kierkegaard, posthumously publ. 1880.)

SUD     *The Sickness unto Death*. Kierkegaard's Writings 19. Trans. Howard V. Hong and Edna H. Hong. Princeton: Princeton University Press, 1980. (*Sygdommen til Døden*, by Anti-Climacus, ed. S. Kierkegaard, 1849.)

TA     *Two Ages: The Present Age and the Age of Revolution; A Literary Review*. Kierkegaard's Writings 14. Trans. Howard V. Hong and Edna H. Hong. Princeton: Princeton University Press, 1978. (*En literair Anmeldelse. To Tidsaldre*, by S. Kierkegaard, 1846.)

TM     *"The Moment" and Late Writings*. In *"The Moment" and Late Writings*, including Newspaper Articles, 1854–55, and *The Changelessness of God*. Kierkegaard's Writings 23. Trans. Howard V. Hong and Edna H. Hong. Princeton: Princeton University Press, 1998. (*Øieblikket*, by S. Kierkegaard, 1855; *Guds Uforanderlighed*, by S. Kierkegaard, 1855.)

UDVS     *Upbuilding Discourses in Various Spirits*. Kierkegaard's Writings 15. Trans. Howard V. Hong and Edna H. Hong. Princeton: Princeton University Press, 1993. (*Opbyggelige Taler i forskjellig Aand*, 1847.)

WA     *Without Authority*, trans. Howard V. Hong and Edna H. Hong. Princeton: Princeton University Press, 1997.

WL     *Works of Love*. Kierkegaard's Writings 16. Trans. Howard V. Hong and Edna H. Hong. Princeton: Princeton University Press, 1995. (*Kjerlighedens Gjerninger*, 1847.)

# CHAPTER 1

# Kierkegaard's Account of Human Beings as "Spirit"

We live in a world that is awash with talk of "spirituality," despite the fact, or maybe because of the fact, that we are often said to live in a world that is "disenchanted." Many people who are disconnected from any traditional religion nevertheless see themselves as "spiritual but not religious." Many of those who are still part of a traditional religious community also give much attention to spirituality, with a steady stream of books appearing that deal with spiritual practices and disciplines of various kinds that are intended to deepen and strengthen the spirituality of the faithful.

I am convinced that the nineteenth-century philosopher Søren Kierkegaard can help us understand the phenomenon of spirituality and why it seems so important in our contemporary culture. Kierkegaard is not commonly seen as a "spiritual writer." He is most often described as the "father of existentialism," who had a deep influence on such writers as Jean-Paul Sartre, Albert Camus, and Martin Heidegger. Others know him as the religious thinker who jolted the complacent liberalism of European theology in the early part of the twentieth century, deeply influencing such theologians as Karl Barth, Paul Tillich, and Rudolf Bultmann. Most scholarly writers, however, do not immediately think of Kierkegaard as a person to look to for spiritual guidance and edification, even though a large portion of his authorship consists of works that were written explicitly for this purpose.

I have, however, met many nonscholars who read Kierkegaard for personal, edifying reasons, something that would have pleased him, and there are some recent signs that Kierkegaard is beginning to be recognized among scholars also as someone with much to teach us about what it might mean to live spiritually. In 2002, George Pattison published *Kierkegaard's Upbuilding*

*Discourses: Philosophy, Theology, Literature.*[1] In this work, Pattison makes a good case for the importance of these early "discourses," both in their own right and for understanding Kierkegaard's whole authorship, although Pattison's own book, as an academic work, did not have as its primary purpose to edify his readers. Then in 2011, Sylvia Walsh published a new translation of Kierkegaard's "communion discourses" and, in a beautiful introduction, argued for the importance of seeing Kierkegaard's work as culminating in the experience of taking communion, finding a place of rest at "the foot of the altar."[2] More recently, Christopher Barnett published *From Despair to Faith: The Spirituality of Søren Kierkegaard* in 2014, shortly after I myself had begun work on this book.[3]

Barnett gives a clear and convincing picture of Kierkegaard as a "spiritual writer," someone deeply influenced by Lutheran pietism and the Moravians, and through them shaped by late medieval Catholic mystical writers, such as Meister Eckhart and Eckhart's follower, Johannes Tauler. Much of Barnett's work is devoted to showing how Kierkegaard uses aesthetic "icons," both from nature and Scripture, to help his readers develop their spiritual lives. That life itself is seen as a journey that has its origins in God's creation. God endows his human creatures with freedom, and humans use that freedom to distance themselves from God. The human task then is to return to one's spiritual home in God.

I agree with Barnett's thesis as I have described it, both in the sense that he accurately describes Kierkegaard's view and in the sense that it is a view about the human condition that is fundamentally sound. I have learned a great deal from Barnett, but I am convinced that there is much more to be said about Kierkegaard's view of spirituality, something that I am confident

---

1. George Pattison, *Kierkegaard's Upbuilding Discourses: Philosophy, Theology, Literature* (London: Routledge, 2002).

2. Søren Kierkegaard, *Discourse at the Communion on Fridays*, trans. Sylvia Walsh (Bloomington: Indiana University Press, 2011), 32–33. The quotation about being at the foot of the altar comes from Kierkegaard himself. Shortly before Walsh's translation appeared, Olli-Pekka Vainio had published a short but insightful article on the spiritual significance of communion for Kierkegaard. See "Kierkegaard's Eucharistic Spirituality," *Theology Today* 67 (2010): 15–23.

3. Christopher Barnett, *From Despair to Faith: The Spirituality of Søren Kierkegaard* (Minneapolis: Augsburg Fortress, 2014). Even more recently than Barnett's book, a work of David Kangas appeared: *Errant Affirmations: On the Philosophical Meanings of Kierkegaard's Religious Discourses* (London: Bloomsbury Academic, 2018). As the subtitle implies, this book is devoted to exploring more the value of this part of Kierkegaard's authorship for philosophy than the spiritual life in its own right.

Barnett would affirm as well. A deeper appreciation of Kierkegaard's view of spirituality will shed light on our age's fascination with the theme and give us a clearer understanding of why so many want to be "spiritual but not religious." For Kierkegaard, human beings are at bottom spiritual creatures. Being a spiritual person is not like being artistic or musical. Art and music belong to what Kierkegaard calls the "differential" aspects of human existence. Some people are musically or artistically gifted, and some are not. Some people are fascinated with art and music, while others think of art and music as frivolous wastes of time. Not so with spirituality. Although it is true that different people achieve different degrees of spirituality, every human being is nonetheless "spirit," and we cannot understand our humanness without an understanding of our spirituality.

An exploration of Kierkegaard's understanding of spirituality is therefore essential to gaining a deeper understanding of Kierkegaard's view of human existence itself. Since Kierkegaard is universally regarded as a "philosopher of existence," this means that thinking about spirituality is central and not peripheral to Kierkegaard's work as a whole. One might object that many atheists have found Kierkegaard's account of human existence to be profound and helpful, even though they have little use for his Christian faith. This is true, but I shall argue that even the atheism of such thinkers would be understood by Kierkegaard as a manifestation of their own spirituality. Before looking at Kierkegaard's view in more detail, I shall pause for a brief review of how the term "spirit" has been used in Western culture, which will shed light on the large range of meanings that the term currently has.


## The History of Spirit: A Brief Look

The English words "spirit" and "spirituality" have a long history and a wide range of meanings. The term "spirit" comes from the Latin *spiritus*, which was the standard translation of the Greek term *pneuma* and the Hebrew word *ruach*. Etymologically, all these terms are linked to wind and breath, understood as the source of motion and life. Spirit was thus thought of from the beginning as that which makes life and movement possible. At the beginning of the creation narrative in Genesis, the "spirit" or "breath" of God hovers or moves over the face of the waters. In the second account of the creation of humans, given in chapter 2, God is said to breathe the breath of life into the man whom God had formed from the dust of the earth. In the Bible, what is "spiritual" is thus linked from the beginning to being animated, and the source of animation is ultimately God.

The term "spirit" acquired a rich range of meanings in the Christian tradition. Most obviously, early Christians used the term "spirit" to refer to the third person of the Trinity, the Holy Spirit. It is also frequently used to refer to an aspect of human persons that is "inner" and "immaterial," often regarded as the part of a human person that can survive death. Thus, the *Oxford English Dictionary* provides, as one of many meanings, "the immaterial part of a corporeal being, especially considered as a moral agent," and also "a disembodied and separate entity . . . regarded as capable of surviving after death." When used in this way, the term "spirit" is often a synonym for "soul" or even "mind."

In the early nineteenth century, German philosophers used the term *Geist*, variously translated as "mind" or "spirit," to refer to a concept that was central to the movement known today as German Idealism, which was by far the most important philosophical movement in Kierkegaard's day. Even though Kierkegaard was very critical of Hegel and this movement, he was also influenced by it. The philosophers of this period used "Spirit" not to refer to one kind of entity that is contrasted with another, but as the key to understanding reality as a whole. G. W. F. Hegel's *Phenomenology of Spirit* provided the classical example: a grand narrative that tried to explain reality as a whole and Western culture in particular as manifestations of Spirit. In this usage, the word "Spirit" does not refer to some particular immaterial entity, the nonphysical part of a human being that is distinguished from the body. Rather, Spirit is a way of describing the *character* of reality. Ultimately, Hegel wanted to show that this category provides us with an understanding of the whole of being.

Hegel's project is in some ways akin to that of his predecessor Spinoza, who had tried to describe the whole of reality as one substance, identified with God, which has both mental and physical attributes. Hegel agrees with Spinoza that reality is ultimately one in some sense, but he argues that Spinoza's concept of substance is too static and impersonal. Hegel claims that in Spinoza "self-consciousness was only submerged and not preserved."[4] So, Hegel claims that "everything turns on describing and expressing the True, not only as *Substance*, but equally as *Subject*."[5] Hegel's project is difficult to

---

4. G. W. F. Hegel, *Phenomenology of Spirit*, trans. A. V. Miller (Oxford: Oxford University Press, 1977), 10.

5. Hegel, *Phenomenology*, 10.

understand, especially in an age such as ours, in which we have been taught to understand reality through the lens of the natural sciences. In talking about "Spirit," Hegel wants to help us see that there is something about reality as a whole, not just the human mind, that is "subject-like." But what makes reality "subject-like"?

There are two features that are especially important. One is that all of reality, like a human person, is something that is in process, something that becomes itself only through development. There is an obvious analogy here to a human person or self, which becomes what it is only through a long process. The second feature is that the process involves a complex series of tensions between apparently contradictory elements. Human life often revolves around the resolving of conflicts and tensions, and Hegel thinks the same is true for reality as a whole. Hegel's term for this is "dialectic." Something that is dialectical is not only a process, but the process is one that involves the development of conflicts that are overcome, only to produce new conflicts as the "dialectic" continues.

## Kierkegaard's Use of "Spirit"

To understand the way Kierkegaard speaks of "spirit," we need to keep in mind both the long Christian tradition and the nineteenth-century philosophical uses of the term. Although Kierkegaard is known as (and was) a fierce critic of Hegel, this does not mean that he was not influenced by Hegel and his philosophical milieu or that he did not learn things from Hegel. Kierkegaard describes human beings as "spirit," and when he does so, he draws on Christian sources, including the Bible, but also from Hegel. His account of the human self is one that sees it as a process, a process that involves dialectical tensions. Hegel's metaphysical monism is foreign to Kierkegaard, but Hegel's understanding of the nature of "Spirit" has echoes in the way Kierkegaard uses the term "spirit."

Often Kierkegaard's writings use the term "spirit" in a way that reflects traditional Christian usage. God is frequently described as spirit, and, of course, Kierkegaard refers at times to the Holy Spirit. He also sometimes uses the term to describe humans as beings who can survive the death of the body. A well-known passage from *The Sickness unto Death*, a book attributed by Kierkegaard to the pseudonym Anti-Climacus, is a good example. I will discuss this work in some detail in the remaining sections of this chapter, as well as in chapter 2. Here what is important to note is that part 1 of the book begins with the claim that "a human being is spirit" (SUD, 13).[6] Part of what this means is that there is an eternal dimension or aspect of the human self, one that will not be destroyed by death: "Socrates demonstrated the immortality of the soul from the fact that sickness of the soul (sin) does not consume it as sickness of the body consumes the body. Thus, the eternal in a person can be demonstrated by the fact that despair [Kierkegaard's term for the sickness of the self] cannot consume his self" (SUD, 20–21).

Besides these more traditional uses, Kierkegaard also commonly uses the term "spirit" in a way that shows the influence of Hegel. Kierkegaard criticizes Hegel's dialectical account of the "World-Spirit," which manifests itself in human history. Hegel had thought this concept was the key to understanding the meaning of human existence. However, Kierkegaard argued that if we find the meaning of our lives in contemplating or understanding world history, we really have abandoned the sphere of existence, which is a sphere of passionate striving, for the standpoint of the disinterested observer or contemplator. However, Kierkegaard appropriates Hegel's understanding of spirit as a kind of being that requires a process of development that is dialectical. The difference is that Kierkegaard sees this dialectical process as applying to individual human beings rather than to reality as a whole or history.

A passage in *Concluding Unscientific Postscript* illustrates this usage beautifully.[7] The pseudonymous author, Johannes Climacus, draws a

6. References to Kierkegaard's writings will be made in parentheses, using a modified version of the sigla developed by Robert Perkins for the *International Kierkegaard Commentary* series. The sigla used can be found at the beginning of this book. Thus, SUD refers to *The Sickness unto Death*. Strictly speaking, this book is attributed to a pseudonym, "Anti-Climacus," with Kierkegaard's name appearing on the title page as editor. However, it is clear that Kierkegaard employs this pseudonym because Anti-Climacus speaks from a high and strictly Christian standpoint, one that Kierkegaard did not think he had a right to portray himself as speaking from. Kierkegaard has no doubts about the truth of what Anti-Climacus says, but does not feel morally entitled to say them in his own voice. I try to honor Kierkegaard's own request to cite the pseudonym when quoting from his pseudonymous books. However, I do not think there is much doubt that Kierkegaard himself believed what Anti-Climacus says in *The Sickness unto Death*. At times in this chapter, when I believe the ideas are clearly Kierkegaard's, I shall refer to the author as just "Kierkegaard," but at other times, when the special character of Anti-Climacus as a "super-Christian" seems relevant, I shall refer to the pseudonym.

7. Although this book is attributed to Johannes Climacus, a pseudonymous character Kierkegaard invented, and not to Kierkegaard himself, it still sheds important light on the meaning of the key term "spirit" in Kierkegaard's writings. Climacus is certainly not identical to Kierkegaard. He describes himself as a "humorist" who wants to know how to become a Christian but is not (at least not yet) a Christian. Nevertheless, there is a close relation between

contrast between human beings, who are spirit, and other animals, such as sheep. "In the animal world, the particular animal is related directly as specimen to species, participates as a matter of course in the development of the species" (CUP 1:345). If a particular line of sheep is improved by selective breeding, later sheep born in this line will share these improvements as a matter of course. It is not so with human beings. "Development of spirit is self-activity; the spiritually developed individual takes his spiritual development along with him in death" (CUP 1:345). This means that later individuals must acquire any similar spiritual development for themselves through "self-activity." As evidence for this view, Climacus points out that Christianity assumes that Christian parents do not give birth to children who become Christians as a matter of course, but to sinful children who must become Christians, even if they are baptized as infants.

A human self is therefore something that one must become, not something that one is by virtue of being born or that happens "as a matter of course." The process by which this happens is frequently described as "dialectical" in the sense that it requires an individual to overcome conflicts and tensions. It is not hard to live one's life in such a way that one has one quality at one time and then later has a different quality. A person can be sad today and happy tomorrow. However, the task of existence demands that a person bring together into one life what appear to be incompatible states:

> One person is good, another is shrewd, or the same person acts as good at one time, and shrewdly at another, but simultaneously to see in the same thing what is most shrewd and to see it only in order to will the good is certainly difficult. One person will laugh, another will weep, or the same person does it at different times, but simultaneously to see the comic and tragic in the same thing is difficult. (CUP 1:354; translation modified)

This dialectical character of individual human existence will be explored in more detail below.

A question naturally arises at this point concerning the consistency of Kierkegaard's usage of "spirit." Kierkegaard constantly describes God very

---

Climacus and Kierkegaard, signaled by the fact that Kierkegaard put his own name on the title page as "editor." For more on the relation between Climacus and Kierkegaard, see C. Stephen Evans, *Kierkegaard's* Fragments *and* Postscript: *The Religious Philosophy of Johannes Climacus* (Waco, TX: Baylor University Press, 2018), 17–32. This is a reprint of the original edition (Atlantic Highlands, NJ: Humanities, 1983), 17–32.

traditionally, as a perfect, unchanging being.[8] However, as we have seen, when Kierkegaard describes humans as spirit, he emphasizes the necessity of a process of development, in which a person must become the self he or she in one sense already is. Does this mean the term is used inconsistently? How can what is spirit (in the case of God) be unchanging if spirit is a quality (in the case of humans) that must be developed?

On the surface, it does seem like the term is used in two radically different senses, but there is an underlying common meaning. The root meaning of "spirit" is connected to its original sense as that which animates or gives life to something. Something that has spirit can move itself. A living animal, for example, is something that has its principle of motion within itself. A rock or a lump of clay is not spirit in this sense, since it moves or changes only in response to external forces. Even nonhuman animals are not really spirit for Kierkegaard. They have the power to move themselves but not the power to define themselves. A reality that is spiritual is something that is more independent and more complete than something that lacks this quality.

God is preeminently spirit because God is completely independent in a way that nothing God creates can be. God needs nothing else, and if God acts, the motivation for God's actions stems completely from God's own nature. This implies that spirit is also linked to freedom in one important sense; God is perfectly free, since there is nothing that can limit his actions or prevent him from realizing his ends.

There is a sense in which God alone is spirit unconditionally or absolutely. Nothing else can possess God's freedom and independence. Nothing else is such that it changes or acts only through its own nature. Nevertheless, Kierkegaard holds that God, by creating humans in his own image, has given them a kind of relative and conditional spirituality, by giving them a kind of freedom and a kind of independence, though in humans these qualities are relative and not absolute. Human freedom and independence cannot be absolute, because humans exist only because God creates and sustains them. However, God has bestowed upon humans a gift by giving them a relative independence. *The Sickness unto Death* describes the relation this way: "God, who constituted man a relation, releases it from his hand, as it were" (SUD, 16). I shall describe below the "relation" referred to here but now

---

8. One of Kierkegaard's last publications was a discourse he published on God's unchangeableness. See "The Changelessness of God" (TM, 263–81), published by Kierkegaard in the middle of his attack on the state church.

want to focus on the idea that God *releases* humans (who are constituted by a relation) "from his hand, as it were."

The wording here is precise. God does not really release humans from his hand metaphysically. Humans continually depend on God, "in whom they live, and move, and have their being" (Acts 17:28). They are not truly released from God's hand, but it is *as if* they were released. Psychologically, there is a kind of independence of God; humans can and do root their psychological identities in things other than God. As we shall see, humans are also created in such a manner that to flourish and fully be themselves, they need to ground their identities in God. God *ought* to be the ground of the self psychologically as well as metaphysically. However, God has given humans the gift of freedom and does not want to force humans to relate to God. God gives humans this freedom so that they can relate properly to God as friends, not simply as puppets or automatons.

It is true that Kierkegaard thinks that this freedom is wasted or squandered if humans do not use it to relate to God. He often uses the term "freedom" in a normative sense, in which it is equivalent to "true freedom." But that does not negate the reality of the gift: "The enormous thing granted a [human] being is—choice, freedom" (KJN 7:64 [NB 15:93]).

We might here distinguish freedom as a formal quality, the ability to choose, from freedom as a positive quality of a flourishing human. The misuse of the formal quality of freedom leads to the loss of this flourishing. The formal freedom is not something possessed by a "pure spirit," but by a bodily, historical being. Our choices have consequences; we are continually being shaped by them. While formally humans may continue to have the power to choose between option A and option B, this power has little value if A and B are both destructive and there is no power to choose anything else.

We can now understand why it is that humans, if they are to be spiritual creatures, must be temporal creatures, who become themselves through a process. It is only in this way that humans can have even a relative degree of independence and autonomy, in which they have a say in who they are by participating in the process by which they become themselves. If God were to create humans as morally perfect beings, complete and finished, they would owe those qualities entirely to God. They would not truly be spiritual, because their actions and changes would be entirely due to something outside themselves. For a finite being to be spiritual, even in a relative sense, that being must go through a process of becoming, in which the being's own choices make a difference.

Kierkegaard thinks that God's gift of freedom is one that requires omnipotence. If a human being gives a gift to another human, that gift in some way creates a dependence of sorts. If I try to transform another human being through some process of conditioning or training, I am really making the person dependent on me. God's power is different:

> The absolutely greatest thing that can be done for a being, greater than anything one could make it into, is to make it free. It is precisely here that omnipotence is required. This seems odd, as it is precisely omnipotence that has the capacity to make something dependent. But if one reflects on omnipotence, one will indeed see that it must precisely also contain the ability . . . to retreat into itself again in such a way as to allow that which owes its existence to omnipotence to be independent. (KJN 4:56 [NB 69])[9]

Kierkegaard thus holds that one of the powers an omnipotent being must have is the power to limit itself.[10]

## Spirit as a "Relation That Relates Itself to Itself"

To give a more detailed account of what it means for humans to exist as spirit, we must undertake a close exegesis of the book in which Kierkegaard describes the human self most explicitly, *The Sickness unto Death*, by Anti-Climacus.[11] We have already seen above that Anti-Climacus says that God constituted the human self as a "relation." The relation is also described as a "synthesis," since it involves a bringing together of elements that stand in some tension with each other. "A human being is a synthesis of the infinite and the finite, of the temporal and the eternal, of freedom and necessity" (SUD, 13). Here we see the "dialectical" character of the process by which human beings become themselves. Human beings strive for ideals that have a kind of infinite character, but they do so as finite beings. They can conceive and strive to actualize what is eternal, but they do so as beings who live in

9. Kierkegaard makes similar claims at several points in his writings.
10. See my essay on kenotic Christology for a defense of this claim. C. Stephen Evans, "Kenotic Christology and the Nature of God," in *Exploring Kenotic Christology: The Self-Emptying of God*, ed. C. Stephen Evans (Oxford: Oxford University Press, 2006), 190–217.
11. I have already discussed the relation of Kierkegaard to Anti-Climacus in a previous note. Since there is a close relation, at times I shall continue to attribute the words of Anti-Climacus to Kierkegaard himself.

time. Their lives contain possibilities, but they are also constricted by necessities they neither chose nor can change.

It is important to recognize human life as an attempt to synthesize these contrasting elements. However, Kierkegaard says that if we consider humans only in this way, we still do not grasp them as "selves," and therefore we will fail to understand them as "spirit" as well. To understand a human being as a genuine self, we must see the person not just as a relation or synthesis but as a "relation that relates itself to itself" (SUD, 13). This may seem mysterious and abstract, but it is not as difficult as it first appears to be. Kierkegaard means that human beings are not just conscious beings who synthesize these contrasting elements. They are self-conscious beings with the power to step back from themselves and reflect on who they are.

Self-consciousness introduces a kind of duality in the self; there is the self that I am, but there is also the self that steps back and looks at itself. (William James makes a similar distinction between what he calls the "I-self" and the "me-self.") This self-consciousness makes possible an evaluative stance that introduces another duality: There is the self I see as my ideal self, the self I want to become, and there is the self I actually am. I am defined both by what I have become and by what I am trying to become. Structurally, both this ideal self and the actual self are composed of a relation or synthesis of the contrasting elements. So it is literally true that a human self is an activity that "relates itself to itself." It projects its actual self, which is a synthesis, toward its future self, the synthesis it wants to become.

How does such a self come into being? Logically, Kierkegaard says that there are two possibilities: "Such a relation that relates itself to itself, must either have established itself or have been established by another" (SUD, 13). It is obvious that the first possibility describes the kind of being God is, one who is completely self-sufficient and dependent on nothing else.

Interestingly, this description of a godlike self that is completely free because it constitutes itself could also be taken as a description of Jean-Paul Sartre's phenomenological account of human existence.[12] For Sartre, when humans are conscious, they always negate what they are conscious of, and thus consciousness can never be defined or captured by any description of itself that it is conscious of. This fact about consciousness applies to self-consciousness as well. When I am conscious of my self, the self I am conscious of is an object of sorts, while the "I" that is conscious of it remains a

---

12. See Jean-Paul Sartre, *Being and Nothingness*, trans. Hazel E. Barnes (New York: Washington Square, 1992), 56–86.

subject. To use Sartre's example, if I am a waiter, as soon as I become conscious of myself as a waiter, I in some way escape just being a waiter.[13] The negativity of consciousness ensures its freedom. Kierkegaard, in describing a self that constitutes itself, is almost certainly thinking of God and not a Sartrean view of human consciousness. However, perhaps it is no accident that there is a similarity, since Sartre himself claims that human consciousness is an attempt to become God, though Sartre admits this is impossible, and therefore "man is a useless passion."[14]

I shall later look at Kierkegaard's own critical account of something that resembles this Sartre-type "negativizing consciousness" that sees itself as completely autonomous. In the opening pages of *The Sickness unto Death*, Anti-Climacus simply announces without argument that we humans are *not* godlike beings: "The human self is . . . a derived, established relation, a relation that relates itself to itself and in relating itself to itself relates itself to another" (SUD, 13–14). Kierkegaard's reputation as a philosopher who embraces "individualism" makes it necessary to linger over this passage and emphasize its significance. Human beings are not totally free, autonomous individuals. They are relational beings through and through. Even their activity of relating themselves to themselves is achieved by being related to "another."

## Who Is the "Other" That Makes Human Selfhood Possible?[15]

It is obvious that if humans do not constitute themselves, then they must be constituted by something outside the self. Many readers of *The Sickness unto Death* have assumed that the only possible "other" that could be the basis of the human self is God. Admittedly, there are factors that support such a reading. To begin, Kierkegaard describes the state of a self that has fully become itself by rooting out "despair," understood as a failure to become the true self, in this way: "In relating itself to itself and in willing to be itself, the self rests transparently in the power that established it" (SUD, 14).

13. Sartre says that the waiter could say that "I am a waiter in the mode of *being what I am not*" (*Being and Nothingness*, 71–73).

14. Sartre, *Being and Nothingness*, 754.

15. This section restates and summarizes something I argue for in more detail in C. Stephen Evans, "Who Is the Other in *The Sickness unto Death*? God and Human Relations in the Constitution of the Self," in *The Kierkegaard Studies Yearbook 1997* (Berlin: Walter de Gruyter, 1997), 1–15.

It is natural to think that this "power" must for Kierkegaard be God. After all, we know that Kierkegaard is a Christian who believes that humans were created by God. What other "power" could be the ground of the self? In addition, as Kierkegaard describes the varieties of despair in the book, he continually argues that the cure for each form of despair lies in a proper relation to God. For example, the "despair of possibility" is a kind of state in which a person is detached from reality and lives in fantasy. Such a person may have grand emotions or grand fantasies about his or her life plan, but those emotions and plans do not make contact with the person's actual life. The "cure" for this kind of despair is a realization that I am a creature of God who is responsible to God, a realization that requires me to accept the necessary elements of my life that I did not choose and cannot change. The same thing is true for the "despair of necessity," the form of despair opposite to the despair of possibility. The despair of necessity is a kind of fatalistic state in which a person is unable to see any meaningful possibilities. The cure is to see that God is the one "for whom all things are possible," and thus if I have a relation to God, the possibility that is essential to a meaningful life will be present. The God-relation provides an antidote to all the forms of despair.

Therefore, it is easy to understand why readers would think that the "other" that makes it possible for the self to "relate itself to itself" must be God. However, I believe that this identification is too hasty. To begin, Anti-Climacus, in part 2 of *The Sickness unto Death*, explicitly says that this is incorrect. In the "preceding section" (part 1), he has pointed out a "gradation in the consciousness of the self" (SUD, 79). But this "previously considered gradation in the consciousness of the self" was one that was "within the category of the human self, or the self whose criterion is man" (SUD, 79). Only now, in part 2, is he going to consider "the self directly before God" (SUD, 79). We must recall that the pseudonym employed by Kierkegaard here is the strictly Christian character of Anti-Climacus. Anti-Climacus is not shy about employing Christian terminology, and it cannot be accidental that in part 1 he uses the abstract language of an "other" or "power" to describe the basis of the self, while in part 2 talks explicitly about God. It is true that in part 1, as we have seen, Anti-Climacus constantly discusses God as the cure for the various forms of despair. However, at the beginning of the book, the term "God" is avoided in favor of abstract language.

To understand what is going on, we should consider again the "formula" that describes the condition of the self when despair is rooted out: "In relating itself to itself and in willing to be itself, the self rests transparently in the power that established it" (SUD, 14). This is an implicitly normative claim, a description of an *ideal* self. In order for a self to achieve this ideal, Anti-Climacus clearly thinks that the "power" that the self must relate to has to be God. A self that is grounded on anything else cannot fully will to be itself and cannot "rest transparently" in the "power" that is its ground. However, on reflection, we can see that the very fact that human selves can and do *fail* to achieve this ideal state shows that the self can relate to some "power" or "other" besides God. In fact, given the fact that despair is claimed by Anti-Climacus to be universal, this is not only possible but pervasively the case. Human persons constantly ground their selves in things other than God. The racist's sense of his self is grounded in the concept of race. People base their sense of identity on such factors as wealth, intelligence, nationalism, or power. They develop these identities through relationships with real or imagined humans who serve as models to be emulated or rejected.

When we look at the "other" that is the basis of the self, we must therefore distinguish factual descriptions from normative descriptions. Anti-Climacus certainly holds that for people to be free from despair and attain genuine or true selfhood, they must relate themselves to themselves by relating to God. However, descriptively he knows that human selves constantly fail to do this; they base their selves on God-substitutes, on what Christians term idols. Nevertheless, *ontologically or structurally, selfhood continues to be relational.* Humans cannot create themselves out of nothing. If they do not ground their identities in God, they will ground them in something else that is a substitute for God.

Metaphysically, humans are indeed dependent on God and are created by God. However, when God gives humans freedom, letting them "slip out of his hand, as it were," he gives them the ability to construct an identity on things other than God. Psychologically, humans have a "self" that is partly constituted by how they conceive of themselves—that is what makes them "spiritual" beings. In fact, when we look at humans from a developmental standpoint, basing one's sense of self on something other than God is actually unavoidable. As infants, humans do not know God. Humans must learn who God is and what it means to "live before God." Spiritual existence is an achievement; it is initially present only as a capacity or potentiality in a human person.

Kierkegaard thinks that the "power" or "other" to which a self relates provides a "criterion" for the self, an ideal that the self strives to realize. Our intended destiny is to become like God himself.[16] However, having

16. The idea that humans are to become like God is one that is common among Chris-

God as one's criterion is an achievement, not something present from the beginning. Kierkegaard makes this very clear in part 2: "The child who previously had only his parents as a criterion becomes a self as an adult by getting the state as a criterion, but what an infinite accent falls on the self by having God as the criterion!" (SUD, 79). The "state" here is a reference to the Hegelian view that the self gains its identity from society. Kierkegaard recognizes that this is true, psychologically and developmentally, but he denies that this is normatively ideal. The person who "lives before God" can have a kind of self that a merely human criterion of selfhood cannot provide. Humans who fail to live before God in this way are in despair; they are failing to be their true selves.

However, they continue to be selves of a sort. I have already noted that Kierkegaard claims that, just as Socrates attempted to show the immortality of the soul from the fact that bodily sickness does not destroy the soul, "the eternal in a person can be demonstrated by the fact that despair cannot consume his self" (SUD, 21). The despairing person "is mortally ill" and "yet he cannot die." Even the person who is spiritually dead continues to exist as spirit.

## Spirit as Both Ontological and Normative

It now should be clearer what Kierkegaard means when he says that a human being is "spirit." The term functions both ontologically and normatively. There is a sense in which spirit describes what a self necessarily is. Ontologically, a spirit is a being that (at least partially) defines itself or helps to create its own identity. Since this is an ontological or structural feature of human existence, it is true of all human persons. Since every human person exists as spirit, it makes perfect sense that someone can be "spiritual though not religious." Ontologically, spirit is not a differential category, but a universal feature of the self.

---

tian writers, but especially prominent in the Eastern Orthodox Christian view of salvation, in which our ultimate state is one of *theōsis* or divinization. Christopher Barnett's account of Kierkegaard's view of the human spiritual journey as a "return to God" emphasizes this point well. See his *From Despair to Faith*, 53. In saying we are to become like God, Kierkegaard obviously does not mean we are to become our own creators, or anything like that. Rather, he argues we become like God through recognizing how unlike God we are and through turning to him in submission and faith. Barnett makes this point well also, in his chapter 2, pp. 25–62.

Furthermore, since we have seen that humans, as finite beings, do not create their identities out of nothing, their spiritual character is essentially tied to relationships to something outside the self. We always "relate ourselves to ourselves" through our relation to some "other." Spirituality goes hand in hand with relationality, and the content and quality of a person's spirituality reflect the content and quality of the relationships that define the self. This may seem surprising, since Kierkegaard is widely known as an "individualist." I shall later examine Kierkegaard's concept of the "single individual," which certainly plays a key role in his thought. At this point, I shall merely say that even the single individual is not an isolated individual, because for Kierkegaard it is impossible for a human self to define itself except through a relationship to something distinct from the self.

The "other" that defines the self is always something "higher," even if it is not God. At least, the self that is defining itself by this "other" *perceives* the "other" as higher. In the ideal, healthy case, in which the self is itself through a relation to God, the relation takes the form of accountability. The human self is created to live "before God," answering to God as God gives to each self its appointed task. However, even when the "other" is something other than God, there is still a sense that this other provides the self an ideal, something the self must measure itself by. Even if a person thinks of the ideal self as grounded in some abstract principle, that principle is seen as something "higher" that exercises a power over the self. There is no true accountability without a person to be accountable to, but there is an analogous sense in which a person who does not consciously believe in God still is defined by "something higher."

The fact that Kierkegaard treats spirit both ontologically and normatively actually fits with everyday usage of the term "spirit" today. We continue to talk at times about "spirit" as a type of entity. In that sense, it is often claimed that human selves are not identical to material objects. They are spirits, albeit bodily spirits, or perhaps we say that humans have spirits. However, we also talk about spirituality in a normative sense, in which one person is said to be unusually "spiritual," in contrast to others who are "worldly." In this normative sense, spirituality is a quality that can be gained or lost, and it comes in degrees.

In *The Sickness unto Death*, Kierkegaard first describes humans from the ontological or structural standpoint. It is the fact that human nature is spirit in this sense that makes it possible for humans to despair, understood as the failure to be one's genuine or authentic self. If the self (ontologically) is the kind of being that must choose to become itself (by "relating itself to itself"), we can see that the possibility of this kind of failure is inherent in the structure of the human self. Having explained the possibility of despair as inherent in our ontological nature, I devote the bulk of the book to a normative account of the ways humans fail to become themselves, and it is to that account that I shall turn in the next chapter.

The most important lesson to draw from this initial account of spirit in Kierkegaard is that spirituality is always relational. The character of a person's spirituality is a function of the "other" to which a person relates himself, and how the person relates to that other. When the "other" is understood as a personal God, the relationship takes the form of accountability. When the "other" is something other than God, it is still seen as something "higher" that exercises what we might describe as a magnetic pull on the self.

# CHAPTER 2

# Spiritlessness and Demonic Spirituality

The normative account of spirit that Kierkegaard provides (through the voice of Anti-Climacus) in *The Sickness unto Death* looks at the way things go wrong in the human self.[1] The book is, as noted in the previous chapter, an account of despair, viewed as a failure to become one's true or genuine self. It thus provides a normatively laden account of spirit that is mainly negative. The positive account of spirit is given only briefly and formulaically. In part 1, the account uses the abstract and formal language that describes the self structurally: "In relating itself to itself and in willing to be itself, the self rests transparently in the power that established it" (SUD, 14). In part 2, the formula is deepened by making it into an account of faith, the quality that the human self must have to be fully spiritually developed in a positive way: "Faith is: that the self in being itself and in willing to be itself rests transparently in God" (SUD, 82). At the time Kierkegaard originally planned *The Sickness unto Death*, he had thought that the material that makes up the bulk of the book would form the first half of a longer book that would also give an account of faith and the positive development of spirituality.[2] The longer book was never written, but some of the content that would have gone into its second half was incorporated into some of Kierkegaard's other

1. Since I am convinced that Anti-Climacus is invented only because Kierkegaard felt personally unworthy to write from a true Christian perspective, I will often omit the cumbersome "through the voice of Anti-Climacus" in the rest of this chapter. I have no doubt that Kierkegaard fully accepts the truth of Anti-Climacus's account.

2. The longer book would have been called *Thoughts That Cure Radically, Christian Healing*. See Hong, introduction in SUD, xiii. It is also likely that Kierkegaard did not originally plan to make this projected book pseudonymous.

late writings, including *Practice in Christianity*. I will examine Kierkegaard's positive account of distinctively Christian spirituality later, in chapters 6 through 8. In this chapter, I will focus mainly on the account given of the ways spirit goes wrong.

Kierkegaard's reason for focusing on the negative description of spirit is quite justified from a Christian perspective, since the Christian doctrine of original sin implies that all humans (with the exception of Jesus and possibly the Virgin Mary) have indeed failed to become the self God intends them to become. The negative account of spirit is thus an account of the human condition as it actually is, and Kierkegaard explicitly affirms the universality of despair: "In any case no human being ever lived and no one lives outside of Christendom who has not despaired, and no one in Christendom if he is not a true Christian, and insofar as he is not wholly that, he still is to some extent in despair" (SUD, 22).

In part 1 of the book, Kierkegaard describes different forms of despair from two different perspectives. He first provides what could be called a symptomatic account of the forms of despair, focusing on the effects of despair on the self. The self is, as we saw in chapter 1, intended to be a synthesis of dialectical qualities. The self that goes wrong and fails to be itself winds up unbalanced in some way. One of the "balancing" qualities is missing or underdeveloped, and the self fails to be what it should be. This perspective thus describes the "what" or content of a life that is lived in despair. One could also say that this first account describes the effects of despair on the self's actual history.

The second account given looks at despair from the point of view of consciousness. A self that is in despair may have a lesser or greater degree of awareness of its own state. Here the focus is not so much on the content of the self's character, but on the degree of awareness that the self has of this character. A greater degree of consciousness of the self means there is a greater intensity to the self's spirituality. Although every human is structurally spirit, this spirituality can be weakly or strongly actualized. As we shall see, however, a greater degree of spirituality in this sense is not completely positive. Kierkegaard believes that there is such a thing as negative spirituality, which he describes at its maximum as demonic. Even this negative spirituality has a kind of value, however, and is not altogether a bad thing, but is "dialectically" closer to salvation than the state of "spiritlessness." In this chapter, I shall try to look at despair from both of these perspectives, the structural or content perspective and the perspective of consciousness. At several places, we will encounter "demonic" spirituality, comparing it with the more common human state of "spiritlessness."

## Despair Understood Symptomatically

In chapter 1, I briefly introduced the idea that Kierkegaard sees human existence as a dynamic process in which seemingly contradictory qualities are unified. Humans are "a synthesis of the infinite and the finite, of the temporal and the eternal, of freedom and necessity" (SUD, 13). In Kierkegaard's *The Concept of Anxiety* (attributed to the pseudonym Vigilius Haufniensis), human existence is also described as "a synthesis of psyche [soul] and body that is constituted and sustained by spirit" (CA, 81). *The Sickness unto Death* does not mention "soul and body," but the accounts of the symptoms of despair this book provides often imply a link between the terms on one side of the synthesis (finitude, necessity, temporality) and physicality.

All of these descriptions of the "synthesis" see human life as a heterogeneous compound of incongruous elements. One pole of the synthesis is expansive and godlike, while the other is limiting and situates human life as creaturely. Kierkegaard is hardly alone in noticing these incongruous qualities. Pascal gives a memorable description:

> What kind of freak then is man? How novel, how monstrous, how chaotic, how paradoxical, how prodigious! Judge of all things, feeble earthworm, repository of truth, sink of doubt and error, glory and refuse of the universe.[3]

A similar paradox is found in Plato's Socrates, in a passage that Kierkegaard's Johannes Climacus cites in *Philosophical Fragments*. According to Climacus, although Socrates was a "connoisseur of human nature," he was "not quite clear about himself," wondering whether he was a "monster" or "a friendlier and gentler being, by nature sharing something divine" (PF, 37).[4]

Kierkegaard sometimes describes these elements of human existence as "contradictory," but it is clear that he does not mean that the elements are *logically* contradictory, which would make human existence logically impossible.[5] Rather, he means that the elements are incongruous; bringing

---

3. Blaise Pascal, *Pensées*, trans. A. J. Krailsheimer (New York: Penguin, 1966), 64.

4. The Plato reference is to *Phaedrus* 229e.

5. For a discussion of how Kierkegaard uses the term "contradiction" (Danish *Modsigelse*), see C. Stephen Evans, *Passionate Reason: Making Sense of Kierkegaard's* Philosophical Fragments (Bloomington: Indiana University Press, 1992), 97–104. Understanding Kierkegaard's usage here is critical to making sense of his claim that the incarnation, like human existence generally, involves a "contradiction."

them together is difficult and arduous, a process that is tension filled and requires struggle. It is important to notice that despair is not simply identical to finitude, and that the fact that the synthesis is ongoing and incomplete is not itself a symptom of despair. As long as a human person is living in time, the incomplete character of the synthesis is a necessary and ineradicable feature. Despair, however, is neither necessary nor ineradicable. Despair is not simply the "synthesis" or "relation" itself, but rather a "misrelation," which is itself made possible by the fact that the synthesis is a self-conscious, free activity (SUD, 14). Despair does not consist simply in the fact that during this life I cannot fully realize my ideals, but in a failure even to be properly directed toward my ideals. Eternity cannot be fully realized in time, but temporality can be oriented toward the eternal. Despair is the condition in which this fails to occur.

As noted above, the descriptions of the various aspects of the two sides of the polarity in human nature naturally align themselves. Finitude, temporality, necessity, and physicality seem to go together as the limiting side, while infinitude, eternity, possibility, and spirituality describe the expansive side. This suggests that the three descriptions of the synthesis do not describe three distinct dualities, but simply different aspects of one basic and fundamental duality. This suggestion is supported by the actual descriptions Kierkegaard gives of the various forms of despair viewed symptomatically. The despair of finitude and the despair of necessity seem very similar, while the despair of possibility and the despair of infinitude are also alike. Interestingly, the third way of describing the synthesis (temporality/eternity) is not even described when Kierkegaard goes on to give concrete pictures of what the different forms of despair look like in real life. I suspect that is because the eternal-temporal polarity is already present, explicitly or sometimes implicitly, in the descriptions he gives of the other forms, and thus there was no need to add anything additional.

## The Despair of Infinitude

As Kierkegaard himself says, the symptomatic descriptions of despair given in *The Sickness unto Death* have an "algebraic" or formulaic character. Kierkegaard looks at the four qualities that make up the two polarities he considers, and describes four forms of despair, one for each of the qualities. In each case, he describes a "misrelation" in the synthesis, in that one element predominates, and its correlative is missing or underdeveloped.

It is important to note that the problem is never that one element is too large. Kierkegaard is no fan of mediocrity and does not think that the "balance" in a human life should be achieved by damping down or diminishing some aspect of human existence. It is not, for example, that a human being can have too much imagination, or too strong an understanding of the necessary elements of his or her life. Rather, the misrelation is due to the weakness or atrophy of the contrasting element that ought to balance the strong quality.

Thus, the "despair of infinitude" is not due to too much infinitude, but to a lack of finitude. To live "infinitely" is to live solely in the imagination, for the imagination is unlimited in a way that actual human life can never be. Kierkegaard says that the imagination is a kind of foundational or basic human faculty, "the capacity *instar omnium* (for all capacities)" (SUD, 31). This foundational capacity shapes the basic human faculties of "feeling, knowing, and willing" (SUD, 30). What emotions a person can have, what a person can know, and what a person can will are all limited by the person's imagination. We might say that all of these capacities are reflective in nature and depend on imagination. Imagination is thus fundamental to human existence, not something limited to art or the aesthetic.

The problem with someone who is in the grip of the "despair of infinitude" is that the person's reflective capacities misfire or abort. The imagination that is intended to help us feel, know, and act becomes an end in itself. The person's life is "fantastic" in the sense that it is lived in fantasy: "The fantastic is . . . that which leads a person out into the infinite in such a way that it only leads him away from himself and thereby prevents him from coming back to himself" (SUD, 31).

Kierkegaard gives examples of this sad fate for each of the three faculties mentioned. The first is the person whose emotions are purely abstract and never become concrete, as in a person who has a great love for humanity but can't stand the actual people he or she comes into contact with. A knower becomes "fantastic" when the person simply wants to know more and more facts but has no conception of the value or meaning of what is known. Perhaps the case of willing is the easiest to understand. Here we might imagine someone who wills some lofty end, say, becoming a neurosurgeon, but never actually enrolls in an organic chemistry class. Many of our human ends are complex and require long periods of time to actualize. Some in fact are such that in principle they cannot be fully actualized or "finished" in time. Nevertheless, if we have a case in which someone imagines that he or she wills an end but the willing never expresses itself concretely in any action, that is a case in which there is something phony or false about the willing.

22

For the infinitude made possible by the imagination to benefit us, it must always embody its output in what is concrete and particular.

We might think that a person who is in the despair of infinitude would be a kind of dreamer, hopelessly cut off from reality and incapable of living in a practical way. This is indeed one form this despair can take, but Kierkegaard maintains that a person who exhibits the despair of infinitude can also appear remarkably ordinary: Such a person can "go on living fairly well, seem to be a man, be occupied with temporal matters, marry, have children, be honored and esteemed—and it may not be detected that in a deeper sense he lacks a self" (SUD, 32). I think that Kierkegaard means that a person who has no real self can get through life by becoming a kind of conformist, making choices by observing how "the others" live. There is a curious similarity between this kind of person and the one described in the next section, the individual who actually lacks imagination almost completely. What we might call "middle-class conformism" thus provides a kind of common strategy for getting through life.[6] Both the despair of infinitude and finitude can use this strategy. The former needs it because the imagination is misfiring and not making contact with reality; the latter because the imagination is simply not working at all. This kind of conformism is central to "spiritlessness," and it shows up frequently in Kierkegaard's descriptions of human existence.

## The Despair of Finitude

The despair of finitude is described by Kierkegaard as a kind of "despairing narrowness" in which a person has become totally "finitized" (SUD, 33). This life most frequently appears, as noted in the previous paragraph, as a kind of conformism in which a self "seems to permit itself to be tricked out of itself by 'the others'" (SUD, 33). The crucial point is not that the person resembles other people in various ways, but that the person has been robbed of a quality that Howard and Edna Hong translate as "primitivity." It is difficult to find a good English word for the Danish term here, which is *Primitivitet*. I do not think "primitivity" succeeds, however. A better term might be "authenticity," though this word also is misleading in some respects.

---

6. Kierkegaard's term for this is *Spidsborgerlighed*, a term the Hongs translate as "philistine-bourgeois mentality." I prefer to translate this as "middle-class conformism" or "bourgeois conformism," since Kierkegaard's stress is not on lack of culture but on lack of primitivity or authenticity.

The idea behind Kierkegaard's claim is one that is central to his view of human existence: It is that God creates individual human beings who are intended by God to have their own unique, individual character. Although Kierkegaard does believe that there is such a thing as a common human nature, he does not think that a human person's identity is exhausted by that common nature. Each person has what we might call a unique role to play in God's great economy, and to play that role God has given each person a specific individual nature.[7] To use a metaphor that Kierkegaard employs more than once, each person has a unique divine name. Each of us has the task of "remembering" that name, of trying to decide what "calling" or "vocation" we have been given, and what gifts and talents we have that must be developed to fulfill that calling.[8]

The relational character of the human self here comes clearly into view. We can also see why, normatively, to build one's self on a relation to something other than God leads to ruin. One's true or genuine self is not simply created by the self out of nothing. By being spirit, a person is given the gift of participating in the process of becoming a self. However, the self that one must become is partly *given*. It is given not as perfected actuality, but as a set of possibilities. However, even those possibilities take shape against the background of a given set of actualities.

The givenness of the self implies that there are two fundamental types of despair. If the human self were a godlike self (as Sartre claims), then this would not be the case: "If a human self had established itself, then there could be only one form [of despair]: not to will to be oneself" (SUD, 14). Since the spirituality of humans has a relational character, things are different. The despair in which one fails to will to be oneself Kierkegaard calls the despair of weakness. However, since the self we are to become is one that is given to each of us, a second form of despair is also possible, the despair of

---

7. Kierkegaard's view here is remarkably similar to that of the medieval thinker Duns Scotus. Scotus's great predecessor Thomas Aquinas had argued that all humans possessed the same essential nature but that this nature was individualized through its bodily history. Scotus agreed that there was a common human nature or essence, and he agreed that the body was important, but he claimed that in addition to this common essence, each individual human had an individual essence (haecceity, from the Latin *haecceitas*). Thus, Socrates, besides possessing human nature, also exemplified what we might call "Socrateity."

8. Here "calling" or "vocation" (*vocare* = Lat. "to call") must not be taken in the vulgarized sense it often has assumed, in which it is limited to a person's job or line of work. One's calling may well include work, but it is fundamentally a calling by God to be a certain kind of person and to live a certain kind of life, a calling that should be expressed in all that one does.

defiance, in which a person does will to be a self, but not the self the person genuinely was created to be. This distinction will play a key role when we look at despair from the point of view of consciousness.

The despair of finitude occurs when a person becomes afraid to take on the task of understanding and actualizing the person's calling. "Surrounded by hordes of men, absorbed in all sorts of secular matters, more and more shrewd about the ways of the world—such a person forgets himself, forgets his name divinely understood, does not dare to believe in himself, finds it too hazardous to be himself and far easier and safer to be like the others, to become a copy, a number, a mass man" (SUD, 33–34). It is easy to read this as a critique of modern society and the "mass man" it has made possible, and it is true that Kierkegaard thinks that this condition has been greatly exacerbated by modern mass media. However, Kierkegaard thinks that this possible way of going wrong can and has occurred in many different societies and ages. This person is in one way the opposite of the individual who is lost in imagination. The despair of finitude embodies a fundamental lack of imagination in which an individual simply cannot conceive of living in a way that diverges at all from the roles assigned to him or her by "the others."

The idea is not that people should try to be different for the sake of being different. After all, if I choose my style of clothing just because it is not what others wear, I am still allowing myself to be shaped by the others. Rather, Kierkegaard thinks that each of us has the task of becoming ourselves, the unique self that God intended each of us to be. The person who refuses this task is not necessarily punished in a temporal or "worldly" way. Rather, just as was the case with the despair of infinitude, "a man . . . in this kind of despair . . . can very well live on in temporality, indeed, actually all the better, be publicly acclaimed, honored, and esteemed" (SUD, 35). We can see from both of these cases that what we might call genuine or authentic spirituality does not always show itself outwardly. Or, to put things more accurately, it does not show itself through conventional worldly achievements.


The Despair of Possibility and the Despair of Necessity

I shall consider these two forms of despair together, since each can be understood only in relation to its correlative. The despair of possibility is grounded in the lack of necessity, just as the despair of infinitude is due to a lack of finitude, while the despair of necessity similarly reflects a lack of possibility.

Kierkegaard illustrates the contrast between the roles of possibility and necessity in human life with two powerful metaphors, one taken from language and one from human physiology. To speak in an articulate way, one needs both vowels and consonants. "Losing oneself in possibility may be compared with a child's utterance of vowel sounds" (SUD, 37). Such a child makes sounds but cannot utter any intelligible words. A person who has no possibilities at all would be like a person who only had "pure consonants": such a person could not speak at all. To speak, one needs both vowels and consonants, and to live in a fully human way, one needs both possibility and necessity.

Possibility is also compared to oxygen. A human person cannot breathe, and thus cannot live, without oxygen, but it is also impossible to breathe pure oxygen. Similarly, the self cannot breathe as spirit without possibility, though it is impossible to live on possibility alone.

The despair of possibility seems, as noted, remarkably like the despair of infinitude. Just as the latter is described as a state in which someone is "carried away from himself," so the former is a state in which the self becomes "an abstract possibility" and is "lost." People would ordinarily describe such a person as living in fantasy, out of touch with reality. This is correct, Kierkegaard says, but the loss of actuality is grounded in the loss of necessity. "Actuality is a unity of possibility and necessity" (SUD, 36). Without contact with the necessary, the self becomes increasingly unreal.

Strikingly, Kierkegaard says that what such a self lacks is "the power to obey, to submit to the necessity in one's life, to what may be called one's limitations" (SUD, 36). This comment clearly presupposes the idea that the self is something given as a task, and the necessary elements of a person's life reflect the structure and content of the task. The fact that a failure to come to terms with necessity is described as a form of disobedience clearly speaks to the relational character of the human self, and we can see why, normatively, a relation to God is required to heal this form of despair. If I recognize myself as a creature who is accountable to God, I will see the constraints of my life that I cannot change as defining the station in which God has placed me and as providing parameters for the calling I have been given.

The despair of necessity, of course, is a state in which one lacks possibility. In its extreme form, this takes the form of fatalism or determinism, a life in which hope has been extinguished. However, this is not the only form of the despair of necessity. The middle-class conformist provides another type that is in fact more common, since fatalism requires a high degree of imagination that few humans have. The fatalist "despairs of possibility" altogether. However, the middle-class conformist is someone who lives in the world of probabilities; such a one thinks he can control possibility by shrewdly playing the odds and relying on probability. Kierkegaard thinks that this state, which is a kind of spiritlessness, is even more wretched than that of the determinist (SUD, 42).[9]

From Kierkegaard's point of view, to rely on worldly probability is a kind of spiritual deadness, in which the meaning and value of a person's life is completely a function of contingencies that are in the end out of our control. Kierkegaard's own ideal of human existence is admittedly high, since probably most humans live their lives in just this way. Most of us think like this: If a person gets cancer and dies young, that is unfortunate and too bad; if I do not suffer that fate, then my life will be a good one. Hence, I will try my best to tilt the odds in that direction. I will eat healthy foods and exercise, keep up with the medical reports, and avoid foolish risks. Such a stance just seems like common sense.

Kierkegaard wants to oppose to this kind of mentality a view of human life that maintains that every human life has meaning and value, regardless of what happens to a person. On his view, it is unacceptable to say that my life has meaning and value because I was one of the fortunate ones. The meaning and value of my life does not depend on the fact that I did not die young, or struggle with excruciating pain, or live through grinding poverty. Kierkegaard rejects a view that implies that if those things had happened to me, then my life would have been without meaning and value. There is a deep commitment to human equality in Kierkegaard's view. It is not a claim that humans are or should be equal in natural gifts or money or status, but a claim that human life should have meaning regardless of a person's worldly status.

The middle-class conformist, who has the "philistine-bourgeois mentality," lives on the basis of probability, and if something happens that is so terrible that the person lacks the imagination even to consider it, such a person despairs (SUD, 41). The event in fact does not even need to be all that terrible; it just needs to be something that the person cannot deal with using the resources of practical common sense. For example, a person might lose a job that was the basis of the person's sense of identity and, as a result, simply see no point in going on with life. It seems as if such a person has been "driven to despair," but for Kierkegaard the person's life was in fact a form of despair all along, an essential despair that is revealed by a contingent event.

9. I provide a longer account of Kierkegaard's critique of probability in chapter 8.

One may think that Kierkegaard here betrays a lack of familiarity with what it is like to deal with tragedy. After all, he was born to a well-to-do family and never even worked for a living. (Though the critic should remember that Kierkegaard suffered grievously from depression and also endured the death of five of his six siblings while he was young. He also used up his inheritance and died almost penniless.) Kierkegaard would surely respond that it is when things look impossible from an earthly point of view that one discovers whether a person really believes in God. "In order for a person to become aware of his self and God, imagination must raise him higher than the miasma of probability, it must teach him to hope and fear" (SUD, 41). The person of faith has the "infallible antidote" to the despair of necessity, regardless of what happens to the person, because "for God everything is possible at every moment" (SUD, 39–40). Faith in God is not like a belief that such and such an event is not likely to happen. It is a faith that God will not allow a life to become wasted, regardless of what happens.

The faith that the believer has in God should not be confused with some kind of "health and wealth" gospel, which makes empirical claims about what God will do for a person. The person of faith makes no such claims. "The *believer* sees and understands his downfall, humanly speaking . . . but he believes. For this reason he does not collapse. He leaves it entirely to God how he is to be helped but he believes that for God everything is possible" (SUD, 39). Such a person believes in miracles, although the miracle may consist in allowing him to be saved in and through what most people would describe as a horror.

The fatalist or determinist is deprived of possibility and therefore deprived of hope. Such a person is "unable to pray," since prayer depends on a belief in possibility. However, the fatalist at least has escaped the "miasma of probability" and shows a degree of spirituality even to envisage his state as one in which all hope is gone. The middle-class conformist who lives on the basis of probability is even more spiritless, because he also lacks hope but does not even recognize this, confusing genuine hope with a shrewdness grounded in probability.


Despair Understood from the Perspective of Consciousness

In the second half of part C of part 1 of the book, Kierkegaard attempts to provide a kind of phenomenological description of what despair looks like from a first-person viewpoint, arranged by "degree of consciousness." As we saw earlier, although spirituality is a structural, ineradicable element in the self, a person's spiritual capacities can be developed to different degrees, and different degrees of spirituality make possible different degrees of despair. The most fundamental distinction is between despair that is conscious of itself as despair and despair that is not conscious of itself, which I shall call unconscious despair. Within the category of conscious despair, a distinction is made between the despair of weakness and the despair of defiance, already briefly discussed above. Finally, with the category of the despair of weakness, Kierkegaard distinguishes despair over the earthly from despair over the eternal. The following chart captures the map Kierkegaard gives:

### THE CONTINUUM OF DESPAIR

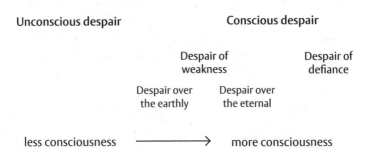

less consciousness ⟶ more consciousness

One might think that unconscious despair would be impossible and that despair is an emotion that must be experienced. However, Kierkegaard does not use the term "despair" simply to refer to a felt emotion, but to a state or condition of the person, one that characteristically gives rise to that emotion we call despair but which can manifest itself in many ways in a person's life. Writing long before Freud or Nietzsche, Kierkegaard was a depth psychologist who recognized many of the ways humans fail to know themselves as they truly are. There are different forms of unconscious despair. The person may simply fail to notice his despair altogether. Or, the person may be aware of despair in some way but in denial about it or even actively repressing the awareness.

Unconscious despair, far from being impossible, is actually the most common form, according to Kierkegaard. This common form is the despair of the individual who is not even aware of his or her spiritual character and thus fails to notice the failure to actualize the self. Someone who is not even aware of a possibility will naturally fail to see the actualization of this possibility as a problem. It is essentially the condition of someone who is "spiritless," in the sense that the person has no knowledge or understanding of his or her spiritual potential.

Kierkegaard often describes such a spiritless person as a "pagan," but he draws an interesting distinction between what we might call the classical pagan, who lived prior to Christianity and had no knowledge of God's revelation, and the person within Christendom, who nonetheless lives in essentially pagan categories. Kierkegaard does appreciate the possibilities that were present in ancient Greek and Roman society. However, although the achievements of the pagans may have been amazing in many ways, Kierkegaard nonetheless claims that any existence

> that is not conscious of itself as spirit or conscious of itself before God as spirit, . . . but vaguely rests in and merges in some dark universality (state, nation, etc.) or, in the dark about his self, regards his capacities merely as powers to produce without becoming aware of their source, regards his self, if it is to have intrinsic meaning, as an indefinable something—every such existence, whatever it achieves, be it most amazing, . . . is nevertheless despair. (SUD, 46)

The spiritual failure of classical paganism, according to Kierkegaard, can be seen in the fact that the pagan saw suicide as morally indifferent, or even praiseworthy, even though the same pagan might pass harsh judgment on stealing or adultery (SUD, 46). (It seems likely that Kierkegaard today would say the increasing acceptance of suicide in Western liberal countries is evidence of a return to pagan ways of thought.)

The classical pagan, although spiritless, is still qualitatively superior to the pagan within Christendom. The former, though lacking spiritual development, is still "qualified in the direction of spirit," while paganism within Christendom is a "departure" or "falling away" from spirit and thus is spiritlessness in a deeper sense (SUD, 46–47). Kierkegaard discusses this kind of spiritlessness at greater length in part 2 of *The Sickness unto Death*, since it presupposes an awareness of Christianity.

## The Distinction between the Despair of Weakness and the Despair of Defiance

Kierkegaard begins his discussion of conscious despair with a reminder that the clean conceptual distinction between the person who is unaware of his or her despair and the person who is conscious of despair does not accurately describe the complexities of actual human life. Many people in despair have a kind of "dim awareness" of their state, and even this dim awareness comes in many different forms and degrees. The awareness that a person does have can be kept at bay through "diversions" such as "work and busyness" (SUD, 48). In general, there is a "dialectical interplay" between "knowing and willing." A person's knowledge shapes his will, but what he can know is also shaped by what he wants to be the case. Kierkegaard says that in general the more a person is conscious of despair, the more intense that despair is. As we shall see, clarity about one's despair characterizes what Kierkegaard calls "the demonic," an intense though negative form of spirituality. Kierkegaard thinks that few humans have much capacity for the demonic; few of us are capable of destroying ourselves with a clear understanding that this is what we are doing. Kierkegaard even wonders whether "simultaneous clarity and despair [about the self] are conceivable" (SUD, 47). At least for most humans, some degree of self-deception is necessary in order to despair.

The basic contrast between the despair of weakness and the despair of defiance is not hard to grasp. In both cases, there is a degree of awareness of a person's true or genuine self. In the despair of weakness, the person fails to actualize that genuine self, the self given to the individual by God as a task. Perhaps the person does not even believe that it is possible to become a self. There is a lack of confidence in the self's power to become itself. In the despair of defiance, the self has confidence in its powers but refuses to accept its creaturely status. Such a self in effect says, "I refuse to become the self I was meant to be; I want to decide for myself who I am and who I am to become."

Again, when stated abstractly, the distinction seems clear-cut, but Kierkegaard once more claims that in actual life the two forms are not so easy to distinguish. The individual in weakness who thinks she is unable to become the self she was meant to be is still showing some defiance of God. If God demands that we become a certain kind of self, then to fail to believe that this is possible shows a lack of faith in God, a distrust of God and what God requires. From the other side, the person who defies God nonetheless is not as strong as the person would like to think. "No despair is entirely free of defiance," but it is also true that "even despair's most extreme defiance is never really free of some weakness" (SUD, 49).

31

## Masculine and Feminine Despair?

Kierkegaard tries to illuminate the difference between the despair of weakness and the despair of defiance with a very controversial claim. The despair of weakness, he says, is "feminine despair," while the despair of defiance is "masculine." Perhaps anticipating the controversial nature of this claim, he attaches a footnote to the remark, in which he tries to explain it.

The footnote does clarify what Kierkegaard means, and in it he does distance himself from some (though not all) of the objectionably sexist ways his claim might be understood. First of all, he makes it clear that he is using the terms "masculine" and "feminine" to designate types of behavior *typically* associated with men and women, but he recognizes that men and women do not always conform to these stereotypes. Many men display what Kierkegaard calls "feminine" despair, and there are many women who show "masculine" despair (SUD, 49–50n). Nevertheless, Kierkegaard does believe that there are typical differences between the sexes. He claims, for example, that women's sense of self or identity is typically bound up with "devotedness" to other human persons. He says that men are also capable of devotion but that typically this is less central to their identity than is the case with women. In effect, he is claiming that the more typical way women fail to actualize their true selves is by being too prone to set aside their own callings, allowing their lives to be determined by what others demand or expect from them. Men, on the other hand, are more prone to think too little about others and the claims that others may rightly have on them.

Many feminists will see this claim as an "essentialist" claim that smacks strongly of sexism and leads to the subordination of women.[10] I am not sure Kierkegaard can be completely cleared of this accusation, since he does sometimes seem to share the stereotypes about women that were dominant in his culture. Nevertheless, there are a couple of things to say in his defense.

First, there does seem to be some psychological truth in what Kierkegaard says. Although, as Kierkegaard says, there are certainly plenty of men and women who are exceptions, it does seem that men are more likely than women to be the kinds of people who dominate groups, paying too little attention to the needs of others while focusing on their own wants, behaving

10. For some of these criticisms, see Celine Leon and Sylvia Walsh, eds., *Feminist Interpretations of Kierkegaard* (University Park: Pennsylvania State University Press, 1997). This book contains both lively critiques and defenses of Kierkegaard's view of women, in light of feminist theory.

aggressively in ways that prioritize themselves.[11] It also seems that women often fail to speak up for themselves or stand up for themselves, fearing to be regarded as "pushy" or "bossy," with a reasonable fear that they may pay a price if they do not act in gender-stereotyped ways. If so, then there may be something right about Kierkegaard's distinction, at least as providing some probabilistic generalizations about gender differences in Western cultures as they actually exist. There is no need to think that these generalizations must always hold true for other times and cultures, however. Kierkegaard is, I believe, describing gender differences as he observes them in his context, not describing them as they must be, much less prescribing how they ought to be.

The second thing to be said on Kierkegaard's behalf here is that he does, at the end of the footnote, espouse a qualified egalitarian view of men and women. Despite the biological and cultural differences between men and women that he believes hold, he nonetheless says that, in relation to God, men and women are equal and have the same basic calling or vocation. Both are equally spiritual and have the task of becoming the selves God intends them to be through faith in God. "In the relationship to God, where the distinction of man-woman vanishes, it holds for men as well as for women that devotion is the self and that in the giving of oneself the self is gained" (SUD, 50n).

Perhaps what Kierkegaard is saying is something like this. As human selves develop in society, shaped by human relations and social expectations,

11. Some support for Kierkegaard is provided by Mary Stewart Van Leeuwen, "Christian Maturity in Light of Feminist Theory," *Journal of Psychology and Theology* 16, no. 2 (1988): 168–82. Psychological research has consistently confirmed, on a statistical and average basis, some differences between men and women, and some of these differences seem consistent with Kierkegaard's view. Men are more likely to be aggressive and commit violent crimes, for example, while women are more likely to suffer from depression. Some of the evidence for these claims can be found in the following articles: Wolfgang Linden et al., "There's More to Anger Coping Than 'In' or 'Out,'" *Emotion* 3, no. 1 (2003): 12–29; and Rachel H. Salk, Janet S. Hyde, and Lyn Y. Abramson, "Gender Differences in Depression in Representative National Samples: Meta-Analyses of Diagnoses and Symptoms," *Psychological Bulletin* 143, no. 8 (2017): 783–822.

Recognizing these claims as correct, however, does not imply anything about why they are correct. Recently, some psychologists have offered evidence that some of the differences are grounded more in social norms and expectations than in biological differences. See Janet Shibley Hyde, "The Gender Similarities Hypothesis," *American Psychologist* 60, no. 6 (2005): 581–92, as well as her more recent "Gender Similarities and Differences," *Annual Review of Psychology* 65 (2014): 373–98.

I am very grateful to Charlotte vanOyen Witvliet for providing me with these references, as well as some others, and for some very good advice about this section.

as well as biological constraints, differences between men and women develop. These have a reality that must not be ignored. After all, the self that a person must become is always a concrete, particular self that must come to terms with the particularities of existence. This may mean that there are differences in the problems that men and women typically face, and differences in the kinds of struggles they often must go through. However, these differences do not alter the fact that the essential task that men and women face is the same: becoming the particular selves God created them to be through the achievement of an identity grounded in God. Men and women are equally spiritual creatures.

## The Despair of Weakness

The despair in weakness, described as "not to will to be oneself," presupposes some conscious awareness of despair but not necessarily an adequate understanding. The lowest degree of this despair Kierkegaard calls "despair over the earthly" or over "something earthly." This kind of person's identity is grounded in some finite good: having money or looks or athletic ability, for example. Typically, such a person invests in some particular goal: I will be somebody if only I get that job, or marry that person, or win that award. If the person fails to achieve the goal, then despair results. If the person's fortunes rebound, then the person would be happy again, not in despair.

That is how the person in this form of despair would describe the situation, but Kierkegaard does not agree. On his view, this person is in despair regardless of whether the person is fortunate or not. Despair is an essential condition, and whether a person is in such a state cannot be a matter of luck. The real problem is that the person has no real self at all; he lives in a purely "immediate" way and does not understand himself as spirit. The person may even wish to become someone else: "If I were so and so, then I would not be in despair." Kierkegaard describes such a stance as almost comical, for it is absolutely impossible for a self to become someone else. If *I* were someone else, I would not be the self I am. I would not exist.

If a person is not purely "immediate" and is more reflective, then despair accordingly becomes more conscious. Such a person does not despair simply because of what actually happens to him, but is capable of despairing as a result of reflection over what *could* happen. This is the beginning of spiritual development; the person is now aware of himself as "essentially different from the environment and external events and from their influence" (SUD,

54). However, instead of advancing to actually willing to become the self it should be, the self may "recoil" from the difficulty of such spiritual existence. The person may actually think he has overcome the despair he felt at one point, by simply pouring himself into "outward life," taking his capacities or talents as givens and simply refusing to think about who he really should be (SUD, 56). This kind of development gives rise to the illusion that despair is a kind of stage that a young person must go through, a kind of adolescent "phase," but which adults usually manage to overcome.

From Kierkegaard's viewpoint, this kind of "victory" over despair is in reality an acceptance of failure. It is a deeper kind of despair, but the despair is well hidden and even repressed. No spiritual development or achievement comes simply with age as a "matter of course." It is not possible to acquire a self the way people grow wisdom teeth or a man grows facial hair after puberty. It is in fact very easy for a person to "sink into triviality," confusing his contentment with the trivial with a victory over despair (SUD, 59).

If a person's reflective imaginative power grows, then the person's despair may become even deeper and more intense. The person may understand that the thing his life was built upon (money or fame or power) was meaningless and that his life would have been just as empty whether he succeeded or failed. Such a person does not just despair over "something earthly" but over the *whole* of the earthly.

Again, the deepening of spirituality brings with it an opportunity. The person who has begun to see that "everything under the sun" is nothing but "vanity" (to echo the stance of Ecclesiastes) is closer in one way to spiritual health. However, if this opportunity is not actualized, a deeper form of despair results: "despair of the eternal" or "over oneself." The person sees that he has squandered the possibilities he was given, but this insight can simply lead to a different form of self-hatred or rejection. As Kierkegaard puts it, the person does not simply despair "in weakness" but now despairs "over his weakness" (SUD, 61). Such a person ought to "humble himself" under his weakness and turn from despair to faith. Instead, the person "entrenches himself in despair and despairs over his weakness" (SUD, 61). Such a self refuses to acknowledge itself because of its weakness.

This kind of person has a degree of spirituality and a kind of self, unlike the more immediate person. Such a self has a greater element of defiance and is closer to "masculine" despair. However, this self that has been developed is kept closely hidden. There is a kind of "false door," and behind that door is the self, but a self that does not reveal itself to others (SUD, 67). The person develops a kind of *persona* that is presented to the world and keeps the actual self locked up inside. Kierkegaard describes this inner hiddenness with a Danish term that is virtually untranslatable: *Indesluttethed*. The Hongs translate this as "enclosing reserve." The idea is that the true self is "shut up" inside itself.

Kierkegaard says that in an odd way this stance is really a form of pride. The person in the grip of this despair will probably not see it that way, since the person is engaged in berating himself over his weakness. But there is a kind of pride involved in refusing to be the actual self one is. The self thinks something like this: "I would be willing to be myself were I not the miserable, weak self I am." This is a form of pride in that the self "cannot bear this consciousness of weakness" (SUD, 65).

A person who is locked up in "enclosing reserve" is in danger of suicide, according to Kierkegaard, and perhaps will need a confidant, someone he can reveal himself to, to avoid such a fate. However, this may not be easy and may not in the end work, since the person may despise himself even more for his inability to bear his state in solitude and for his need of a confidant (SUD, 65).

## The Despair of Defiance

The last form of despair Kierkegaard considers in part 1 of *The Sickness unto Death* is the despair of defiance, the kind that he has already described as "masculine." Calling this despair "masculine" does not mean that most men have this quality. Kierkegaard thinks that most people, men as well as women, are too spiritless to be capable of this kind of robust conscious despair, in which the person wills to be a self, but not the self the person was meant to be. He calls this form of despair masculine because those who exemplify it are more likely to be men, or to exhibit stereotypical masculine characteristics, but he does not think many humans of either sex are capable of this.

This person is someone who has developed enough spirituality to have a sense of what it means to have a self, and to understand that the self must be freely chosen. This person has an awareness of his own freedom and his own responsibility. However, the attitude is one of defiance, in that the individual refuses to become the self that I have been calling his true self, and instead wants to decide for himself who he will become. This person has become aware of the self's freedom as a formal quality, which Kierkegaard calls "the infinite self." This infinite self is made possible by its negativity, its ability to negate or withdraw itself from all the labels by which it could be defined. With the help of this negative, infinite form, the self attempts to take a godlike stance: "With the help of this negativity, the self in despair wants to be master of himself or to create himself, to make his self into the self he wants to be, to determine what he will have or not have in his concrete self" (SUD, 68). Kierkegaard makes the godlike aspirations of this kind of despair very explicit by a reference to Genesis 1: This kind of self does not want to begin "at the beginning" or "with the beginning," but rather "in the beginning" (SUD, 68).

Kierkegaard struggles to find a name for this kind of self who wants to be his own creator. In some ways this self is seeking a kind of absolute self-sufficiency of the type sought by the ancient Stoics, who tried to achieve contentment by becoming indifferent to whatever might happen to a person. The Stoics withdrew their identity from the concrete details of life and even relationships, viewing the true self as the inner self that could be completely controlled and mastered. Stoics, however, are not the only ones who seek this kind of autonomy. Hence, Kierkegaard says that "if a generic name for this despair is wanted, it could be called stoicism, but understood as not referring only to that sect" (SUD, 68).

If Kierkegaard were writing today, he would have a better name for this stance. He would doubtless call it "existentialism." This is ironic, given that Kierkegaard is often described as the "father of existentialism." However, if the paradigm of existentialism is the French thinker Jean-Paul Sartre, it is clear that Kierkegaard was describing what most people think of as existentialism in this section. For the Sartrean self is indeed defined by negativity; consciousness for Sartre is a kind of negative activity whereby the self secures its freedom. Kierkegaard describes this kind of despair in very similar terms. The "infinite form" of this self is essentially "a negative self." Furthermore, Sartre explicitly says that the conscious self is implicitly seeking to become God.[12]

The similarity between Sartre's view of the self and Kierkegaard's description of the active despair that wills to be the self it wants to be can also be seen in the weaknesses of the view. Sartre's ethic, in which it is up to the self to create right and wrong, and good and evil through its choices, is often accused of making choices arbitrary. After all, I cannot choose some course of action *because* it is right or good if it is my choice that *makes* the course

---

12. See Jean-Paul Sartre, *Being and Nothingness*, trans. Hazel E. Barnes (New York: Washington Square, 1992), 724.

of action right or good. Hence, Alasdair MacIntyre famously criticizes such choices as "radical choices" that are ultimately arbitrary.[13] Kierkegaard, writing over a century before MacIntyre, makes essentially the same criticism.

The problem with the despair of defiance is that the "choices" of the self can always be undone: "the negative form of the self exercises a loosening power as well as a binding power; at any time it can quite arbitrarily start all over again" (SUD, 69). The commitments of such a self cannot give the individual a genuinely stable identity because the choices themselves lack stability. On this view, "the self is its own master" and seems to be absolute, but "this absolute ruler is a king without a country, actually ruling over nothing." His position is undermined by the fact that "rebellion is legitimate at any moment" (SUD, 69). I cannot really believe that something is good or right if I am conscious that I could at any moment make its opposite good or right by an arbitrary act of will. Meaningful choice requires some kind of power or "other" that in some way makes a *claim* on a person, a claim that the person does not arbitrarily invent but recognizes. The absolute freedom of the despair of defiance makes this recognition impossible, and this in turn leads to a self that is empty, that lacks concreteness. The relational structure of the human self means that it is not really possible to be a completely autonomous self, creating itself all by itself. In the final chapter, I shall return to this fundamental contrast between a self that is accountable and a self that tries to claim an absolute autonomy.

The despair of defiance is not spiritlessness but a form of negative spirituality that is approaching what Kierkegaard calls demonic spirituality, in which someone consciously and clear-headedly embraces what is bad. Such a person is miserable and knows himself to be miserable and yet chooses to remain in that misery. Kierkegaard compares a person in the grip of such despair to an author's error that somehow becomes conscious and confronts the author:

> Figuratively speaking, it is as if an error slipped into an author's writing and the error became conscious of itself as an error—perhaps it actually was not a mistake but in a much higher sense an essential part of the whole production—and now this error wants to mutiny against the author, out of

13. See Alasdair MacIntyre, *After Virtue* (London: Bloomsbury, 2011), for this criticism. Ironically, MacIntyre claims that Kierkegaard himself is the inventor of radical choice, failing to recognize that Kierkegaard clearly foresaw the problems with such choices long before the twentieth century.

hatred toward him, forbidding him to correct it and in maniacal defiance saying to him: No, I refuse to be erased; I will stand as a witness against you, a witness that you are a second-rate author. (SUD, 74)[14]

The person who is in the despair of weakness is not interested in "any consolation eternity has for him," because that person is simply "immediate" and only interested in finite goods (SUD, 74). The person in the grip of the despair of defiance also does not want to hear about eternity's consolation, but for a different reason. Such consolation might undermine the stance of the despairer, who spitefully wills his own ruin as a proof of God's lack of goodness.

## Despair as Sin and the Problem of Paganism

In part 2 of *The Sickness unto Death*, Kierkegaard reviews the different forms of despair, but from a higher, still more intense perspective. Despair is now explicitly described as sin. "Sin is: *before God, or with the conception of God, in despair not to will to be oneself, or in despair to will to be oneself*" (SUD, 77). As I will try to show in the next chapter, Kierkegaard does not think humans are ever totally lacking in an awareness of God. However, this awareness can be more or less conscious, and everything changes when there is an explicit awareness of God as God really is. Suppose I really understand who God is and know that I was created by God and am responsible to God to become the self God created me to be. In that situation, if I weakly fail to become myself or defiantly will to become some self I myself have created, the situation is much more intense and serious. Thus, when God reveals himself and his purposes for humans, the stakes are raised. Despair is transformed into sin, and the cure for despair is explicitly described as faith, ultimately faith in Christ who offers forgiveness for sin.

For the most part, I shall postpone my discussion of these important themes to chapters 6 through 8, where I will discuss the various forms of Christian spirituality. However, in the conclusion of this chapter, I want to look at Kierkegaard's discussion of paganism. Paganism poses a problem for

---

14. Interestingly, the Spanish author Miguel de Unamuno, who read *The Sickness unto Death* carefully and in fact underscored this very passage in his copy, did something like this in his novel *Mist*, in which the chief character, Augusto Pérez, confronts and challenges the author Unamuno.

Kierkegaard and his understanding of spirituality, and he clearly is drawn toward some apparently conflicting viewpoints.

The problem stems from the fact that sin is defined as a form of despair that involves a consciousness of God. Paganism, which for Kierkegaard means the classical Western world that did not possess the Christian revelation, lacks such a consciousness. Sin is a spiritual condition, but a human person who lacks spiritual development may not be capable of sinning. Kierkegaard poses the problem sharply:

> What a strange problem! Christianity regards everything as under sin; we have tried to depict the Christian point of view as rigorously as possible—and then this strange outcome emerges, this strange conclusion that sin is not to be found at all in paganism but only in Judaism and Christendom, and there again very seldom. (SUD, 101)

The problem is grounded in the fact that most people seem to live lives "almost too spiritless to be called sin" (SUD, 101).

Kierkegaard sees that there is an apparent contradiction between this and traditional Christian teachings. After all, the Scriptures clearly teach that pagans are lost, mired in sin, and in need of redemption. However, Kierkegaard sees paganism as "despairing ignorance of God." The pagan did not realize that humans exist before God; "paganism is 'to be without God in the world'" (SUD, 81). Kierkegaard admits that this implies that "in the strictest sense the pagan did not sin, for he did not sin before God, and all sin is before God" (SUD, 81).

However, Kierkegaard is reluctant to admit that the pagan gets a free pass, "even though in one sense it is also quite true that frequently a pagan is assisted in slipping blamelessly through the world simply because he is saved by his superficial Pelagian conception" (SUD, 81). The solution to the seeming contradiction is to see that this "superficial Pelagian conception" is itself a form of sin. From a Christian point of view, sin cannot be ignorance, as Socrates thought. What Socrates lacked was "a dialectical determinant appropriate to the transition from having understood something to doing it" (SUD, 93). Socrates assumes that someone who really understands what is good and right will act accordingly. If a person does not act accordingly, it shows that the person really did not understand. Christianity, however, has learned from revelation that sin is rooted in the will. The Greek mind was "too happy, too naïve, too esthetic, too ironic, too witty—too sinful—to grasp that anyone could knowingly not do the good, or knowingly, knowing what is right, do wrong" (SUD, 90). Christianity understands that sin is rooted not in the intellect but in "the will, defiance" (SUD, 90).

The solution to Kierkegaard's difficulty about paganism is this. Paganism does indeed manifest a kind of ignorance of God and, in comparison with the paganism in Christendom, has a lesser degree of guilt and a greater degree of naïveté and innocence. However, the pagan does have a capacity to know God; spirituality is an ontological quality of the human self. Hence, the pagan's ignorance is not total innocence. It is a willed ignorance and thus sinful, even if the sinfulness is less intense than someone who has a true understanding of God but is willing to defy God. How does it happen that a person is spiritless? "Is it something that happens to a person? No, it is his own fault. No one is born devoid of spirit, and no matter how many go to their death with this spiritlessness as the one and only outcome of their lives, it is not the fault of life" (SUD, 102).

Kierkegaard makes the above comment chiefly with the spiritlessness within Christendom in mind. But he clearly believes that those who do not have access to the Christian revelation of God nonetheless possess the possibility of some kind of knowledge of God. The sin of the pagan is the willful repression of the possibility of this knowledge. Kierkegaard here agrees with Paul in Romans 1, who says that there is a natural knowledge of God that is possible for everyone, a knowledge that makes humans to be "without excuse," even though it is a knowledge that sinful humans willfully turn away from.

This will be surprising to many readers, since there is a widespread view that Kierkegaard does not think God's existence can be known at all. Belief in God is supposed to require a "leap of faith," since the traditional proofs of God's existence all fail. This widespread view is simply mistaken. Kierkegaard never describes belief in God as the result of a "leap of faith." It is true that Kierkegaard does not think one can prove God's existence, but he also thinks that one needs no proof of God's existence. The leap of faith has nothing to do with believing in God; it has solely to do with belief in Jesus of Nazareth as the God-man.[15] It is the idea that God became incarnate that is for Kierkegaard "the absolute paradox," which poses a huge difficulty for human reason.

---

15. Strictly speaking, the phrase "leap of faith" does not appear anywhere in Kierkegaard's writings. However, he does clearly describe faith in Christ as something that requires a leap, but he never says anything like this about belief or faith in God. The metaphor of faith in Christ as requiring a leap comes from Lessing. See Kierkegaard's discussion of Lessing in CUP 1:93–105.

Kierkegaard believes that there is a natural knowledge of God, an awareness of God that does not depend on the Christian revelation. In the next chapter, I will spell out the nature of this awareness and the kind of spirituality that it makes possible in those who actualize it. I shall call this kind of spirituality "Socratic spirituality," since for Kierkegaard Socrates is the preeminent example of someone outside of Christian faith who nonetheless lived a spiritual life. An understanding of Socratic spirituality should give us a better grasp of non-Christian forms of spirituality, those forms both in other religions and in those that do not think of themselves as religious at all.

# CHAPTER 3

# Natural Knowledge of God

We have seen that spirituality is an ontological quality of the human self for Kierkegaard. It is, however, a quality that is given as possibilities that must be actualized. The self we are becoming is shaped by an ideal self that is a function of a relationship to something outside the self, something that is "other." No finite human is capable of inventing a self out of nothing. For the self to be fully itself, the "other" to which it relates must be God. We must ground our identities in God to become the selves God intends us to become.

However, we have also seen that the freedom we have as spiritual creatures allows us to ground our selves in things other than God: God-substitutes or idols. The usual idols are things such as wealth and fame. When the "other" that gives us our identity is taken from our society or culture, these are the kinds of ideals on offer, and the cultural and social forces that shape us naturally push us toward such ideals. This kind of idolatry could be called the spirituality of paganism, whether it be found in ancient Greece or modern Christendom, since Kierkegaard often describes it this way. We saw in the last chapter that Kierkegaard thinks that the common forms of despair, understood as loss of selfhood, involve this kind of devotion to finite, "worldly" goods.

Although Kierkegaard thinks that a genuine self must be rooted in a God-relationship, he does not think that genuine selfhood is possible only for Christians. Despite the negative use of the term "paganism," Kierkegaard does think that there are forms of spirituality outside of Christianity that have value or worth. Kierkegaard's pseudonym Johannes Climacus asserts this plainly: "A person existing religiously can express his relation to an eternal happiness (immortality, eternal life) outside Christianity, and it certainly has also been done" (CUP 1:559).

Kierkegaard agrees with Climacus about this, as can be seen from his treatment of Socrates. Kierkegaard greatly admires Socrates and continually holds him up as a model that even Christendom—especially Christendom—can learn much from. Kierkegaard is clear that Socrates was not a Christian thinker, although he says (perhaps humorously but also seriously) that he is "definitely convinced that he has become one" (PV, 54). Even though Kierkegaard says that he has faith in or "believes in" only one person, the Lord Jesus Christ, he nonetheless calls Socrates "my teacher" (PV, 55). In this chapter, I shall try to describe how it is possible to have a kind of spirituality that Kierkegaard finds admirable, one that shows a genuine religiosity, one that can be found in non-Christian religions and even in people who do not possess anything that resembles traditional religious faith. It is, I think, appropriate to call this "Socratic spirituality," since Socrates was for Kierkegaard an exemplar of it.

Since Kierkegaard sees genuine or authentic spirituality as something that requires a relation to God, this will require an account of what kind of relation to God a person can have outside of Christianity. In this chapter, I shall try to describe the knowledge of God that is the basis of this kind of spirituality. Then in chapters 4 and 5, I will try to describe the spirituality that this knowledge of God makes possible.

As I briefly asserted at the end of the last chapter, giving an account of how ordinary people might know God outside of the Christian revelation will require us to attack a commonly held myth about Kierkegaard, who is supposed to regard faith in God as something made possible by an irrational leap of faith. This myth has been popularized in books like Albert Camus's *The Myth of Sisyphus*, where Camus says that Kierkegaard recognized the absurdity of human existence but could not live with this absurdity and had to take recourse in a "leap."[1] This myth about Kierkegaard is doubly wrong. First, Kierkegaard never thinks of belief in God as irrational, though he often claims that it is irrational for people who claim to believe in God to live as if God did not exist. Second, Kierkegaard does not think this kind of faith in God requires anything like a "leap"—the leap specifically refers to faith that God became incarnate in Jesus of Nazareth.

Kierkegaard's view is in fact close to that of John Calvin, who famously says no proof of God's existence is necessary, because God has given hu-

1. See Albert Camus, *The Myth of Sisyphus* (New York: Penguin, 1979), 39–40.

mans a *sensus divinitatis*, a cognitive faculty whereby they naturally recognize God's reality.[2] In the remainder of this chapter, I shall try to give an account of what this knowledge of God outside of the Judeo-Christian revelation is like. In the next two chapters, I shall describe the kind of spirituality it makes possible, as well as provide illustrations of how such spirituality can be developed, by looking at some of Kierkegaard's *Upbuilding Discourses*.

## Natural Knowledge of God and "Subjectivity"

If our spirituality requires a relation to God as the "other" intended to be the ground of our identity, then it seems impossible for there to be healthy or authentic spirituality without some awareness of the divine. Kierkegaard believes, however, that humans do have a natural capacity to know God. Kierkegaard recognizes that our human knowledge of God is faulty and that people have many mistaken ideas about God. This does not, however, make it impossible for people to have a relation of sorts to God.

One reason this is so is that Kierkegaard does not value accurate propositional knowledge about God as highly as some religious thinkers, for two reasons. First, there are many people who have accurate propositional knowledge about God who really have no personal or existential relation to God. Second, there are also people who may have seriously mistaken ideas about God who nonetheless have a real relation to God.

This is surely the point Kierkegaard tries to make in the famous discussion of "truth as subjectivity" in *Concluding Unscientific Postscript*. In this section, the pseudonymous author, Johannes Climacus, makes a famous comparison between two characters:

> If someone who lives in the midst of Christianity, with knowledge of the true idea of God, enters the house of God, the house of the true God, and prays, but prays in untruth, and if someone lives in an idolatrous land but prays with all the passion of infinity, although his eyes are resting upon the image of an idol—where, then, is there more truth? The one prays in truth to God, although he is worshipping an idol; the other prays in untruth to

2. See John Calvin, *Institutes of the Christian Religion*. Calvin's view has been vigorously defended by Alvin Plantinga and other "Reformed epistemologists." See Alvin Plantinga, *Warranted Christian Belief* (Oxford: Oxford University Press, 2000).

the true God, and is therefore in truth worshipping an idol. (CUP 1:201; translation modified)[3]

The first thing to notice about this passage is that Kierkegaard is not denying the objectivity of propositional truth. On the contrary, his descriptions of the person in Christendom and the pagan make no sense unless there is objective truth. The pagan's beliefs about God are wrong, while the person in Christendom is said to have correct beliefs. Nor does Kierkegaard say or imply that propositional truth is unimportant or has no value at all. In fact, later in the same chapter, Climacus makes it clear that he understands that propositional truth is indeed significant, even though he still wants to put more emphasis on the importance of how truth is appropriated: "Exactly as important as the truth, and if one of the two must be preferred still more important, is the manner in which the truth is received" (CUP 1:247; translation modified).

What the passage about "truth as subjectivity" implies is that humans can have a kind of direct awareness of God even when their understanding of the God they are aware of is faulty. This is not surprising. We sometimes have direct experience of something without realizing precisely what it is we are experiencing. I might, for example, come into a dark house and bump into a furry animal, thinking it is a cat, when in fact it is a dog. A person can still learn from such an experience, and what is learned may be valuable in how the person responds. If I bump into a strange animal, thinking is it a cat when it is a dog, I still may be wise to back away and refrain from threatening gestures that might provoke the animal to attack me.

Philosophers sometimes use the Latin terms *de re* and *de dicto* to distinguish knowledge of reality from propositional knowledge. To know something *de re* is to know an object, something real. To have knowledge *de dicto* is to have knowledge through a "dictum" or through words. Normally, the two kinds of knowledge go together, and each seems to enrich the other. We understand more about reality when we have the right conceptual understanding; we understand our concepts better when they are put to use to get us in touch with reality through experience. However, sometimes

---

3. Here and going forward, where I have indicated "translation modified," I give the Hong pagination, but the translation is my own from the Danish *Samlede Værker*, 1st ed. (in this case vol. 7), the corresponding pages for which can be found in the margins of cited Hong edition (in this case CUP).

the two are distinguishable, and that seems especially true for knowledge about God.

The point or value of knowing about God is that such knowledge may make possible a personal relationship to God. Even though propositional knowledge about God can make this possible, and should do so, it does not create such a relationship unless the person who has the knowledge has the right kind of concerns or "subjectivity." The person in the example in Christendom who prays to God in "untruth" is for Kierkegaard someone who has only a verbal or rote knowledge about God, a knowledge that makes no difference to the way the person lives. The situation of the pagan who worships the idol is far from ideal, and Kierkegaard does not mean to say that it is ideal. However, at least this pagan's understanding of God, flawed as it may be, is reflected in his actions. Kierkegaard thinks that the pagan in this situation may in fact be praying to the actual God and therefore may have a relation of sorts with God, however faulty his understanding of God may be. The passion of the pagan, who is pictured as someone who yearns for God and longs to connect with God, is in fact an openness to God, and perhaps something of God's character is still reflected in the unconditional character of the pagan's passion.

Kierkegaard's view that it is possible to have a relationship with God even if one lacks accurate propositional knowledge of God is controversial. One can see this from the debates that erupted in America after the 9-11 terror attacks over whether Christians and Muslims "worship the same God." It is certainly true that Christians and Muslims have some different beliefs about God. For Christians, God is a Trinity, and Jesus of Nazareth is one of the persons of the Trinity. Muslims say that this is an abandonment of monotheism. Despite these disagreements, Kierkegaard would say that from a *de re* perspective, if a Christian and a Muslim pray to God, understood as the one God who created the universe, they must be praying to the same God. What other God could they be praying to? There is only one such God; no other deities exist. Once one sees the possibility of *de re* awareness of God, it is easier to understand how Kierkegaard, as a Christian thinker, nonetheless thinks that non-Christians may have an awareness of God and even a relationship of sorts with God, despite the fact that their understanding of God may be faulty. It may even be possible for someone who believes there is no God, or at least someone who thinks that this is what he or she believes, to have a kind of relation to God.

## Kierkegaard's Account of Natural Religious Knowledge[4]

How is this knowledge of God possible? There is an obscure footnote in Kierkegaard's *Philosophical Fragments* in which Johannes Climacus, the pseudonymous author, describes a man who wants to prove the existence of God as "a superb theme for crazy comedy!" (PF, 43n). In Kierkegaard's *Papirer*, we find a much a longer version of this footnote that was deleted from the final manuscript of the book. In the long version, Kierkegaard (and at this stage of composition the book is attributed to Kierkegaard himself rather than the pseudonym) explains why the situation is comical by imagining "a man deluded into thinking that he could prove that God exists—and then have an atheist accept it by virtue of the other's proof" (PF, 191; translation modified). This is comic because both the man producing the proof and the atheist are "fantastic" figures, that is, figures that cannot exist in real life: "Just as no one has ever proved it [God's existence], so there has never been an atheist, even though there certainly have been many who have been unwilling to allow what they know [that God exists] to have control of their minds" (PF, 191–92).

Did Kierkegaard really think that there has never been an atheist? Since the long version of this footnote was deleted before publication, one might think that Kierkegaard thought better of this extravagant claim before publishing the book. However, a more plausible explanation of the deletion is this: Kierkegaard made the change to the book at the last minute, when he decided to attribute the book to the humorist Johannes Climacus, removing his own name as author and inserting it as editor. Since Climacus as a pseudonymous character does not claim to be a Christian, it is plausible to think that the footnote accurately expressed Kierkegaard's own viewpoint, but he recognized that it did not fit with the views of the enigmatic Climacus, who does not tell us (in *Fragments*) what his own religious commitments are.

I shall argue that it is precisely the longer version of the footnote that expresses Kierkegaard's own view of what I shall call natural religious knowledge. That view can only be called a forthright version of Platonism, as a later passage in the deleted footnote makes clear: "With respect to the existence of God, immortality, etc., in short, with respect to all problems of immanence,

---

4. This section of this chapter is largely taken, with significant revisions, from my article "Kierkegaard, Natural Theology, and the Existence of God," in *Kierkegaard and Christian Faith*, ed. Paul Martens and C. Stephen Evans (Waco, TX: Baylor University Press, 2016), 25–38.

recollection applies; it [the knowledge that can be recollected] exists altogether in every man, only he does not know it" (PF, 192).

## Kierkegaard: Platonist or Existentialist?

Of course, the idea that Kierkegaard was a kind of Christian Platonist fits poorly with the popular conception of Kierkegaard as the father of existentialism. That popular conception goes something like this: Kierkegaard recognized that the traditional rational arguments for God were a failure and thus that belief in God has no rational basis. However, because life without God would be meaningless and absurd, he taught that humans, through an heroic act of will, ought to take "a leap of faith" and believe in God anyway. Writers such as Camus thought that this "leap" was weak and unmanly; the truly heroic figure is like Sisyphus, who ceaselessly pushes the rock up the mountain, while knowing how hopeless his task is. The rock is fated to roll down the mountain again. Despite the pointlessness of his life, Sisyphus refuses the leap and simply embraces the absurdity of existence.[5]

Oddly, even some Christian writers have embraced Camus's view of Kierkegaard. Francis Schaeffer, for example, in his comprehensive story of the intellectual history of Western culture, credits Kierkegaard with the invention of a "two-story universe," with upper and lower spheres separated by "the line of despair."[6] On this view, Kierkegaard saw that the universe as understood by modern thinkers was meaningless, and so he postulated an irrational "upper story" of religious truth to provide meaning and purpose.

This popular conception of Kierkegaard as an existentialist who gave up on reason because reason offers us only a meaningless and hopeless world is completely false. Kierkegaard is suspicious of what modernity calls "reason" not because it leads to a meaningless and absurd view of life. Rather, "reason" is suspect because, for Kierkegaard, it is closely tied to a kind of worldly shrewdness that makes humans all too content with a life that is shallow and meaningless. This kind of "reason" has no difficulty with belief in God *per se*. The problem is that all too often it produces a belief in a God who is perfectly suited to rationalize a life of middle-class conformity that undermines a person's spiritual dignity. However, it is not inevitable that

5. Camus, *Myth of Sisyphus*, 108.
6. Francis Schaeffer, *The God Who Is There* (Downers Grove, IL: InterVarsity, 1968).

the natural awareness of God should take this form. The figure of Socrates shows that, even apart from Christianity, a person can be aware of God in a way that makes the person's life noble and risky.

I shall try to show that Kierkegaard thinks that God's reality is or should be obvious to every human person. He is opposed to proofs of God's existence primarily because they make something that could be known by anyone appear to be doubtful. On his view, a person who attempts to prove God's existence is actually working against himself. He is like a man who announces he wishes to give the other people in his village a large sum of money but first offers them an elaborate argument that he is doing a good thing. Their natural reaction will be suspicion, both of his argument and of his offer.

### Natural Theology and Natural Religious Knowledge

Kierkegaard's critique of arguments for God's existence has given him the reputation of a critic of natural theology. Does he reject natural theology? Well, it depends upon what we mean by natural theology. If one thinks that natural theology necessarily involves an attempt to argue for God's existence from some kind of objective, detached standpoint, then Kierkegaard certainly rejects natural theology. He rejects the idea of a proof of God's existence, partly, as I said, because it makes it appear that there might be some doubt about the matter, but also because the stance of the one who constructs the proof, one that Kierkegaard sees as objective and detached, takes one's gaze away from the factors that make it possible for actual humans to know God.

Suppose, however, that someone thinks that natural theology could consist of an account of how a natural knowledge of God is possible, a plausible story about how an awareness of God's reality could be acquired that is not dependent on God's special revelation in the history of Israel that culminates in Jesus of Nazareth. If that is what natural theology is or could be, then Kierkegaard is not opposed to natural theology at all. It is true that he does not focus very much on epistemological issues and spends little time giving an account of how natural religious knowledge is possible. He thinks that a person can have an awareness of God's reality without having a *theory* about how such awareness is possible. Nevertheless, one can see embedded in his writings an account of how ordinary people know that God is real. Kierkegaard both accepts the reality of natural religious knowledge and has a view about how such knowledge is possible. On my view, Kierkegaard thus offers something that could reasonably be described as natural theology.

Before proceeding, let me first say something about the use of the word "knowledge" in this context. I want to speak of natural religious knowledge as a form of knowledge because I think it satisfies all the epistemological *desiderata* one might have for something to count as knowledge. If God exists, then when ordinary people believe there is a God, their belief is true. Furthermore, I would argue that, at least if my preferred epistemological views are right, they are sometimes justified in holding the belief; I would then argue further that it is even possible for them to have a degree of confidence or certitude in their belief. To me this sounds like knowledge, though clearly it is nothing like knowledge in the modern scientific sense of the word. However, nothing important hinges on my use of the word "knowledge," and if someone thinks that these religious beliefs would be better described as something like "justified beliefs," that person may just substitute that terminology for mine.

## Kierkegaard's Analysis of Modernity and the Decline of Religious Faith

It is well known that Kierkegaard's pseudonymous authorship has a novel-like quality. The pseudonymous writings are attributed to characters with outlandish names: Victor Eremita, Constantine Constantius, Hilarius Book-binder, Johannes de Silentio, and Johannes Climacus, to mention just a few. Furthermore, many other characters appear as part of the volumes, including Johannes the Seducer and some other aesthetes who make drunken speeches about women in the first part of *Stages on Life's Way*, the young man from *Repetition*, Judge William, and so on. One remarkable fact that is seldom noticed is that in this amazing panoply of characters there is not a single atheist. Even the Seducer from *Either/Or I* speaks in a matter-of-fact way about God: "After all, my God is not the God who belongs to me, but the God to whom I belong" (EO 1:406). It is true that the Seducer seems not to care very much about God and can even take a cynical view of God, as he takes a cynical view of everything. But he never denies the reality of God. He is no Sam Harris or Richard Dawkins.

Why should this be so? I suspect it is because Kierkegaard simply does not take the figure of the vehement atheist seriously. Of course, Kierke-gaard knows that there are people who *describe themselves* as atheists or free-thinkers and mentions them from time to time, sometimes comparing them favorably with people who claim to believe in God but have little concern or passion for God. Unlike conformist representatives of Christendom, the "evangelical atheist" feels some passion about the matter, and Kierkegaard sees this as a good thing. However, Kierkegaard feels no need to respond to the challenge to religious faith posed by the evangelical atheist. The closest he comes to a response is the diagnosis given in *The Sickness unto Death* about the person who declares Christianity to be false. Such a person is described as one who is in the grip of offense, seen as the most intense form of despair (SUD, 125–31). From Kierkegaard's perspective, someone who claims to be an atheist is truly a person who "is unwilling to allow what he knows [that God exists] to have power over his mind" (PF, 191–92; translation modified). To take the arguments of such people too seriously is to fail to recognize that their own unbelief is a motivated unbelief, involving what a Freudian would call repressed knowledge.

Kierkegaard's pseudonym Johannes Climacus surely speaks for Kierkegaard as well when he criticizes the idea of proving God's existence: "To prove the existence of one who is present (*er til*) is the most shameless affront, since it is an attempt to make him ridiculous; . . . For how could it occur to anyone to prove that he exists, unless one had permitted oneself to ignore him, and then makes matters worse by proving his existence right before his nose" (CUP 1:545; translation modified). God is (or ought to be) present to a human being, and if a person feels the need to argue for God's existence, that is a reliable sign that the person is ignoring the ways God is present to that individual or has lost or never acquired the skill whereby one recognizes God. Climacus goes on to compare God to a king and says that if a person who was in the "majestic presence" of a king tried to prove the king's existence, he would in effect be making a fool of the king. No, one indicates an awareness of the king by an appropriate expression of submission. Similarly, one "proves" God's existence by worship (CUP 1:545–46).

But how is God present to human individuals? The answer is that God is present as the moral lawgiver, the one with authority who demands of us that we become a certain kind of person. God is the Lord, and if he is not known as the one who must be obeyed, he is not really known at all. We know that there is a God because we recognize that we are beings who are accountable for how we live our lives. God is known simply as the one to whom we are accountable. Climacus makes this point by arguing that God cannot clearly be discerned in world history, because "as it [world history] is seen by humans, God does not play the role of Lord; as one does not see the ethical in it, therefore God is not seen either" (CUP 1:156; translation modified). We see God when we see the world through ethical lenses.

For Kierkegaard, anyone who has a moral conscience has an awareness of God's requirements, for to have a conscience is simply to have a "relationship in which you as a single individual relate yourself to yourself before God" (UDVS, 129). Similarly, *The Sickness unto Death* explains that God's judgment, unlike the judgment of a human judge or authority, cannot be evaded by humans mutinying as a group or crowd, because God judges humans as single individuals. Kierkegaard actually says that God's judgment in eternity will be easy (he says "a child could pass judgment in eternity" [SUD, 124; translation modified]) because human persons through conscience make a "report" about their guilt each time they sin. Thus, Kierkegaard believes that anyone who has a conscience has a *de re* relation with God, even if the person is unaware that God is the source of the authority of conscience, indeed, even if the person believes there is no God (SUD, 123–24).

Support for this view is also found in *Works of Love*, where Kierkegaard also claims that God is the source of our ethical duties. God has a justifiable claim on our obedience, because he is the one who created us out of nothing and has destined us for a life of love and happiness in relation to himself and others. Just as human lovers acquire obligations to each other through their history of interactions, so God has a claim on us due to our history with God: "But that eternal love-history has begun much earlier; it began with your beginning, when you came into existence out of nothing, and just as surely as you do not become nothing, it does not end at a grave" (WL, 150). Because of this debt to God, we must obey God: "But you shall love God in unconditional obedience, even if what he requires of you might seem to you to be to your own harm, indeed, harmful to his cause; for God's wisdom is beyond all comparison with yours. . . . All you have to do is obey in love" (WL, 20).

Modernity is understood by Kierkegaard as a kind of concerted mutiny against this divine authority, an attempt to depose God as our moral ruler and usurp his role as moral lawgiver. The modern world is "a more or less open intent to depose God in order to install human beings . . . in the rights of God" (WL, 115). We think that morality's requirements can be determined either by individual humans or by some kind of social agreement. The latter proposal is one that Kierkegaard mocks: "Or should the determination of what is the Law's requirement perhaps be an agreement among, a common decision by, all people, to which the individual has to submit? Splendid—that is, if it is possible to find the place and fix a date for this assembling of all people (all the living, all of them?—but what about the dead?), and if it is possible, something that is equally impossible, for all of them to agree on one thing!" (WL, 115). The result of the mutiny is moral confusion and moral disintegration. The only solution to the problem, according to Kierkegaard, is for "each one separately, [to] receive our orders" from God (WL, 117).

Of course, modernity sees this mutiny not as a revolt but as liberation, the achievement of full human autonomy. Kierkegaard steadfastly rejects such a view of human freedom. An absolute freedom turns out to be a meaningless freedom, since meaningful choices require a world where there are real distinctions between good and evil, right and wrong. The "vortex" unleashed by modernity makes meaningful choice impossible. Being accountable to God is not incompatible with genuine freedom, since it is only when we are "infinitely bound to God" that we can be genuinely free (WL, 147–49).

This idea that true freedom is linked to being accountable is central to Kierkegaard's thought, but it is often ignored, because such a claim is so contrary to the prevailing ethos of contemporary Western culture. We think that freedom means being completely autonomous. We talk about "holding people accountable" for their actions, but what we really mean is that we want them to be punished when they do what we do not like. We like to see *others* held accountable for their behavior, but we ourselves do not like being responsible to others.

This is not a new way of thinking, of course. In Plato's *Republic*, Thrasymachus notoriously says that the freest and happiest person is the tyrant who answers to no one and decides what is "just" or "unjust" to benefit himself. Thrasymachus argues that those who must obey authorities are always at a disadvantage in comparison with those who are not accountable to someone.[7] The biblical story of the fall of Adam and Eve provides an even better illustration of how much we humans seek to evade accountability. When the serpent tempts Eve to eat of the fruit of the forbidden tree, the enticement offered is that, by disobeying God's command, the humans will themselves "become like gods."

This human aversion to accountability is sometimes justifiable. The authorities to whom we are accountable are frequently corrupt, self-serving, manipulative, or just plain evil. It is reasonable to seek to be free from accountability to such people. However, it does not follow from this that the best condition is to be accountable to no one at all. Kierkegaard believes that what makes human life truly human is the fact that humans find themselves subject to what we might call a claim to live in particular ways, a claim that

7. Plato, *Republic* 336–56.

comes from beyond the self. (If the self were itself the source of the claim, then the self could release itself from the claim.) To be free from this claim is not to be liberated, but to be cast into a nihilistic vortex where choice itself becomes meaningless.

Kierkegaard believes that only God can be the source of this claim. We cannot make sense of its unconditional character or its objectivity if we think it is grounded in some kind of social agreement or in self-interest. It is true that people who are aware of this claim may not recognize its true source. Kierkegaard himself says that divine authority has sometimes been called by "thinkers" something else: "the idea" or "the true" or "the good" (WL, 339). True to his view that people can have a *de re* awareness of God without an adequate *de dicto* understanding of God, he is thus open to the idea that a person can be aware of God's claim on his or her life without realizing that the claim comes from God. God is, however, the true source of authority.

Kierkegaard thus holds a divine-command view of moral obligations.[8] The demands of duty are literally God's requirements for us, and the voice of conscience is the voice of God. The fact that our moral duties are divine commands does not mean that morality is in any way arbitrary. Kierkegaard is not a radical voluntarist who thinks that God simply decides what is good and makes it good by his will. God himself is the good, and God is love. His commands are necessarily aimed at fostering love in us. Nevertheless, the acts God commands acquire a new status by virtue of the fact that God commands them. When we violate his commands, our actions are not only bad because our actions no longer aim at the good. They are wrong because they constitute a failure to acknowledge the debt we owe to God. They disrupt our relation to God, who has a rightful claim on our love and obedience. All sins are therefore sins against God (SUD, 80).

One might object here that this cannot be so, because the dictates of conscience are heavily shaped by contingent cultural factors. Some people believe that morality demands that dead human bodies be buried; others think that morality demands that dead human bodies be cremated, or exposed to vultures. Surely such contradictory duties cannot all be the voice of God. Are not our human consciences too obviously all too human in their origin to stem from God?

Kierkegaard agrees that conscience is highly shaped by contingent historical factors. He completely rejects the Kantian fable that human morality

8. For a full explanation and defense of this, see C. Stephen Evans, *Kierkegaard's Ethic of Love: Divine Commands and Moral Obligations* (Oxford: Oxford University Press, 2004).

is something we come to know by pure, *a priori* reason. We come to know right and wrong through history; we are taught what is right and wrong by our parents and elders. And there are indeed large differences in the moral traditions of various cultures. But this fact does not disturb him, for two reasons. One is a distinction between the form and content of our moral lives. The most important fact about our moral lives is that we recognize that we have duties; we are morally accountable beings. If we have mistaken views about the *content* of some of our moral duties, we still rightly recognize ourselves as morally accountable beings. Second is a conviction that, even with all the cultural chatter, some genuine information about what God requires gets through. There is a quality in humans that Kierkegaard calls "primitivity," which refers to an authentic awareness of God's requirements that, despite the distractions of cultural relativity, is possible for humans to recognize (TA, 129).[9]

Once we recognize that the claims of conscience come from God, then the way is open to recognizing that accountability to God is not a curse but a blessing. Accountability to someone who is selfish or corrupt may indeed be a bad thing. However, it cannot be bad to be accountable to someone who is completely good, who is perfectly knowledgeable, and who desires only your own good. Therefore, when the right conditions are met, accountability is not an evil to be avoided but a gift to be welcomed. In such a situation, accountability is a virtue.

## Kierkegaard on the Crisis of Faith in Western Culture

We should now be able to understand why Kierkegaard is not enthusiastic about a certain kind of apologetic argument for religious belief. Many apologists for religion implicitly accept what I would call the "standard narrative" about why religious faith has declined among intellectuals in Europe and North America in the last two hundred years, the same narrative that is accepted by many religious skeptics. The narrative is simple, memorably expressed in Bertrand Russell's famous quip about what he would say to God if, after death, Russell discovered that he had been wrong and that God was real after all. Russell said he would simply tell God, "Not enough evidence."[10]

9. I discuss this concept briefly, as well as the difficulty of translating Kierkegaard's *Primitivitet* into English, in chapter 2.

10. As attributed to Russell by Wesley C. Salmon, "Religion and Science: A New Look at

On this account, religious belief has declined primarily for intellectual reasons. Hume and Kant undermined the rational case for God by showing that the proofs for God's existence do not work. Modern science has shown that the natural world can be explained without reference to theology. Historical biblical criticism has undermined belief that the Bible is an inspired revelation from God. All such accounts presume that modern intellectuals have rejected belief in God because of their intelligence and intellectual honesty. Belief has declined because we have become more intelligent and less credulous. The apologist attempts to save the situation by showing that Russell was wrong. We do have enough evidence, and the attacks on faith can be answered.

Kierkegaard simply does not buy this narrative. He thinks it gives an overly flattering view of secular intellectuals; it presumes that they would be quite willing to believe if only their intellectual problems were solved. On Kierkegaard's view, religious faith has declined among some intellectuals not because they are so smart, but because their imaginations are weak and their emotional lives are impoverished. If intellectuals do not believe in God, it is either because they do not want to believe or because the natural human capacities that ought to allow them to recognize God at work in their lives have atrophied and are no longer working properly.

I think it is because Kierkegaard does not accept the standard narrative for why religious faith has declined that he does not ascribe to epistemology the importance it has had for most modern Western philosophers. Modern Western philosophy begins with Locke and Descartes and is inspired from the beginning by the anxieties fueled by religious disagreements and the scientific revolution. Most modern philosophers have, as John Dewey thought, been engaged in a quest for objective certainty; they have sought a method that will vanquish uncertainty and give us truth that is final and sure. For this reason, modern philosophy is dominated by epistemological concerns.

---

Hume's Dialogues," *Philosophical Studies* 33 (1978): 176. The source of this quotation appears to be Leo Rosten's interview with Bertrand Russell in the *Saturday Review/World* (February 23, 1974): 25–26. Rosten recounts asking Russell, "'Let us suppose, sir, that after you have left this sorry vale, you actually found yourself in heaven, standing before the Throne. There, in all his glory, sat the Lord—not Lord Russell, sir: God.' Russell winced. 'What would you think?' 'I would think I was dreaming' [Russell replied]. 'But suppose you realized you were not? Suppose that there, before your very eyes, beyond a shadow of a doubt *was* God. What would you say?' The pixie wrinkled his nose. 'I probably would ask, "Sir, why did you not give me better evidence?"'"

Kierkegaard does not share this obsession with epistemology. To be sure, he has epistemological views.[11] However, Kierkegaard does not think that knowledge depends on epistemology. He rejects the idea that until we have the right theory of knowledge, we can't know anything. Philosophy of knowledge is like philosophy of art; we could not begin to theorize about art if we did not have recognizable examples of art. Similarly, we could make no progress in giving an account of knowledge if we did not already know some things prior to philosophizing about knowledge.

Knowledge does not have to wait for epistemology, and religious knowledge is not dependent on apologetics. Kierkegaard does not embark, as did so many modern Western philosophers, on a quest for a method that will give us humans objective certainty about the questions that concern us the most. Such a method would give all normal humans, regardless of their abilities and concerns, a guaranteed access to the truth. Instead, Kierkegaard thinks we must accept and embrace our finitude. We are historically situated creatures. The path to truth for us is not one that leads us to the "view from nowhere," that perspective Spinoza put forward as the human ideal, by which we seek to see the world as God sees it, "under the aspect of eternity." Rather, we must see the world as God has created us to see it, as finite, fallible (and sinful) creatures. We can achieve the truth we need by becoming the creatures we were created to be. If we fail to grasp truths we ought to know, we must not assume the problem lies in the evidence rather than in ourselves. We must not assume that a failure to know is always a result of a lack of evidence. Knowledge may not always depend on evidence at all.[12] Even when knowledge does depend on evidence, a failure to gain knowledge may be a result of a person's inability to understand and appreciate evidence, or an inability to have the experiences that might provide the evidence.

11. Marilyn Piety has published a fine book on Kierkegaard's epistemology: *Ways of Knowing: Kierkegaard's Pluralist Epistemology* (Waco, TX: Baylor University Press, 2010).

12. The view that knowledge is not always the result of evidence but is what happens when humans are related to reality in the right way is called "externalism" in epistemology. Having evidence is just one way such a relation can be established. For some defenses of externalism, see William Alston, *Epistemic Justification* (Ithaca, NY: Cornell University Press, 1989); D. M. Armstrong, *Belief, Truth, and Knowledge* (Cambridge: Cambridge University Press, 1973); Fred Dretske, *Knowledge and the Flow of Information* (Cambridge, MA: MIT Press, 1981); Alvin Goldman, "What Is Justified Belief?" in *Justification and Knowledge*, ed. G. Pappas (Dordrecht: D. Reidel, 1979); and Alvin Plantinga, *Warrant and Proper Function* (New York: Oxford University Press, 1993). For a short defense of such a view directed at theologians and biblical scholars, see chapter 9 of C. Stephen Evans, *The Historical Christ and the Jesus of Faith: The Incarnational Narrative as History* (Oxford: Oxford University Press, 1996).

## Subjectivity and Religious Knowledge

What does this mean? Partly, it means recognizing that we are not purely thinking things, but embodied persons whose lives, including our intellectual lives, are deeply shaped by our hearts. What a person knows and believes is intimately connected to what a person desires and fears and hopes and loves. Our emotions and passions are not just distorting filters that must be peeled away if we are to see reality as it is; they are—sometimes—factors (skills or capacities) that allow us to connect with the world in the right way.

Once we understand that our natural religious knowledge comes to us through conscience and our knowledge of the ethical, we can see why Kierkegaard is the great philosopher of subjectivity. For the emotions and passions play an essential role in becoming aware of what is good and what is bad, what is right and what is wrong.[13] We cannot see the need to help another if we cannot feel compassion for the suffering of the other. We cannot aspire to live courageously if we are not inspired by courageous actions. We cannot value honesty if we cannot feel the shamefulness of a shabby lie told to save a few bucks.

It is in and through the passions and emotions that we become aware of God's claim on our lives. The person who lacks this sense of the ethical lacks "primitivity." People who lack this quality will not be helped simply by acquiring more information or becoming scientifically educated. These "remedies" may only make the problem worse, by strengthening a person's "objective" attitude toward human life. What such a person needs is not primarily apologetical arguments. Rather, the person needs to care more deeply about the point of living a human life, a caring that will lead to that kind of deep thinking that Kierkegaard calls "subjective thinking."

The concept of subjective thinking has nothing to do with being arbitrary. It is not tied to wish fulfillment, and it is fully compatible with a searing honesty and concern for truth. It centers on the passionate kind of thinking that grips a person when a person thinks such thoughts as this: "I have but one life to live, and that life is finite. Death looms ahead for me. What then

13. For a defense of the role emotions play in acquiring moral knowledge, see Adam C. Pelser and Robert C. Roberts, "Religious Value and Moral Psychology," in *Handbook of Value: Perspectives from Economics, Neuroscience, Philosophy, Psychology, and Sociology*, ed. Tobias Brosch and David Sander (Oxford: Oxford University Press, 2015); as well as Adam C. Pelser, "Philosophy in *The Abolition of Man*," in *Contemporary Perspectives on C. S. Lewis's* The Abolition of Man: *History, Philosophy, Education, and Science*, ed. Timothy M. Mosteller and Gayne John Anacker (London: Bloomsbury Academic, 2017).

should I do with my life? What is its purpose and meaning?" Such a person will be open to hearing the voice of conscience, and conscience will have for that person the kind of authority that testifies to its divine origin. Subjective thinking of this sort is the foundation of a healthy spiritual life.

## Natural Religious Knowledge and Christian Revelation

Far from denying that humans have a natural knowledge of God, it would be closer to the truth to say that Kierkegaard simply takes for granted that humans can know that God exists through their awareness of God's claim on their lives. He takes this for granted, but it never becomes a major or central theme in his works. If spirituality is primarily something that arises out of a relation to God, this means that there is a kind of natural spirituality, something that can and does exist outside of Christianity. In the next chapter, I shall go on to describe the nature of this form of spirituality.

Nevertheless, I think it is correct to say Kierkegaard is not primarily interested in this natural knowledge of God or the spirituality it makes possible, for their own sake. He gives a lot of attention to them, but he is primarily interested in them as possible precursors to Christian faith and Christian spirituality. He does not make the natural knowledge of God or Socratic spirituality the main focus of his writings because he believes that in comparison to the knowledge of God and the kind of spirituality made possible by Christianity, they are poor things. Kierkegaard discusses this "Socratic" spirituality for two reasons. The first is that, even if it is "pagan," it is often far above the kind of spirituality (or lack thereof) to be found in contemporary Christendom. It provides a measuring stick that shows how shallow the spirituality of people who think they are Christians actually is. The second point is that it provides a starting point for the development of "subjectivity," providing the soil that must be present if genuine Christianity is to be understood and accepted. Kierkegaard thinks that the development of "inwardness" and "subjectivity" in contemporary people would do far more to revitalize Christian faith than apologetics.[14]

14. I should like to say at this point that, while I fully agree with Kierkegaard that apologetics alone will never produce a healthy Christian church and that the church needs many things more than it needs apologetics, I do not agree with him that apologetics is not valuable. In fact, I believe that Kierkegaard himself practices a type of apologetics. See C. Stephen Evans, "Apologetic Arguments in *Philosophical Fragments*," which appears as chapter 8 in C. Stephen Evans, *Kierkegaard on Faith and the Self: Collected Essays* (Waco, TX: Baylor University Press,

So why does Kierkegaard think that this natural religious knowledge, and the spirituality it makes possible, is not very valuable when compared with what genuine Christianity offers? The real answer to this question will not be clear until I have described in detail the character of both Socratic and Christian spirituality. However, I can say at this point that one major problem with our natural religious knowledge of God is that this knowledge is highly unreliable, shot through with mistakes. In the very footnote in which Kierkegaard claims that there are no atheists, he makes this point. In claiming that all humans know about God and immortality, Kierkegaard says that all this knowledge is obtained by "recollection," clearly signifying that this knowledge is gained through natural human capacities and not through a supernatural revelation. Though everyone has this knowledge, at least implicitly, Kierkegaard adds that the conceptions of God and immortality that people have "may be very inadequate." In other words, people may rightly know that there is a God but have very mistaken ideas about what God is like, and these mistakes can and do distort the forms of spirituality connected to this knowledge of God.

I think Kierkegaard is right about this. Religious belief may indeed be something that humans are hardwired to have. Evolutionary psychologists today are increasingly drawn to the view that humans have an innate tendency to form a belief in God or gods, as can be seen by the ubiquity of religious belief in every tribal culture. However, the wild diversity of the beliefs this natural disposition produces shows that it cannot be reliable in its content. Kierkegaard himself is very aware of the Feuerbachian point that we humans have a strong tendency to create a God in our image. Our natural knowledge of God is thus riddled with error, distorted by wish fulfillment and self-deception. We have an inveterate tendency to soften God's requirements and to create for ourselves a God who will baptize and sanctify our own desires and demands instead of holding us accountable to his laws. The resulting spirituality will be one that too often flatters us or is invented to satisfy our wishes, although Kierkegaard does not think that this must always be the case. There is always the splendid example of Socrates to show what is possible.

The fact that our natural religious knowledge is unreliable in its content does not mean it has no value at all. C. S. Lewis says somewhere that he was asked whether he does not worry that England was becoming a pagan

---

2006). Also relevant is chapter 9, "The Relevance of Historical Evidence for the Christian Faith: A Critique of a Kierkegaardian View."

country, and his answer was "Would that it were so." The reason is not hard to discern. Missionaries have always found cultures that adhere to "pagan" or tribal religions to be fertile ground for converts. Such people already know that there is a God or gods and often know that there is a supreme or "high God." They know the importance of the spiritual realm and want to have the right kind of relation to the gods. They bear a sensitivity to the divine in ways that middle-class conformist people in Christendom often do not. The missionary's task is then to help the "pagan" people come to understand God's true nature and how to respond to him.

Natural religious knowledge, when it is motivated by a passionate desire to know and please God, can then have genuine value as a preparation for the gospel. This is clearly what Kierkegaard has in mind in *Concluding Unscientific Postscript* when he has Climacus describe "Religiousness A," a kind of natural religiousness that is possible outside of Christianity, which I will discuss in chapter 4. The spirituality of the pagan, while it may be a poor thing in comparison with genuine Christianity, can also be the starting point for the kind of personal development that is necessary for people in contemporary culture to understand and appreciate Christian faith. The pagan is wrestling with deep and genuine existential questions, and if someone wishes to become a Christian, he or she will have to acquire the ability to wrestle with those questions as well. This capacity does not come automatically as a result of knowing a lot about science or history, especially if that knowledge is "objective" and detached.

Kierkegaard never confuses Christian faith with natural religious knowledge, and no one has a deeper appreciation of the necessity for God to reveal himself to us via special revelation if we are to know God truly and relate to him as we ought. However, to say that the true knowledge of God requires us to hear and respond to God's Word addressed to us does not mean that, apart from Christian faith, atheism would be the most rational view of the universe. The natural knowledge of God made possible through subjectivity still retains value. Even those who have not come to know God in Jesus can still recognize that there is a transcendent reality and that they are accountable to that reality. Without some natural religious knowledge of this sort, we would not even be able to understand the gospel. The gospel is the answer for the human condition and its central problem, but if we do not understand the problem, we cannot understand how the solution can be the solution. Natural knowledge of God is not the gospel, and it is not the solution to the human problem. It can, however, be the starting point of a journey that will enable a person to grasp the power of the gospel.

# CHAPTER 4

# Socratic Spirituality (1):
# Religiousness A and Upbuilding Spirituality

There are two places in Kierkegaard's writings where Socratic spirituality is described in detail. One is in *Concluding Unscientific Postscript*, attributed to the pseudonym Johannes Climacus, a book that plays a key role as the turning point in Kierkegaard's authorship, according to Kierkegaard himself. The other place that we must look is the many *Upbuilding Discourses* that Kierkegaard wrote under his own name.[1] In this chapter, I shall discuss the account of the spiritual life given in *Postscript*, where a kind of spirituality is described under the label of "Religiousness A." In chapter 5, I will then discuss a similar account of spirituality, found in the *Upbuilding Discourses*.

*Postscript* claims to be a kind of sequel to *Philosophical Fragments*, also attributed to Climacus. In *Fragments*, Climacus had pretended to invent an alternative to the Socratic view of the "Truth," a concept that in the book is a kind of philosophical analogue to the religious concept of salvation. On the Socratic view, the capacity for gaining the Truth is one that humans possess within them; the Truth is something to be "recollected" through "immanence" (PF, 192). In the invented alternative, Climacus describes a view that says that the Truth must be given to humans by a God who has himself become human. This humoristic "invention" is obviously something that suspiciously resembles Christianity. Climacus admits this, saying, near

---

1. In the older translations, these works are called *Edifying Discourses*. Howard and Edna Hong preferred "upbuilding," because it is a more literal and perhaps earthy translation of the Danish *opbyggelige*. Since the Hong translations are currently the standard scholarly edition, I shall defer to their choice in this case.

the end of the book, that "if he ever writes a sequel," he will call this invention by its right name and "clothe the issue in its historical costume" (PF, 109).

*Postscript* purports to be this half-promised sequel, and the first section of this massive book does fit this description. Most of the book, however, does something quite different. Having described in *Fragments* the view that humans lack the Truth and even the ability to gain the Truth on their own, most of *Postscript* pursues a different question. The pseudonymous author Climacus still assumes, hypothetically, that the thesis of *Fragments* is correct: Christianity affirms that the Truth must be given to humans by God through the gift of faith that is made possible by God's historical incarnation. However, even if this is so, is there anything humans can do to prepare themselves to receive this gift? It turns out that the answer is yes. If a person is even going to understand Christianity as an answer to the human dilemma, that person must have a degree of ethical and spiritual development. Most of *Postscript* describes this process of spiritual development, not as part of Christianity, or even as something that makes becoming a Christian inevitable or more likely, but as something that is a necessary precondition for becoming a Christian.

What Climacus is doing is describing a kind of spirituality that is possible independently of the Christian revelation. When fully developed, he calls this form of spirituality "Religiousness A" and distinguishes it from Christianity, which he calls "Religiousness B." *Postscript* offers what might be called a phenomenology of natural religious life, the kind of religiosity that is possible apart from God's special activity in Christ and the church. This is an audacious thing to attempt to do. If one thinks of the multiplicity of non-Christian religions, as well as the forms of spirituality found in those people who do not identify with any traditional religion, it might seem impossible to say anything illuminating about religiousness in general.

If Kierkegaard were attempting to summarize all of the world's religions and religious quests, the task would indeed be impossible. However, there are two important qualifications to the description I just gave that make the task less impossible, even if still daunting. One is that Kierkegaard does not try to describe the various religious views concretely, capturing all the differences. Rather, he attempts to focus on what he sees as central concerns and aims that are present to some degree in anything that looks like religion. The other qualification is that Kierkegaard's account is not really descriptive but normative. He is trying to give an ideal account of human religiousness at its best. Some of what is called "religion" may be very different from what he describes, but where this is the case, Kierkegaard would, I believe, say "so much the worse for that form of religion."

The methodology he follows is not empirical or historical but philo-sophical and phenomenological. The evidence for his view will not be found in empirical descriptions of world religions, though it would be a strike against his view if one could not find anything in those religions that fits his account. Rather, the evidence will be found in the reflective judgments about human existence that readers make who are attempting to understand their own lives. The judgments that count will be those made by readers whose lives can plausibly be described as a kind of religious quest. The reactions of shallow readers who have no religious inclinations will not matter to him, because he is not writing for such people.

We have already seen that human selves are ineradicably spiritual in the sense that they embody a temporal attempt to actualize ideals. However, re-call that many people's lives are shaped by ideals that wholly consist of finite and worldly concerns. Such people want only to be wealthy or erotically successful or famous or to achieve some other kind of finite distinction. It is obvious that such ideals have no essential connection to what is morally good. In fact, recently in the United States, a horrible new version of the person who wants to be famous has emerged: the person whose ambition is to be in the news by becoming a mass murderer, perhaps by killing many in a school shooting. Such an ideal of selfhood seems genuinely to fit what Kierkegaard calls demonic despair.

Of course, becoming a mass murderer is a relatively rare ideal, though clearly not as rare as it used to be. Nevertheless, it belongs in the category of finite worldly goods that function as idols. Most people whose lives are defined by finite, worldly goods have more prosaic ideals. Still, all such lives lack a genuine or authentic religious character; their lives are at best devoted to idols and thus form a kind of counterfeit form of spirituality. However, there are many people who recognize the shallowness of such a life. They want their lives to have a different kind of meaning, and they want something more than pleasure or riches or power.

Many people who hold such a deeper view of human life are members of traditional religions, but some are not. Some of those who are not partic-ipants in a traditional religion might reject the label of "religion" altogether, but some want to hold that they are religious, even if they do not believe in a God or gods. For example, Ronald Dworkin, in *Religion without God*, claims that people who have what he calls the "religious attitude" accept the following view of human life: "Each person has an innate and inescapable responsibility to try to make his life a successful one: that means living well, accepting ethical responsibilities to oneself as well as moral responsibilities to others."[2] Dworkin knows that many Christians, Jews, Muslims, and members of other faiths have such a view, but he says that people such as himself, who do not believe in God and who do not accept the teachings of any religious faith, can accept such a view as well. Although such people are often described as "nones," who are "spiritual but not religious," I think it would be more accurate to describe them as "spiritual though not adherents of any traditional religion." Dworkin is right that there is something fundamentally religious about people who have such a view. The religious character they embody is at least one form of what Kierkegaard has in mind when he describes "Religiousness A."

Dworkin is certainly not alone in thinking this way about human life. Socrates is represented by Plato as having a very similar view. In the *Crito*, Socrates argues with his friends that he must remain in prison and accept his sentence of death. The main premise of his argument is that it is not simply living that is important, but "living well." Socrates then gets his friend Crito to agree that living well means to live "honorably and rightly."[3] Once Socrates shows Crito and his friends that it would be wrong and not honorable to bribe the jailors and escape, then it is clear that Socrates must stay, even though it will lead to his death. For Socrates, the good life simply is the ethical life. He recognizes that not everyone thinks that way, but he nonetheless seems completely certain that his view is correct.

## How Are the Ethical and the Religious Related?

We saw in chapter 3 that for Kierkegaard the natural knowledge of God that we possess is grounded in morality. The natural religious life begins in the moral life. This is perfectly clear in the account of the religious life presented by Johannes Climacus in *Concluding Unscientific Postscript*. Climacus, for example, says that it is a requirement of all genuine religiousness that it "has passed through the ethical" (CUP 1:388). However, the religious life does not "pass through" the ethical in the sense of leaving the ethical behind. We can see this in Climacus's claim that the ethical is the "mother tongue" of the "religious realm" and that someone who does not continue to "speak" that mother tongue is not a true citizen of that realm (CUP 1:390; translation modified).

2. Ronald Dworkin, *Religion without God* (Cambridge, MA: Harvard University Press, 2013), 10.
3. *Crito* 48b–d.

One might object to this by appealing to Kierkegaard's most famous work, *Fear and Trembling*. In that book, the pseudonymous author Johannes de Silentio argues that the "knight of faith," the exemplar of the religious life, must be sharply distinguished from the "tragic hero," who is the "beloved son of ethics." The person with genuine religious faith must be willing to "teleologically suspend the ethical," sacrificing his son if God commands it, as Abraham was willing to sacrifice Isaac, even though such an act is contrary to ethics. So it might appear that there is a contradiction between *Fear and Trembling* and *Postscript* on the relation between the ethical life and the religious life. *Postscript* says that genuine religiousness grows out of the ethical and never abandons it, while *Fear and Trembling* seems to see the religious person as someone whose life can come into conflict with what ethics requires.

Since the two books are attributed to two different pseudonyms, it is certainly possible that the views of Silentio and Climacus might differ without implying that Kierkegaard's own views are contradictory. However, though there is certainly a difference between the two books, I do not think there is any contradiction between what is taught about the relation of the ethical to the religious. The reason this is so is that the phrase "the ethical" does not have the same meaning for the two authors. For Silentio, "the ethical" is exhausted by our human social roles and the responsibilities that come with those roles. Thus, he says that Agamemnon's willingness to sacrifice his daughter Iphigenia is not truly similar to Abraham's willingness to sacrifice Isaac. It is true that Agamemnon also performs the sacrifice at the request of a god, but in his case, what he does is fully ethical. It is assumed that his role as king trumps his role as parent. He must sacrifice his daughter because the needs of the nation require this. Agamemnon's action is in fact perfectly in accord with Hegelian ethics, in which the social duties of the state outrank those of the family.

Silentio says that the actions of Agamemnon are perfectly understandable and justified; they are actions that cause the maidens of Greece to "blush with enthusiasm" (FT, 50). Abraham's actions, however, cannot be justified by an appeal to "the universal," since he does not act "to save a people, nor to uphold the idea of the state" (FT, 52). Abraham's act cannot be ethically justified, according to Silentio, because Abraham is stateless; he has no higher social institution than the family. Given this conception of the ethical as something that is grounded in human social institutions, it is easy to understand how a person's duty to God could come into conflict with the "ethical."[4]

---

4. For a more extended argument that this is how *Fear and Trembling* ought to be read,

By "the ethical," Climacus means something entirely different from the kind of Hegelian sense of the "ethical" that pervades *Fear and Trembling*. While the life of the ethical person in *Fear and Trembling* is defined by the social roles that define the individual's identity, Climacus sees the ethical life as one that begins only when a person sees that there is *more* to the life of an individual human than the fulfillment of such roles. Climacus satirizes people whose lives are exhausted by such roles as people who live their lives the way a child who does not know table manners behaves at a party, always watching to see how "the others" do things (CUP 1:244). For Climacus, the authentic ethical life begins only at the point where a person commits to an ethical requirement that is absolute in character, which relativizes all such social roles. If I am to live ethically, I must seek to become the unique self God created me to be, taking into account the "primitivity" God has placed in me.

Kierkegaard himself affirms a similar view in *Upbuilding Discourses in Various Spirits*:

> At every person's birth there comes into existence an eternal purpose for that person, for that person in particular. Faithfulness to oneself with respect to this is the highest thing a person can do, and as the most profound poet has said, "Worse than self-love is self-contempt." (UDVS, 93)[5]

Living well is then a matter of seeking to achieve "the highest." For Kierkegaard, as for Socrates and Dworkin, the "highest" means living a life that is committed to morality. This moral task, for Kierkegaard, is very personal and stems from God. However, as we shall see, someone like Dworkin, who does not believe in God, may nonetheless have a *de re* awareness of God. He may be aware of God by being aware of God's requirements, even though he does not realize the requirements come from God and thus is not aware of God as a personal being.

---

see chapter 3 of C. Stephen Evans, *Kierkegaard's Ethic of Love: Divine Commands and Moral Obligations* (Oxford: Oxford University Press, 2004); and also my introduction in the Cambridge edition of *Fear and Trembling*, ed. C. Stephen Evans and Sylvia Walsh (Cambridge: Cambridge University Press, 2006).

5. The "most profound poet" is Shakespeare; the reference is to *King Henry V*.

## Achieving an Absolute Relation to What Is Absolute

The fact that Kierkegaard's pseudonym Climacus uses abstract language to describe the quest of the person who has embarked on this kind of deep religious quest is evidence that Kierkegaard himself wants to recognize the possibility that people can have a kind of awareness of God without being aware of God as a personal reality. A person who sees the moral life as "the highest" is aware of what Kierkegaard would call God's call or claim on his or her life. The divine character of the call is recognized when it is seen to be something that is not merely one good among others, but something that is absolutely good. The formula that describes the ideal to which a person ought to be committed is to have "an absolute relation to the absolute," while maintaining a "relative relation to the relative" (CUP 1:393–94). Socrates again provides the model, since he would not go against what he believed to be right even to save his life.

Climacus makes clear that to have this kind of relationship to the divine, it is not enough merely to affirm the existence of God. Nor is it enough to live a conventional religious life, whether that life be Christian or lived within some other religious community. What is required is a recognition of the absoluteness of the requirement. Climacus claims that most of his contemporaries do not seem to realize this. They think of moral character as merely one good among others, something that one would like to have if it does not cost too much. If one merely sees morality as one good among others, then it is not really absolute, and only what is absolute can really be "highest."

If something is really absolute, then it cannot be just one good among others, something to weigh in a cost-benefit analysis to determine the best course of action. Climacus imagines a "gentleman" who is interested in his "eternal happiness," understood as what is absolute (I will discuss below why the absolute is here described in this way), but who demands that this good be described in terms that he can understand: "Can't you describe it to me 'while I shave,' just as one describes the loveliness of a woman, the royal purple, or distant regions?" (CUP 1:392). To want to be an alderman, a crack rifle-shot, and *also* to want an eternal happiness is not to want an eternal happiness absolutely. To find out whether a person really wants an absolute good, he needs to examine the way he exists; it is not sufficient for a person to *say* or *think* that he wants an eternal happiness, if that is the absolute good. "If it [an eternal happiness] does not *absolutely* transform his existence . . . , then he is not relating himself to an eternal happiness" (CUP 1:393).

KIERKEGAARD AND SPIRITUALITY

The idea that the highest good can be viewed as one good among others is described by Climacus as "mediation." Mediation is simply a finitizing of the absolute good, making it commensurable with other finite goods. For all finite goods, mediation makes sense. I can reasonably deliberate about whether the expensive automobile I am tempted to buy is worth the cost. With the money I spend on the car, I could buy new furniture or some exotic vacation or even perhaps acquire a reputation as a generous person by making a large gift to charity. However, what is infinite cannot be "mediated" in this way (CUP 1:419).

For Kierkegaard, the person who recognizes the absolute character of "living well" in the Socratic sense is someone who has an awareness of the divine, even if the person does not realize this. Such people may describe what they are committed to as "the absolute," or they may use other abstract terms rather than traditional religious language, but the divine character of what is referred to can be seen in the unconditional nature of the claim the person recognizes.

## The Absolute and an Eternal Happiness

The account that Climacus provides of the religious life thus begins with the idea of "an absolute relation to the absolute." However, as we saw in the previous section, Climacus immediately begins describing this absolute as "an eternal happiness." What is the justification for this, and is it compatible with the view that the achievement of moral character is the highest end or good that a person can seek? One might think that one must choose between the view that moral character is itself the highest good and the view that the highest good is a kind of reward. If I seek the good for the sake of a reward, surely I do not really view the good itself as what is highest.

The same problem that faces Kierkegaard here is often raised as a difficulty for Immanuel Kant. Kant, like Kierkegaard, posits the achievement of moral character as the absolute good that people ought to seek, but he also claims that the highest good includes the possession of eternal happiness. We all desire happiness, and Kant says we ought to seek a world in which people are both morally good and happy, with the proviso that our happiness should not be sought by infringing the moral law. However, Kant says we can only rationally hope to achieve such a world if that world is created and ruled by God. Faith in God is thus something that a moral person who is rational should have. Critics of Kant sometimes allege that Kant here betrays his own recognition of the absolute value of morality. If Kierkegaard equates the highest good with an eternal happiness, it might seem he is open to the same kind of objection.

Kierkegaard is well aware of this problem, and he confronts it in his own name in *Upbuilding Discourses in Various Spirits*. In the first section of this work, he argues that a person who truly wills the good must will the good as "one thing." To escape "double-mindedness" one must will the good and only the good in truth (UDVS, 36). Two forms of double-mindedness are to will the good for the sake of a reward (UDVS, 37) and to will the good out of fear of punishment (UDVS, 44). Kierkegaard argues that someone who has the "reward disease" does not really will the good at all. Such a person is like a young man who wants to marry a woman because she is rich. In that case, it is clear that the young man does not really love the woman. In the same way, someone who loves the good only because of a reward does not really love the good.

Notice, however, that the young man who really does love the woman can be said to be seeking a reward as well. However, in his case the reward is simply to be able to love the woman. The reward is not something external to the love but is internally related to the love. The young man's joy and satisfaction in loving the woman does not taint the love; rather he has this joy and satisfaction only because he is a genuine lover. In a similar way, the person who really loves the good and wills the good can also be said to be seeking a reward, but again this reward is not an external bribe but simply the satisfaction and joy that the person will have by achieving the good and becoming the kind of person he really wants to be.

The kind of reward that undermines the good is a reward that is distinct from the good and could be had without the good. If I seek the good because I think it will help me become rich and prosperous, then I am not really seeking the good. Kierkegaard therefore rightly rejects external rewards. However, Kierkegaard does not shy away from reward language altogether. There is a reward when one wills the good, but the reward is the good itself. He says that this is "the reward that God has eternally joined together with the good" (UDVS, 37). There is nothing dubious or uncertain about such a reward, because "the good is its own reward, yes, that is eternally certain" (UDVS, 39). It is not even more certain that there is a God, because in the end that God exists and that the good is rewarded turn out to be "one and the same" (UDVS, 39).

We can now understand why Climacus can describe what is absolute in all the various ways he does. The absolute is a commitment to living morally as the highest good. However, it turns out that this commitment to moral goodness is also at the same time both the achievement of a relation to God and a quest for eternal happiness. God is the source of the moral demand, and someone who fully wills the good is seeking, whether the person knows this or not, to be related to God, who is himself essentially good and the source of all that is good. Such a relation to God (or the good) is at the same time the highest happiness imaginable, at least to the person who is committed to the good.

We can now understand why, as we saw in the last chapter, Kierkegaard uses the language of "recollection" and "immanence" to describe the natural knowledge of God. In *Upbuilding Discourses in Various Spirits*, Kierkegaard continually uses the language of God and the good interchangeably. He is a good Christian Platonist, like Saint Augustine, who does not simply think of goodness as an adjective that one can properly apply to God, but thinks of the good as an ontological reality that is identical to God itself.[6]

The account of the "reward" that is part of the moral life that we see in *Upbuilding Discourses in Various Spirits* is precisely the view held by Johannes Climacus in *Postscript* as well. Climacus makes it clear that the eternal happiness he speaks about cannot be understood as some kind of finite good that is externally related to the quest for moral goodness. Rather, Climacus says that an eternal happiness has "the remarkable quality that *it can be defined only by its mode of acquisition*" (CUP 1:426–27; translation modified). One cannot describe an eternal happiness as a set of finite goods, whether those be streets of gold or unending sensuous pleasures. If such images are used, they are used to symbolize a state that cannot really be captured in ordinary human language, because it transcends ordinary human experience. To attempt to describe eternal happiness in such terms is to revert to an aesthetic conception of life. Rather than advance from the ethical to the religious, such a person has slid backward. Eternal happiness can be described only, if at all, by using the language of morality: "Ethically it is entirely consistent that the highest pathos of the essentially existing person corresponds to what esthetically is the poorest idea, and that is an eternal happiness" (CUP 1:393). Climacus even humorously concedes that, from an aesthetic point of view, eternal life appears to be the most boring thing imaginable.

Climacus here touches on an issue that was much debated in the late twentieth century: whether immortality is something that is even worth de-

---

6. For a recent defense of a similar Platonism, see Robert M. Adams, *Finite and Infinite Goods: A Framework for Ethics* (Oxford: Oxford University Press, 1999).

siring. The debate was stirred by a classic article by Bernard Williams, "The Makropulos Case: Reflections on the Tedium of Immortality."[7] Williams argues in this article that eternal life would be impossibly tedious and not worth having. Kierkegaard might concede that this is so if eternal life is conceived in aesthetic terms, as a kind of external reward for the achievement of goodness. However, if we think of eternal life as the realization of moral goodness, seen as something that has infinite value, it seems irrational to welcome the idea that such a life would come to an end. For how can one will something that has infinite value and then will the extinction of that which has this value?

In any case, in connecting the religious life to a desire for immortality, Kierkegaard is surely siding with the vast majority of humans and linking his vision of the religious life to something that every major religion confronts. In some way, every religion must confront the reality of death and the meaning of death. Contrary to Bernard Williams, virtually all human cultures have embodied a hope that physical death is not the end of human existence. Kierkegaard believes that such a hope makes sense if it is conceived as a hope for the achievement of unending moral goodness, understood as something of absolute value.

## Resignation, Suffering, and Guilt

The account of the religious life that Climacus calls Religiousness A has three elements. Having described the religious life as an attempt at "an absolute relation to the absolute," Climacus goes to describe such a life in more concrete ways. The religious life he is describing is a form of "existential pathos." The "initial expression" of this pathos is resignation. The "essential" expression of this pathos is suffering, and the "decisive" expression of it is guilt. This account of lived religiousness, while not a summary or compendium of human forms of religiousness, surely does highlight central issues that lie at the heart of human religions. Every major religion in some way asks questions about suffering and seeks to find meaning in suffering, and every major religion confronts the question of guilt and what to do about it.

7. Bernard Williams, "The Makropulos Case: Reflections on the Tedium of Immortality," in *Problems of the Self: Philosophical Papers, 1956–1972* (Cambridge: Cambridge University Press, 1973), 82–100.

*Resignation*

The necessity of resignation follows directly from the rejection of mediation. Climacus assumes that, although one's absolute commitment can certainly express itself in particular actions, it cannot be exhausted by some set of actions that are required or forbidden. All of us desire other things than moral goodness, and it is easy to see that some of those things can come into conflict with the absolute commitment. To be truly absolutely committed to the absolute means one must be always committed to it and must be willing to sacrifice any finite good that is in tension with what is absolute.

The test for whether I have an absolute relation to the absolute is then whether I am willing to resign or give up some finite good if it stands in the way of my relation to what is absolute. The account of the religious life that Climacus offers here provides a recognizable connection to the prominence of ascetic practices in the great religions of the world, which have often demanded strict disciplines, including the renouncing of forms of food, or alcohol, or sexual activity. Such practices are evidence of religious seriousness on the part of those who engage in them, and certainly can have value. One can hardly argue credibly that one would be willing to give up everything for the sake of the highest if one is not willing to give up anything.

However, Climacus does not want resignation to be identified with a particular list of things that must be done or not be done. His account of resignation is more formal than that. If one asks what a religious person should give up, the answer is that one should give up whatever is a barrier to achieving the highest for any given person. Climacus illustrates this view with an interesting discussion of monasticism within the Christian tradition. (Actually, the discussion of monasticism he gives is included as part of the discussion of suffering, to be discussed below. However, I shall go ahead and introduce the topic here, since the issue of ascetic practices is already present when one considers resignation.) The monk, as Climacus describes him, is someone who thinks that his religious commitment can be identified with a particular lifestyle, a distinct form of "outwardness."

Climacus thinks that this is a mistake, for several reasons. One is that whatever one's outward lifestyle, tensions between the goods that one desires and the absolute good are always possible. The monastic life does not offer immunity from the temptation to value the finite over the infinite. Having a determinate list of things one must do and must not do does not satisfy the demands of resignation. A second problem is that those who adopt such an ascetic lifestyle may be regarded as more holy and devout than other people, an obvious temptation to pride. However, living a genuinely religious life outside the walls of the monastery might actually be more difficult and thus a more significant achievement. At least this would be so if someone actually succeeded in living an authentic religious life in this manner, a possibility Climacus sometimes seems skeptical about.

However, Climacus credits the monastic life as one that shows genuine seriousness and passion, something that the life of the middle-class conformist in Christendom often conspicuously lacks. In comparison with nineteenth-century Christendom, the monasticism of the Middle Ages would be far preferable.


## Suffering

The "initial" description of the religious life as one of resignation is an idealized account. The task of resignation is not one that can be finished or completed in a moment or even in a lifetime. Actual human beings are always immersed in relative finite goods. We are always seeking to find such things as a spouse (or keep one), or a good job, or a nice house or apartment. We are seeking to be recognized for some accomplishment or distinctive quality. It is not easy to give such things up even if we can see that this is what a commitment to the highest requires of us. If we actually put ourselves to the test of resignation, we discover that we fail time and time again, and this discovery is painful. Thus, the religious life, when one actually seeks to live it out on a day-to-day basis, takes the form of suffering, the "essential" expression of the religious life. The religious life involves suffering because a person who is immersed in finite goods must free herself from them by "dying to self," or "dying to immediacy" (CUP 1:460–61).

Dying to immediacy does not mean that one actually severs all ties to what is immediate or ceases to have desires altogether. That would simply mean that one has ceased to exist as a finite creature. It does mean that one must have a *willingness* to give up anything that is an impediment to achieving the highest. This requires a change in the nature of a person's attachment to the finite. The attachments are still there; however, one might say that one's identity is no longer essentially tied to them. If I lose some good, I may be sorrowful, but I will not cease to regard my life as valuable and meaningful. Transforming one's identity in this way is still difficult and involves suffering.

Once more, it is clear that in connecting the religious life with suffering, Climacus is clearly linking such a life with actual religions. Buddhism, for example, begins its reflection on human life by zeroing in on suffering and how it can be defeated. However, the religious suffering that Climacus focuses on is not perhaps what one might expect. He does not focus on poverty, illness, pain, or even untimely death. It is true that these are features of human life that everyone must face, and it is also true for Kierkegaard that a religious life has resources for giving meaning to such suffering. (This is particularly true for Christian spirituality, and this theme will be discussed in later chapters.)

The problem with thinking of suffering in this common way is that it lends itself to an "aesthetic" view of life, which identifies happiness with good fortune. The aesthete thinks that if he or she is fortunate enough to be relatively healthy, to have a long life, in which one possesses the resources and goods that make life satisfying, then one has lived well. On this view, suffering is something contingent or accidental. Some people (the unfortunate ones) have more than their share of suffering. Others who are more fortunate skate through life without much in the way of cares. Suffering is thus seen as something contingent and accidental. The person who has the quality of shrewdness or "worldly wisdom" attempts to tilt the odds of being fortunate in his favor by a knowledge of probabilities.[8] If I choose the right kind of career, marry well, make the right investments, eat healthy food, and exercise, perhaps I will increase my chance of being one of the fortunate ones.

This kind of aesthetic life is one that is "spiritless," devoid of authentic spirituality. The illusion that one can guarantee a good life through shrewdness is just that: an illusion. Even clever people cannot guarantee that they will not face financial disaster if the economy collapses. Even the people most dedicated to healthy food and exercise may lose the genetic lottery and succumb to an early death from cancer or heart disease. A healthy spirituality begins to take root only when a person renounces such illusions and faces the fact that, as Danish humorists are fond of saying, no one gets out of life alive.[9] The fact that even ordinary suffering cannot ultimately be avoided by anyone ought to be enough to show the bankruptcy of such an aesthetic lifeview.

8. Kierkegaard often uses the term *Kloghed*, which means "cleverness" or "shrewdness," for this quality. The Hongs chose to translate this word as "sagacity," which I think has the wrong connotations, since it is connected to the idea of a sage. I often tell my students that when reading the Hong editions of Kierkegaard, they should always think "cleverness" when they see the word "sagacity."

9. I was told that joke by a Dane very soon after arriving in Denmark in 1977 and have heard it from Danish friends many times since.

A genuinely religious person understands this ordinary, common suffering as an inescapable and universal feature of human existence. Such a person recognizes our calling to live for "the highest" and believes that this is possible both for the fortunate and the unfortunate. It may indeed often be easier for the *unfortunate*, since it will be much harder for them to live on the basis of the illusion that one can avoid suffering. Perhaps this is why Jesus says, in the New Testament, that it is difficult for a rich person to attain the kingdom of God.[10] It is easier for a rich person to think that his riches provide immunity from suffering.

What we might call ordinary human suffering is given religious significance by the way it is accepted. I do not mean that the religious person takes a fatalistic view of life and simply thinks that we should not seek healing for illness or avoid danger when we can. Kierkegaard does think the religious person should seek to do what is possible to ameliorate human suffering. Nevertheless, when all is done that can be done, there will always be suffering that must be accepted and endured. The religious person seeks to view such suffering as an opportunity to manifest one's commitment to the highest: to seek to develop such qualities as patience and courage, as well as compassion for others who suffer.

In any case, even the most fortunate people can experience the special kind of suffering that Kierkegaard calls religious suffering, the suffering that one undergoes when one "dies to self" or "dies to immediacy." The honest religious person, having recognized that the test of resignation has failed, understands the need for this kind of suffering and understands that the task is an enduring one, a task for a lifetime.

At this point, some readers may begin to think that the common description of Kierkegaard as "the melancholy Dane" has some truth in it. Does Kierkegaard's discussion of the place of suffering in the religious life show that he favors some kind of masochism? Climacus claims his view is not masochistic: "Suffering as dying away from immediacy is therefore not flagellations and the like; it is not *self-torture*" (CUP 1:463; translation modified). Part of the evidence that this is right can be seen in the account of asceticism given in the critique of monasticism discussed in the previous section. Climacus makes clear there that religious suffering is not simply living a particular kind of life in which one denies oneself normal good things. However, to see that religious suffering is not

---

10. Jesus famously says that it is "easier for a camel to go through the eye of a needle" than it is for a rich person to become part of the kingdom of God. See Luke 18:23.

religious masochism, we must give a deeper description of what dying to immediacy is.

To give this deeper account, I must now alter the religious perspective we have been examining. Up until now, I have attempted to include in my account the perspective of the person who is "spiritual but not traditionally religious" and who may not consciously believe in God. As we have seen, Kierkegaard thinks such people, if they truly are aware of the need for an "absolute relation to the absolute," in fact have an awareness of God's call on their lives, even if they do not know that it is God they are encountering. Authentic spirituality always involves a relation to God, who is the "other" from whom I acquire the "ideal self" I am struggling to become. However, at this point in the discussion of the religious life, Climacus gives up abstract talk of the "highest" and begins to talk explicitly of God. Perhaps Kierkegaard thinks that for one to have the deeper kind of spirituality, one must not only be aware of God, but be aware of God *as* God. Spirituality takes on a new character when a person recognizes the "other" from whom my identity is derived as *personal*. The "other" in this case is someone I can consciously relate to and am accountable to.

Climacus therefore now begins to describe the task of dying to immediacy by explicitly bringing God into the picture. It is not that he wants to deny that it is possible to have an awareness of God without consciously being aware of God as God. We have already seen that this is possible. However, he now wants to describe the situation from the point of view of the person who does have this kind of conscious awareness of God. This kind of person has a clearer understanding of the religious life, and so this person's perspective is the one to take if we want to have that understanding. From this point, God is explicitly part of the story.

If I want to die to immediacy, what I must do is "express existentially the principle that the individual can do absolutely nothing by himself" (CUP 1:401; translation modified). The person who lives in immediacy is a person who has the illusion of control. Of course, the control a person possesses is limited, but the person thinks that it is nonetheless real. Such a person thinks like this: "There are many things I can do, and some I cannot do. I can go out to dinner at a nice restaurant if I wish, since I have the funds. I cannot buy a Caribbean island; for that I lack the capital."

If God exists and is our creator, not just in the sense that God brought the world into existence out of nothing, but in the sense that God continuously maintains everything in existence, then it is literally true that a person can do nothing apart from God. It is only because of God's sustaining and providential power that anyone exists and has the power to do anything. In one sense, anyone who claims to believe in God and understands God's relation to the world knows this. However, it is one thing to know something like this intellectually, quite another to live as if it is true. Genuine spirituality requires that the truth that I know be embodied in my life. The person who understands that "without God I can do nothing" has given up the illusion of control. Such a person is prepared to let God be God and accept his own creaturely status.

Recognizing God as God and accepting one's own dependence on God is really the same thing as worshiping God (CUP 1:413). When we worship, we acknowledge God as God and recognize the implications of our relation to God for how we live our lives. If we understand worship in this way, it is not simply something one does in a church or at a particular time, even though it is valuable to have special times and occasions in which the obligation to worship is fulfilled in a special way. A person's life as a whole can be seen as a form of worship. This idea is not only present in Climacus. Kierkegaard himself saw his own life in those terms: "it was religiously my duty that my existing as an author express the truth, which I had daily perceived and ascertained—that there is a God" (PV, 72n).

In *Postscript*, Climacus spends many pages describing in concrete terms what this kind of religious existence looks like. He argues against the view that a person relates to God only when that person does special religious activities or performs some momentous action. Rather, a truly religious person literally believes that he or she can do nothing without God and thus has dealings with God in every action. The religious individual attempts "to express existentially the principle that the individual can do absolutely nothing by himself, but is as nothing before God" (CUP 1:461; translation modified). To illustrate the way in which the whole of life involves a relation to God, Climacus intentionally chooses as his illustration an insignificant and innocent action: an act of recreation in which a person who feels the need of relaxation decides to go for a carriage ride in the Deer Park.[11] The very insignificance of the example shows that there is no aspect of a religious person's life that can be isolated from the God-relation.

One might think that going out for a nice outing in the Deer Park hardly counts as suffering. However, this is not the case. Even going for a ride in the

11. "Deer Park" here is a translation of *Dyrehaven*, a former royal hunting preserve north of Copenhagen that was a public park in Kierkegaard's time and remains a popular area. In 1978, I was myself able to enjoy a carriage ride there.

Deer Park requires an individual to overcome the illusion that we humans are purely autonomous and in control. It is indeed difficult and even painful to be reminded that one constantly lives "before God" and that the whole of one's life should be devoted to God.

The contrast with the aesthete who thinks that he or she is "in control" of life with the aid of probability is stark. The religious individual is the one who gives up control, who says yes to God and acknowledges God as God:

> And this is the miracle of creation, not the bringing forth of something which is nothing over against the Creator, but the bringing forth of something which is something, and which in true service of God can itself use this something in order to become nothing before God. (CUP 1:246; translation modified)

Metaphysically, humans (and everything else) are indeed totally dependent on God. Nonetheless, humans are not "nothings" but "somethings." Human persons play a genuine role in their own formation, as spiritual creatures, as we saw in chapter 1. For them to become what they are intended to be by God, they must give themselves to God. It is true that God allows the relation to himself to "slip out of his hand, as it were" (SUD, 16; translation modified). However, this makes it possible for the relation to God to be something that humans themselves play a role in establishing.[12]

Climacus says that his religious individual does indeed succeed in going out to the Deer Park. Having conquered the illusion that he can do this on his own, he must then "with God be able to do it" nonetheless (CUP 1:486; translation modified). We might still think that such a religious individual does not really have a good time. There is a stereotype of the religious individual as dour and humorless, and one might think that a continual awareness that one lives before God would make life grim. However, Climacus denies that this is the case:

> Our religious individual chooses the way to the Deer Park. . . . "But he does not enjoy himself," someone perhaps says. Oh, yes, he certainly does.

---

12. One might worry here that Kierkegaard is moving toward Pelagianism. However, that is not the case. The context here is not Christian theology but natural religiousness. The Christian doctrines of sin and grace, which are the preconditions for seeing the error of Pelagianism, are not in view, since on Kierkegaard's view they can be known only through special revelation.

And why does he enjoy himself? Because it is the humblest expression for his God-relationship to confess his humanity, and because it is human to enjoy oneself. (CUP 1:493; translation modified)

We can now see that religious suffering is not a form of masochism at all. It certainly does not embrace painful experiences simply because they are painful, but is willing to undergo a "dying to immediacy" because this is necessary to achieve a great good: a relation to God.

The nature of religious suffering is perhaps clearer to Kierkegaard's Danish readers than it is to those who read him in translation. The Danish term for suffering that Kierkegaard uses is *Lidelse*, and it has as its root the verb *at lide*. Although this verb does mean "to suffer," it has strong connotations of "allowing" or "accepting" something. The English term "passion" has the same kind of connection to what must be received or accepted, etymologically linked to being "passive," and it originally also meant "suffering." (This meaning is still present when one talks about the "passion" or suffering of Christ.) In Danish, one way of saying that one likes something is to say that one *kan lide* that thing. Literally, one is saying that one "can suffer" the thing, can accept it. Understood in this way, religious suffering is strongly linked to giving up control, accepting one's dependence on God. This can, of course, be painful in the more common sense of the word, especially for people who are prideful, but it is not a masochistic desire of pain for its own sake. It is rather essential for the attainment of spiritual health.

Such a religious life is strenuous, to be sure. Climacus at this point adds a discussion of a particular type of experience that is possible only for the person who is spiritually advanced: spiritual trial (CUP 1:458). A spiritual trial (Danish *Anfægtelse*) should not be confused with a moral temptation. A spiritual trial is a temptation of sorts, but not a temptation to do what is morally evil. Rather, it is occasioned by a kind of irritation or exasperation at the strenuousness of what one is being asked to do. The person in the grip of spiritual trial does not want to lie or cheat or steal. Rather, the person would like to slip back into the kind of "comfortable" or ordinary life most people live. Our human weakness comes up against the difficulty of living one's whole life before God. Perhaps the individual thinks, "Why me? Why am I called to live in such an extraordinary way, to become 'the individual'?" Such an experience is a kind of test, and if one passes the test, then the value of the God-relation becomes more evident and more precious, precisely because of its costliness. God allows spiritual trials as a way of deepening a person's spiritual character.

*Guilt*

The account Climacus gives of the religious life has, as he says, a "backward" direction (CUP 1:526–27). Such a life begins with resignation, but when a person attempts to do this, she realizes that she must "enter upon the immense detour of dying to immediacy" (CUP 1:526; translation modified). However, when a person attempts this task, Climacus thinks that if she is fully honest, she will recognize that she has failed at this task as well. Thus, the "decisive" expression of the religious life turns out to be the consciousness of guilt.

Guilt, like suffering, certainly plays a prominent role in human existence and is surely central to many religions as well. However, just as was the case with suffering, there are various ways of understanding guilt, and these must be distinguished from a genuinely religious understanding of the concept. Climacus discusses a number of these nonreligious understandings of guilt, each of which goes hand in hand with a strategy to deal with the problem of guilt. He assumes throughout that guilt does indeed confront us with a problem.

One view he does not consider at all is the view that guilt is simply a subjective feeling that never gives insight into any objective state of affairs. This is the kind of view that some psychotherapists embrace, in which the problem of guilt is simply identified with feelings of guilt, which are unpleasant, and the task of the therapist is to help the individual get rid of such feelings.

Climacus does not take this view seriously for reasons that will become clear. Guilt feelings are indeed unpleasant, but they can be valuable because they can provide insight. Of course, feelings of guilt are not always reliable. A person may feel guilty for something the person has no responsibility for, and there are people with hardened consciences who can do evil without feeling any guilt at all. However, sometimes we feel guilty because we are guilty. For Climacus, the problem is the guilt, not the feeling. Guilt-consciousness is a good thing, a sign that we still care about "the highest" and therefore have a relationship to it, whether that be understood as an eternal happiness or God. (For Climacus, as we have seen, these are really the same thing.)

Climacus says that "the essential consciousness of guilt is the deepest possible plunge into existence" (CUP 1:531; translation modified). There is little doubt that many people will object to this view because they think that the significance of guilt is here being exaggerated. People will admit that people are often guilty of various acts, but still think that dwelling too much on guilt is unhealthy and unreasonable. Many may think that there are indeed "bad" or "evil" people who are truly guilty. (Hitler often comes to mind when one thinks this way.) However, such a person thinks, "surely I myself and my friends and family are not in this category. We are among the good people, who may fail morally now and then, but whose failings are not really very big or important."

Climacus thinks such a perspective on life is simply a manifestation of spiritual shallowness. One might wonder how the dispute between the critic and Climacus could be resolved? Why think that Climacus is right and the critic wrong? It is hard to see how an "objective" argument could be mounted to resolve this dispute. As I said earlier, the method Climacus follows is phenomenological: he simply wants the people he is addressing honestly to examine their own experience as individuals. The error that lies behind the view of the objector is that guilt is being viewed quantitatively and comparatively. Those who think this way have a strong tendency to assess their own guilt by comparing themselves with others, or with others as they imagine them to be.

Climacus thinks that the morally serious and honest person does not think in this quantitative and comparative way. The morally serious person has a sense of the person he or she ought to become, and also is aware of how far from that ideal self the person actually is. The question whether other people are closer or farther from their ideal selves simply does not interest such an honest thinker. For such a person, guilt is a qualitative concept, not a quantitative or comparative one. This concept of guilt arises "when the individual puts his guilt . . . together with the relation to an eternal happiness" (CUP 1:529; translation modified). The person who thinks this way does not think of guilt as a quality that is attached to particular acts and episodes of his life but to the person as a whole, as a "total predicate" or "total quality" (CUP 1:529).[13] The person is aware of the self he ought to be and would like to be, and is acutely aware of his failure to actualize that self. Taking comfort from invidious comparisons with others seems like a shabby evasion of the moral requirement: "It is simply unethical to have one's life in the comparative, the relative, in the external, and to have the police court, the conciliation court, a newspaper, or some of Copenhagen's dignitaries . . . be the highest court with regard to oneself" (CUP 1:530).

One thing that could be said on behalf of Climacus (and Kierkegaard, who surely shares this view) is this: The people we generally most admire for their moral character, the people we regard as saints, do not usually

---

13. The Hongs term this a "total qualification."

think of themselves as superior to others. Rather, they have a deep humility, which makes them oblivious to comparison with other people. People such as Mother Teresa or Dietrich Bonhoeffer don't think like this: "I am a pretty good person, much better than average." Rather, they tend to be acutely aware of and concerned about their own failings and shortcomings.

Climacus anticipates one other common strategy for minimizing the significance of human guilt. Since guilt is a pervasive feature of human existence, it is tempting simply to identify guilt with finitude. As we often say after making a mistake, "Well, we are only human." The pervasiveness of guilt in human existence tempts us to think it is something we really cannot be blamed for: "From the fact that guilt is explained by existing, it appears that the exister is made innocent; it appears that he may be able to throw the guilt over on the one who has brought him into existence or upon existence itself" (CUP 1:528; translation modified).

Climacus agrees, of course, that we humans are finite beings. He admits that it can be very difficult at times to determine the boundary between finitude and selfishness (CUP 1:496). However, he also thinks that morally serious people who are really honest will admit that finitude cannot be blamed for all their failings. This certainly is true for my own case. When I look within myself and think about my life, I have to confess that some of my failings are due to my own bad choices. The "moral gap" between my actual self and the self I know I should be is not due solely to finitude.[14] It is true that people are dealt "different hands," so to speak, and some hands are easier to play than others. What is possible for one person may not be possible for another. (This is one reason why comparisons to other people are worthless.) Still, regardless of the hand I was dealt, if I am honest, I will admit I could have played it better.

Having established guilt as a "qualitative" category that arises from a comparison between our actual and ideal selves, Climacus tries to clarify the concept by distinguishing it from other, nonreligious senses of guilt that are "lower," because they do not embody a consciousness of guilt as a form of alienation in which I am separated from my true self. Each of these lower forms can be described by looking at the solution they offer to the problem of guilt, the form of "satisfaction" for guilt seen as appropriate.

---

14. For a profound treatment of this idea, see John Hare, *The Moral Gap: Kantian Ethics, Human Limits, and God's Assistance* (Oxford: Oxford University Press, 1996). In this work, Hare discusses in depth the strategies humans have employed to attempt to narrow the gap, including both puffing up our capacities and whittling down the demand.

One such lower concept is the civil conception of guilt as lawbreaking, appropriately punished by the state (CUP 1:541). It is obvious that this way of thinking does not see guilt as a "total quality" of the person, but is stuck in the comparative. On this kind of view, I am not guilty if I have not been arrested or charged with a crime, and if I am guilty, I can satisfy the debt by accepting the punishment the state hands out.

A second possibility can be seen in what Climacus calls the "esthetic-metaphysical concept of Nemesis," understood as a kind of natural justice (CUP 1:541). The idea here is perhaps caught in the common maxim one hears when someone who has done something bad suffers bad consequences: "What goes around comes around." The concept of karma found in some Eastern religions would perhaps be another good example. Climacus himself offers the ancient Greek concept of the Furies as an illustration of this. What is wrong with this view of guilt is that the satisfaction provided for guilt seems external and not really related to the inner self of the one who suffers punishment.

A more respectable, but still lower, conception of guilt connects it with self-inflicted penance (CUP 1:542). The problem with such a view is that it "makes guilt finite by making it commensurable" (CUP 1:542).[15] At this point, Climacus refers again to monasticism and other ascetic practices. Although such a view, from the point of view of true morality, is "childlike," there is still something to be said for it. Medieval monasticism may share in this childlikeness, but Climacus nonetheless says it was "an enthusiastic venture in greatness" (CUP 1:542). The practice of penance at least shows that the person has a degree of passion and earnestness, qualities that Kierkegaard thinks are often lacking in contemporary Christendom. Interestingly, Climacus here notes the parallel between such practices in the Christian tradition and in other faiths:

15. A Roman Catholic theologian might here object that Climacus does not really understand the role of penance in those Christian communities that emphasize the practice. Climacus (and doubtless Kierkegaard as well) seems to think of penance as a self-inflicted punishment that provides satisfaction for guilt. This may be how the practice is often understood in the popular mind. When I was fifteen, I met an older man who told me that as a Catholic, he could enjoy having illicit sex and thought the "penance" imposed by the priest when he confessed was a small price to pay for the enjoyment! It is obvious that this man did not understand his own religion. Catholic theologians rightly insist that it is Christ who makes satisfaction for sin and that penance is not a way of "paying the debt," but rather a way of symbolizing and expressing the person's sorrow over sin and repentance.

No, all respect for the penance of the Middle Ages and for what outside of Christianity is analogous to it, in which there is always the truth that the individual does not relate himself to the ideal through the generation or the state or the century or the market price of the human beings in the city where he lives. (CUP 1:543)

The highest form of spirituality that is possible for humans "immanently" (that is, outside the Christian special revelation) is simply to hold fast to the "recollection" of guilt-consciousness in relation to an eternal happiness. The position seems paradoxical. The person comes closest to the achievement of an eternal happiness precisely by recognizing how far away from the achievement he is! Climacus, like Kierkegaard himself, consistently says that when it comes to spirituality, "the negative is a mark of a higher positive" (CUP 1:534). A person comes closest to God by humbly confessing how far away from God he is. In effect, he is saying that the highest form of spirituality possible is one in which we admit the reality of the moral gap and refuse any solutions that cheapen or minimize the gap.

This is a deep form of spirituality, and it does mean the person has a real relation to God, something that propositional knowledge about God by itself does not guarantee. The "first basic principle" of religion is that "one must fear God" (CUP 1:544; translation modified). However, this is precisely what is missing from contemporary Christendom.

An objective religious person in the objective human mass does not fear God; he does not hear him in the thunder, because that is a law of nature, and perhaps he is right. He does not see him in events, because they are the immanental necessity of cause and effect, and perhaps he is right. But what about the inwardness of being alone before God? Well, that is too little for him; he is not familiar with it, he who is on his way to accomplish the objective. (CUP 1:544)

The highest form of spirituality possible for immanence is then a kind of life in which one is conscious of "living before God" and sees oneself as accountable to God. Indeed, Climacus goes so far as to claim that guilt-consciousness simply is a consciousness of God (CUP 1:546). (Again, we must consider the possibility that this might be true, even though some people who have this awareness of God may not realize that it is God they are conscious of.)

One might object that this perspective provides a rather bleak view of the religious life. Maintaining an honest view of one's moral failures may be important, but if there is no way of dealing with these failures, then the religious life begins to look very unattractive. Indeed, it might seem that this form of spirituality is itself a form of despair, since it seems to condemn a person to the perpetual consciousness of guilt, with no way of dealing with the guilt.

Climacus is aware of the problem and argues that the genuine religiousness he is describing is not a form of despair. "Eternal recollection of guilt is not despair . . . , for despair is continuously the infinite, the eternal, the total in the moment of impatience, and all despair is a type of bad temper" (CUP 1:554; translation modified). Instead, the religious person does have a kind of hope, one grounded in the fact that he still has a relation to an eternal happiness and is still connected to it. Even if the person sees no way the problem of guilt can be resolved, he still has "an obscurely sensed possibility" that there is a "way out," some way that guilt can be resolved (CUP 1:541; translation modified).[16] The religious person may not know how the problem of guilt will be resolved but still somehow can hope that it will be.

The final position of the religious person here is strikingly like the account of the religious life provided by Immanuel Kant, in his book *Religion within the Limits of Reason Alone*. The parallel should not be surprising, since both Kierkegaard and Kant are engaging in the same project here: to describe the religious life in a way that does not presuppose any insights that depend on a supernatural revelation. Both are trying to describe the religious life from a moral point of view, which Kierkegaard calls immanence.

In *Religion within the Limits of Reason Alone*, Kant develops an account of the human condition very similar to that offered by Climacus. Honest human self-examination reveals that human nature is in the grip of "radical evil."[17] Furthermore, Kant agrees with Climacus that humans can do nothing to solve the problem of guilt that this presents, since even if we live a perfect moral life from the present onward, we would simply be doing what we ought to do—the bare minimum—and that cannot erase the guilt from before. One might think that what is needed is something like the Christian doctrine of atonement, and Kant agrees that something like this is necessary. However, he rejects the idea that God's grace can be gained through specific

16. For an explanation of this use of the expression "the way out," see the discussion of humor below.

17. Immanuel Kant, *Religion within the Limits of Reason Alone*, trans. Theodore M. Greene and Hoyt H. Hudson (New York: Harper & Row, 1960), book 1, especially pp. 27–34, "Man Is Evil by Nature."

ecclesiastical practices or through belief in historical events such as Jesus's death and resurrection. Rather, he says that what a human must do is strive to do what is right, doing "as much as lies in his power to satisfy his obligation," perhaps by way of a continual approximation to that ideal. Such a person, Kant says, may "hope that what is not in his power will be supplied by the supreme Wisdom *in some way or other,*" even though reason cannot determine the manner in which this help will be given.[18] Kant then agrees that in the end, the truly religious person must rest on a hope that is indeed obscure. It is a hope that the problem of guilt can be resolved even though the person has no clear idea how this might be possible.

## Humor

The optimistic hope that prevents the religious life from becoming a form of despair also links the religious life to something that Climacus calls "humor." Contrary to the usual stereotype of the religious person as humorless, Climacus sees the religious life as closely connected to humor. Humor is described both as a kind of "boundary zone" to the religious life and also as a kind of "incognito," an outward disguise that the genuinely religious person may adopt to avoid appearing to be self-righteous or superior.

Humor is a kind of life that includes a deep appreciation of what is comic. Indeed, the humorist (among whom Climacus includes himself) sees human existence itself as basically comical. All comedy, according to Climacus, involves a kind of perception of a "contradiction."[19] Obviously, he does not mean a logical, formal contradiction; there is nothing funny about affirming "p and not p."[20] Rather, a contradiction here means an incongruity, a situation in which there are diverse elements that seem to be in tension. Climacus gives as an example a comedian who takes a pratfall while gazing upward. The "contradiction" is between the upward gaze and the falling body. Of course, a contradiction of this sort can be painful as well as funny. It is funny only when it is painless. It is not funny when a

18. Kant, *Religion within the Limits of Reason Alone*, 159.

19. For a deeper account of humor and the comic, see C. Stephen Evans, "Kierkegaard's View of Humor: Must Christians Always Be Solemn?," *Faith and Philosophy* 4, no. 2 (1987): 176–86.

20. Commentators who think that Kierkegaard's description of the incarnation as a contradiction means that he believes it is logically contradictory have not paid sufficient attention to how Kierkegaard uses the term.

comedian who takes a fall breaks his leg. A contradiction that produces pain is not comic but tragic.

Human existence itself involves a massive "contradiction" between the ideals we humans strive for and the actuality of our lives. Is this contradiction comic or tragic? Climacus says that it depends on whether the person perceiving the contradiction knows a "way out" (CUP 1:541). If there is no solution to the contradiction, then human life will be seen as tragic.

It is the element of optimistic hope in the religious person that connects the religious life to humor. The belief or the hope that the problem of guilt will ultimately be resolved means that for the religious person, tragedy does not have the final word. The difference between the genuinely religious person and the person Climacus calls the humorist lies in their existential orientation. The humorist has a kind of intellectual comprehension that existence is not a tragedy but a comedy, and then relies on this intellectual perspective to take a relaxed view of human life. From this perspective, existence does not have to be taken with great earnestness, because regardless of what a person does, "we all get equally far" (CUP 1:582; translation modified). The genuinely religious person knows that this is true as well but still feels compelled to strive for the ideal. Socrates, like the humorist, can jest about human life, but the jest is never an excuse for evading his moral vocation.

# CHAPTER 5

# Socratic Spirituality (2):
# The Spirituality of Kierkegaard's *Upbuilding Discourses*

In this chapter, I will provide a deeper and more concrete account of what I am calling Socratic spirituality, by looking at some of Kierkegaard's early *Upbuilding Discourses*, as well as one discourse from *Upbuilding Discourses in Various Spirits*. Kierkegaard first published his original upbuilding discourses in 1843 and 1844 in six small volumes, with each volume containing two to four of these sermon-like "talks." During Kierkegaard's own lifetime, they were collected and published as *Eighteen Upbuilding Discourses*, and they have appeared under that title in English as well.[1] Kierkegaard himself is careful not to call them sermons, because he was never ordained, though he had completed all the qualifications needed to become ordained. They are "talks" or "discourses" in the sense that they address the reader very directly, and Kierkegaard himself expresses the hope that his ideal reader, the "single individual," would read them aloud. *Upbuilding Discourses in Various Spirits*, as the title implies, contains discourses written from different points of view, some of them very Christian in content. However, "On the Occasion of a Confession" (also translated as a separate book in English with the title *Purity of Heart Is to Will One Thing*) is very similar in character to the *Eighteen Upbuilding Discourses*, and so I shall treat it in this chapter as well.[2]

These discourses embody and flesh out the kind of spirituality that Johannes Climacus describes in a more philosophical and formal manner in

---

1. EUD in the sigla. These discourses were also published earlier in a four-volume set under the title *Edifying Discourses*, trans. David Swenson and Lillian Swenson (Minneapolis: Augsburg, 1943–53).

2. I discuss the nature of the book later in this chapter.

*Postscript.* That means they offer us a spirituality that is grounded in a kind of generic theism. Readers of the discourses sometimes miss this, because the discourses have a superficial Christian form. All of them take Scripture verses as their starting point. They are addressed to people in Christendom who think of themselves as Christians, and thus they allude to biblical stories and texts. However, this does not mean that they are essentially Christian or significantly different from Socratic spirituality. Kierkegaard himself stresses that these early discourses carefully and consciously refrain from any decisive use of distinctively Christian categories.[3] They do not, for example, focus on original sin or Christ's atonement. One could easily imagine versions of these discourses written for Jewish or Muslim audiences, or for that matter, a theistic Hindu audience. These alternative discourses would take different texts as their occasion and would allude to different stories, but the central points made would not have to be different at all.

Although Climacus says that the kind of spiritual life he describes as Religiousness A can be found outside of Christianity, he also says that it is a form of religiousness that can and does exist in Christendom as well. So it is not really surprising that essays that develop this kind of spirituality can take on Christian forms.

Nor does Kierkegaard want to attack or impugn such a form of religiousness, even though it is not really Christian in the decisive sense. Christianity for Kierkegaard is not a religion of "immanence." It cannot be understood as a development of some natural human capacity but requires a supernatural act of grace on the part of God. Religiousness A does, however, stem from our natural human capacities. Nonetheless, Religiousness A can be seen as preparation for becoming a genuine Christian or becoming a Christian in the decisive sense. In fact, Climacus says quite explicitly that something like Religiousness A must be present in a person before that person can even understand the Christian gospel (CUP 1:556).

---

3. Actually, Kierkegaard draws attention to the character of the upbuilding discourses by using his pseudonym, Johannes Climacus. Climacus, as a "third party," makes the case by calling attention to the character of the writings and does not have to rely on any appeal to authorial intention. Here is Climacus's comment: "Magister Kierkegaard most likely knew what he was doing when he called the upbuilding discourses *Upbuilding Discourses* and also knew why he refrained from using Christian-dogmatic categories, from mentioning Christ's name, etc. . . . the categories, thoughts, the dialectic in the presentation are only those of immanence" (CUP 1:272). "Immanence" is Kierkegaard's favorite word for what can be known through human reflection, and he often presents Socrates as the paradigm of such knowledge.

In some ways, these discourses embody a spirituality that is similar to that found in nineteenth-century liberal Protestantism, which tended to emphasize Jesus's role as an ethical teacher. The liberal-Protestant type of view was sometimes summarized in the slogan "the fatherhood of God and the brotherhood of man." Of course, such a slogan greatly oversimplifies liberal Protestantism, as slogans are wont to do, but it nevertheless accurately captures the liberal emphasis on the worship of God and serving God through ethical striving. It is not surprising that such views provided the theological milieu for the development of what was called "the social gospel" in the late nineteenth and early twentieth centuries.

Kierkegaard's *Upbuilding Discourses* are similar in their emphasis on a relation to God, which is expressed primarily through ethical striving. However, there is a big difference between Kierkegaard's account and the later social-gospel views. Kierkegaard's discourses are not focused at all on social changes or resolving social problems. They are entirely focused on the development of "inwardness" in individuals, addressed as they are to the "single individual" whom Kierkegaard "with joy and gratitude" calls his reader (EUD, 5).[4] The focus is not on transforming the world but on the transformation of the character of individuals. Many of the discourses can be read as an exercise in what would today be described as a religious form of "virtue ethics," since they focus on the development of such qualities as hope, patience, and humility.

Obviously I cannot give, in one chapter, a comprehensive reading of all the *Eighteen Upbuilding Discourses*. However, I shall try to discuss some major themes and topics that are especially illustrative of the character of this form of spirituality, drawing on several of the discourses.

### The First Two *Upbuilding Discourses*: "The Expectation of Faith" and "Every Good and Every Perfect Gift Is from Above"

The character of the *Upbuilding Discourses* is clear from the very beginning. "The Expectation of Faith,"[5] written as a talk to be given on New Year's Day, sounds many of the themes that are found throughout these discourses. The

---

4. This formulaic description of the ideal reader is included in the prefaces for each of the six volumes in the Hongs' *Eighteen Upbuilding Discourses* (EUD, 5, 53, 107, 179, 231, 295).

5. I have slightly altered the Hong title. The Hongs translate the Danish term *Forventning* as "expectancy." However, this is a very unusual term in English, and "expectation" seems preferable to me. *Forventning* is a perfectly ordinary Danish word for what a person expects or anticipates.

first point to be made is that the term "faith" here does not refer to faith in a specifically Christian sense, as it usually does in Kierkegaard's late writings and sometimes even in his earlier pseudonymous writings. It makes no reference to Christ as the object of faith and does not discuss Christ as God incarnate, the absolute paradox. Faith is not here a response to particular historical events. Rather, faith in this discourse refers to a religious quality that presupposes only human nature. Faith is "not only the highest good, but it is a good in which all are able to share, and the person who rejoices in the possession of it also rejoices in the innumerable human race" (EUD, 10; translation modified). This is so because the person who possesses faith has something that "every human being has or can possess" (EUD, 10).

It is also clear that this great good of faith has the Socratic character that no human being can give it to another. Faith is not a gift of fortune, something that some people can attain through favorable circumstances but that others, less favorably situated, cannot. Every person has the capacity for faith and only has to will to have faith to realize this capacity. But all individuals must do this for themselves (EUD, 15). If faith were something that could be given by one person to another, then it could also be taken by a person from another. The highest good must be a good that every person can achieve, and such a good cannot depend on the goodwill of other people.

There is a deep commitment to a kind of human egalitarianism here, one that permeates Kierkegaard's entire authorship and that he continues to maintain in his more strongly Christian writings. It is not a political egalitarianism; Kierkegaard was no great fan of democracy and had little faith in schemes to rearrange human societies to eliminate inequalities of wealth and position. Nevertheless, Kierkegaard had a deep love for "the common man," and he took great pains to treat people of all social classes with the same kind of respect.[6] In seeking an account of the meaning and value of human existence, he sees views that make only some human lives meaningful as immoral, even contemptible. This is actually one of the reasons Kierkegaard finds Hegelian (or Marxist) views of human history unacceptable. Views such as these see the meaning of human history as found in its culmination, whether that "end of history" be a society where "absolute knowledge" has been gained (Hegel) or one in which a classless society has been achieved (Marx). Such views are immoral because they see most human lives (those lived prior to the culmination) as empty of meaning. Most people have lived

---

6. See Jørgen Bukdahl, *Søren Kierkegaard and the Common Man*, trans. and rev. Bruce Kirmmse (Grand Rapids: Eerdmans, 2001) for a penetrating discussion of this egalitarianism.

and died only as instruments that make historical progress possible. They may have lived as "cannon fodder" or objects of oppression, and, even if the process eventually produces a glorious end, that will be no comfort to them. Kierkegaard demands that all human lives, throughout history, have meaning and intrinsic value.

A conviction that all human lives have this kind of value is intrinsic to Socratic spirituality. The person who wishes the highest good for himself "wishes it for every human being, because that by which a person has faith is not that by which he is different from . . . others but is that by which he is altogether like all" (EUD, 10). The only qualification to this Kierkegaard makes is that, it turns out, the highest good is not something to be "wished for" but something that must be *willed* (EUD, 13).

Because faith depends only on the capacity of every human to will to have faith, it is thereby something that each person must obtain for himself or herself: "no human being can give it to another, but . . . every human being has what is highest, noblest, and most sacred in humankind" (EUD, 14). This claim fits precisely with a Socratic view of the ultimate Truth that humans are seeking, that Truth that makes life worth living. In *Philosophical Fragments*, Johannes Climacus stresses that Socrates is a "maieutic" teacher, a kind of "midwife" who believes that every person already has the Truth within and must "give birth" to that Truth individually. The Truth then only has to be "recollected" by each person, and thus the person who has learned this from Socrates recognizes that he or she really owes Socrates nothing. Similarly, Kierkegaard says in "The Expectation of Faith" that the person who helps another gain faith really does not wish to be thanked, because in reality the person who gains faith owes the "helper" nothing at all (EUD, 15).

Since the title of the first discourse is "The Expectation of Faith," one naturally looks for an answer to what exactly it is that faith expects or antici-pates. In answering this question, Kierkegaard strikes a fine balance between two types of answers that he rejects. On the one hand, the expectation of faith cannot be defined in terms of specific empirical events or outcomes. The person of faith cannot count on receiving temporal goods such as wealth and fame. The person of faith cannot count on living a long life or being healed from diseases or being protected from disasters. Faith also cannot be identified with a "cheerful disposition that has not yet tasted life's adversities, that has not been educated in the school of sorrow" (EUD, 19). This kind of orientation toward life is not faith but simply youthful naïveté. Kierkegaard does not think faith is what today is often called a "prosperity gospel," nor is it a naïve optimism.

If faith does not expect any particular temporal outcome, one might think that what faith expects then would be some kind of good that will be obtained after death in eternity. However, Kierkegaard does not go down this path either. Faith must offer a good that can be possessed in this life, even if it also promises life beyond death. So what exactly does faith expect?

The answer given is that faith expects "victory" (EUD, 21). Obviously, Kierkegaard does not mean that the person of faith will be victorious over other people in some kind of contest; that would be the kind of particular temporal outcome already rejected. Rather, the victory that faith expects is a victory over the *future.*

But what does that mean? The answer seems cryptic, and it is indeed somewhat vague. That is not surprising, since Socratic spirituality has a kind of vagueness inherent in it. It embodies a relation to "the eternal" or to "God," but the nature of the eternal and God is not altogether clear.

Nevertheless, I think we can see what Kierkegaard has in mind by talking of a victory over the future. The future is a collection of possibilities. The future is open-ended and uncertain. The future thus naturally calls forth anxiety. We imagine various possibilities, many of which may seem terrible, and the person is undone by all these nebulous possibilities. Perhaps if one of these possibilities became actual, it could be faced, but when confronted by this multiplicity of possibilities, people may be overwhelmed. "This is why we frequently see people who have been victorious in all the battles in life become helpless when they encounter a future enemy. Accustomed, perhaps, to challenge the world to combat, they had now found an enemy, a nebulous shape, that was able to terrify them" (EUD, 18). The problem is that these possibilities all reside in the imagination of the person, and, although the person seems to be battling external dangers, the real enemy is one's own self.

How does faith win victory over this anxiety? Kierkegaard provides an illustration to make it clear:

> When the sailor is out on the ocean, when everything is changing all around him, when the waves are born and die, he does not stare down into the waves, because they are changing. He looks up at the stars. Why? Because they are faithful; they have the same location now that they had for our ancestors and will have for generations to come. (EUD, 19)

The sailor conquers what is changeable by fixing on what is unchangeable. In the same way, Kierkegaard affirms, the person of faith conquers the future by focusing on the eternal. Faith is itself the "eternal power in a human being"

(EUD, 19). I think this means that faith is the means whereby the power of the eternal takes root in a person. The content of faith and what it expects is still somewhat indeterminate. There is nothing here comparable to the Christian hope that Christ will someday return and that believers will be bodily resurrected. However, though it is somewhat vague, faith does have content. It could be described as a belief that, whatever happens to us in time, we are still connected to God and the eternal, and thus our lives are not meaningless or worthless.

This answer to the question of what faith expects actually connects the first discourse to the second, "Every Good and Perfect Gift Is from Above." This discourse takes as its text James 1:17–22, which says that "every good gift and every perfect gift is from above and comes down from the Father of lights, with whom there is no change or shadow of variation."[7] The book of James is Kierkegaard's favorite book of the Bible, and James 1:17 was his favorite verse.[8] It is precisely the unchangeableness of God that allows the person who has faith in God to gain a victory over the anxieties of temporal existence.

Kierkegaard poses a kind of "aesthetic" interpretation of this text, which, of course, he ultimately rejects. He imagines heaven as a "vast storeroom" of good gifts, from which God selects goods now and then, sending various gifts in various amounts to various people (EUD, 40). Kierkegaard affirms that this reading of the text cannot be correct, since it would imply that God changes, precisely what the text denies. We should not read the passage simply as telling us to try to discern what things we have been given in life are good, so that we can properly attribute them to God. That is a stance in which "doubt has craftily concealed itself" (EUD, 41), for how can we be sure what things in life will ultimately be for our good? Instead, we should realize that everything we have is a good gift, if it is recognized as coming from God and is received with thankfulness (EUD, 42). If we do this, we are thereby united to God, the one in whom "there is no change or shadow of variation" (EUD, 40), and will realize that nothing that happens to us in life

7. The English given here is a translation of the Danish version of the text cited by Kierkegaard.

8. For a very insightful discussion of Kierkegaard's view of James and use of James, see Richard Bauckham, "Kierkegaard and the Epistle of James," in *Kierkegaard and Christian Faith*, ed. Paul Martens and C. Stephen Evans (Waco, TX: Baylor University Press, 2016), 39–54. Two more of the *Eighteen Upbuilding Discourses* also are based on this text, and Kierkegaard also used it for one published in 1855, during the middle of his attack on the state church of Denmark.

can take away this good. It is true that the future is unknowable, but we can have confidence that whatever happens will not undermine the value and significance of our lives.

This is, however, extremely difficult for us humans. We strongly desire certain goods and fear their loss. We want to tell God what is good for us and then expect that God will satisfy our desires. Kierkegaard speaks directly to the reader who thinks this way: "You wanted God's ideas about what was best for you to coincide with your ideas, but you also wanted him to be the almighty creator of heaven and earth so that he could properly fulfill your wish" (EUD, 37). The problem with this is that a God whose ideas coincide with ours about what is good would not be God. The person who wants God to think as he thinks fails to see that God, "if he were to share your ideas," would thereby "cease to be the almighty Father," who must know better than we do what is for our true good (EUD, 37).

The difficulty here can be seen as another way of describing the tasks of resignation and suffering discussed in the previous chapter. The task here is the same as it was there: to recognize that God is God and that we are not God. We thereby must give up control, "suffering" or allowing God to be God in our lives and having faith in God's goodness. Our task is to give up the "childish" view of God, in which we want God simply to affirm our own desires. We must stand firm against the temptation to evaluate God's actions critically, instead receiving whatever God gives with thankfulness.

## "Strengthening in the Inner Being"

One of the clearer pictures of what a spiritual relation to God looks like for Socratic spirituality can be found in a discourse published as the last of the four presented in the second collection that appeared in 1843. This discourse is clearly connected to the last one discussed above, since it begins with a prayer to the "Father in heaven" who "holds all the good gifts in [his] gentle hand" (EUD, 79). Toward the end of the discourse, Kierkegaard returns to James 1:17 by making a remarkable claim about what it means to call God "Father."

The discourse tries to show that a relation to God cannot be defined by external events or external actions and can be had by anyone, regardless of what his or her life is like.[9] A genuine relation to God is one that resides in

9. Here I remind the reader that Kierkegaard is expounding a Socratic spirituality that

KIERKEGAARD AND SPIRITUALITY

one's "inner being," and such a relation strengthens one's inner being (EUD, 87). Indeed, one can argue that it does more than that: it is only through a relation to God that the inner being of a person "awakens" and comes to life (EUD, 91). When this happens, Kierkegaard says that the person discovers "the explanation" of life, and also that the person will hear "the witness" that provides assurance of God's reality (EUD, 95). The witness is the good gift of God, from whom all good and perfect gifts come. More precisely, perhaps the witness is God himself, who is himself the gift.

The discourse describes a number of different characters whose lives take very different courses. The main lesson Kierkegaard wants to teach is that no one of these circumstances guarantees a relationship to God, but none makes such a relation impossible either. Whether one finds God depends entirely on how those circumstances are understood and received. First, Kierkegaard describes a person who lives in prosperity, who is one of the "fortunate ones" (EUD, 89–90). If such a person does not understand the source of his prosperity, then it is in a sense illegitimate (EUD, 88–89). He can only gain an "explanation," if he is indeed "strengthened in his inner being." To do this, he must learn not to be attached to his prosperity; he must acquire resignation, though Kierkegaard does not here use that term. But the idea is certainly present: "He who has the whole world and is as one who does not have it has the whole world—otherwise he is possessed by the whole world" (EUD, 90). The person who is deeply attached to wealth and possessions will be consumed by anxiety over what might happen to them and thus to himself. However, the person who has these possessions "as if he did not have them" can use and enjoy them as gifts from God. Such a person is strengthened in his inner being.

A similar story is told about the person who has much power. The person with power who has a proper relation to God will know "to whom the honor is due and to whom it legitimately belongs" (EUD, 91). Such a person "rejoices every time his efforts are crowned with success," but when this is not the case, he is undaunted, since his external achievements do not "possess his soul" (EUD, 91–92). Similar accounts are given for the person who suffers adversity in life and for the individual who is "tried" in the "distress of spiritual trial" (EUD, 95–97). It is never what happens to a person that

---

is not really Christian. In his later Christian writings, Kierkegaard himself rejects the view that people can have a full, complete relation to God that is grounded solely in "immanent," Socratic qualities, in favor of the view that to know and relate to God properly a person must become a disciple of Jesus of Nazareth.

determines spiritual health, but how what happens is understood. What we must strive to do is to receive whatever happens as gifts from a loving Father.

One might here object that this may be very difficult for some people, particularly those who did not enjoy a good earthly father or who do not have a good relation with a father. Kierkegaard is very sensitive to this issue; his relation to his own father was very complicated. He loved his father deeply and yet also believed that much of his own suffering and "melancholy" was due to his father's well-intentioned but misguided parenting. Kierkegaard rejects the idea that we call God "Father" because our earthly fathers provide an appropriate model for God. He knows that earthly fathers are not always ideal, and even those who are good fathers are far from perfect. The metaphor goes in the other direction, so to speak. God is, one might say, the Platonic form of fatherhood, the perfect exemplar that all other fathers imitate or participate in to the degree that they are good fathers. All the good qualities that earthly fathers may have (or lack) are derived from the true Father, who has "the fatherliness from which all fatherliness in heaven and on earth derives its name" (EUD, 100).

## Gaining and Preserving One's Soul in Patience

In the very first chapter of this book, I explained Kierkegaard's view that, although in one sense every human person is a self, in another sense the self is an achievement. This view that the self must become what it already is lies at the center of Kierkegaard's understanding of human spirituality. This achievement of selfhood is not something that happens in a flash and then endures as a settled accomplishment. Rather, it is a gradual, lifelong process. Even the person who has a dramatic conversion faces the task of continuing to be the new person he or she has become. We can thus understand why patience is a central virtue in the spiritual life. Becoming one's true self requires, to borrow a phrase from Nietzsche, a "long obedience in the same direction."[10]

The key role patience plays in becoming one's true self is highlighted in two discourses, "To Gain One's Soul in Patience" and "To Preserve One's Soul in Patience," the first from *Four Upbuilding Discourses* from 1843 and the second from *Two Upbuilding Discourses* from 1844. In both, we see selfhood as

10. Friedrich Nietzsche, *Beyond Good and Evil*, trans. Helen Zimmern (New York: Macmillan, 1907), 107.

an achievement, something that must be gained, but that is gained by being continually preserved, or, said more clearly, constantly renewed. In the first discourse, Kierkegaard stresses that one does not gain a self by great worldly achievements. To the contrary, the person who "gains the whole world" is really possessed by that world and thus loses his soul (EUD, 165–66). If the world owns one's soul (or self), then you are really held in thrall by an alien power with no rightful ownership claim. To gain one's soul, one must be willing to give up the world by giving one's self to God, the rightful owner of the soul.

"To Preserve One's Soul in Patience" strikes similar themes but from a slightly different angle. Early in the discourse, Kierkegaard notes that it is easy to see the difficulty of preserving what one has, since "life is uncertain" (EUD, 184). However, when we ask what must absolutely be preserved, nothing that is temporal is satisfactory (EUD, 185). Rather, what must be preserved is the self: "to be even the most insignificant and inferior of human beings and to be true to oneself is much more than to become the greatest and most powerful by means of the shabby partiality of the wish" (EUD, 190). The self one must be true to is simply the self God calls one to be: "what God has intended him to be, neither more nor less" (EUD, 190).

That calling, though it certainly includes individual tasks, also has a universal component. We are all called "to love God and human beings," and this task gives us all "enough to do" (EUD, 198). Patience demands faithfulness to this task in any and all circumstances, whether those be favorable or unfavorable. Even as a person "lies down to die," one ought to ask, "Do I love God just as much as before, and do I love the common concerns of human beings?" (EUD, 198). The love of God and the task of becoming one's true self are connected, since I show my love for God by becoming the self God desires me to become. That self that God wills me to become is a self that is committed to moral goodness and thus one that "loves the common concerns of human beings."

## "On the Occasion of a Confession" (*Purity of Heart*)

I shall conclude this chapter on the spirituality of Kierkegaard's *Upbuilding Discourses* by looking at the long discourse "On the Occasion of a Confession," which constitutes the first part of *Upbuilding Discourses in Various Spirits*, published by Kierkegaard in 1847. This discourse was translated by Douglas Steere and published separately in English under the title of *Purity of Heart Is to Will One Thing.* Since that edition may be more familiar to English readers than the longer book from which the discourse is taken, I will refer to the discourse in this chapter using the title *Purity of Heart*, although the references will be taken from the Hong translation in the longer book.[11] As the title *Upbuilding Discourses in Various Spirits* implies, the various parts of the whole book are not done from the same perspective. The last part of the book, titled *The Gospel of Sufferings: Christian Discourses,* is clearly an expression of Christian spirituality and will be treated later in this book when explicitly Christian spirituality is described.

*Purity of Heart,* however, seems strongly linked to the earlier *Eighteen Upbuilding Discourses* and is appropriately treated as an expression of Socratic spirituality. To be sure, the discourse does have a Christian frame. The whole talk is directed to someone who is about to go to a church service in which sins are confessed. Strangely, however, there is nothing in the discourse about forgiveness and pardon, and no mention is made of the atonement of Christ. At one point, Kierkegaard makes plain that this omission is intentional by addressing his hearer in a very personal way: "If you, my listener, know much more about confession than has been said here, as indeed you do, know what follows the confession of sins, this delaying discourse may still not have been in vain, provided it actually has *halted* you, has *halted* you by means of something that you know very well, you know even much more" (UDVS, 153).

Of course, what "follows the confession of sins" in a Christian service of worship is a pronouncement of pardon and absolution. This is the "more" that the listener knows, but which Kierkegaard has here suppressed by reminding the listener of something else that the listener already *knows* "very well": we need to confess our sin because of how far short of the ideal we all fall. Kierkegaard does not want a mere *knowledge* of sin to be taken for granted, because the knowledge we already have about the forgiveness of sin can make us jump quickly past the need to confess and repent. He thus confronts the listener with the need to "halt" and take guilt seriously.

*Purity of Heart* thus does not really go beyond the spirituality of Religiousness A, which culminates, as we saw in the last chapter, in a consciousness of guilt that understands that there is nothing that humans can do that will solve the problem of guilt. By postponing any discussion of grace and forgiveness, Kierkegaard wants to make sure that his listener fully appreciates

---

11. The Steere translation is available as a Harper Torchbook in paperback (New York: Harper & Brothers, 1956).

the seriousness of guilt. Such a person is ready to hear the Christian story, in much the same way that Johannes Climacus says that the person who possesses Religiousness A is ready to hear the proclamation of the good news about Christ. However, merely focusing on guilt is not yet to move to that Christian proclamation.

The account of guilt given in *Purity of Heart* is, as I shall show, fully consonant with the kind of ethical religiousness that we found in *Postscript*. The guilt of the person is presented strenuously in light of the ethical demand, but it is not really described in Christian terms. There is, for example, no discussion of original sin. From a Christian point of view, sin is fundamentally disobedience, a rebellion against God. In *Purity of Heart*, guilt is connected to God as well, but God is there described in ethical (and Platonic) language: as the Good.

*Purity of Heart* develops its account of the ethical life in a way somewhat similar to Kant: beginning with a formal description of that life and then trying to show that the content of the ethical life can be derived from its form. The ethical task is understood as the task of becoming a genuine or true self, and the formal description of the task is simply this: To be a true or genuine self, the self must be unified. It cannot be a self at war with itself; such a self would not have a coherent identity. So to be a self, a person must "will one thing." It is clear, I think, that this does not mean a person must will one finite thing (such as money or fame) instead of other finite things, but rather must have a unified will. The only object of the will that allows this is the Good as such, which is not a particular finite thing, but something that "is one thing in its essence" (UDVS, 30), even though it expresses itself in many different ways. A unified will therefore requires that one will something that is absolutely or infinitely good. One can here see that, although the language used is different, Kierkegaard has in mind something very much like the description Climacus gives of the task of selfhood: to be absolutely committed to what is absolute.

Instead of speaking of the absolute, Kierkegaard speaks about "the Good" as what the self must be committed to.[12] One might think that this

---

12. Nineteenth-century Danish capitalized all nouns. Thus, the English translator must decide when a noun is a common noun and when it is a proper noun that ought to be capitalized. The Hongs chose to translate the Danish *det Gode* as "the good." However, I think that Steere was correct to translate this phrase as "the Good." Kierkegaard is not speaking about the good as a collection of good things, but as one thing: *the* Good. Part of the evidence for this can be seen in the way Kierkegaard uses "the Eternal" synonymously with "the Good." The allusions to Plato are intentional, I believe. One might compare Kierkegaard here with

is a significant difference, but Kierkegaard makes clear that by "the Good," he has in mind something very similar to what Climacus describes when he speaks of the task of becoming a self. To be committed to the Good turns out to consist of being committed to becoming the self God intends one to be:

> At every person's birth there comes into existence an eternal purpose for that person, for that person in particular. Faithfulness to oneself with respect to this is the highest thing a person can do, and as that most profound poet has said, "Worse than self-love is self-contempt." (UDVS, 93)[13]

This task, though it is individualized for every person, is nevertheless part of our universal human duty. A person who carries it out "is participating in the great common enterprise of humankind; . . . even if no human being sees him, humankind feels with him, suffers with him, is victorious with him" (UDVS, 117).

This account of human existence is fully consistent with the egalitarianism we saw in both Religiousness A and the earlier upbuilding discourses. What gives human life meaning and value must be something that every person can realize: "With respect to the highest, with respect to willing to do everything, it makes no difference at all, God be praised, how big or little the task" (UDVS, 81). The requirement of "the Eternal" is "equal for everyone, the greatest who has lived and the lowliest" (UDVS, 81).[14] What makes this equality possible is that God individualizes the task. Each of us is called to become the particular individual God makes possible, in the particular circumstances of one's own life.

*Purity of Heart* begins with a prayer, but, unlike the prayer that begins the explicitly Christian book *Works of Love* (WL, 3–4), it is not a Trinitarian prayer, but one that is simply addressed to "Father in Heaven." The prayer asks God to make it possible for human beings to carry out the task of becoming themselves by "willing one thing." However, midway through the prayer, there is a lament that the task has not been carried out: "But, alas, this is not the way it is. Something came in between them" (UDVS, 7). Sin has come in between the person's resolution to become a true self and the

---

Robert M. Adams, in *Finite and Infinite Goods* (Oxford: Oxford University Press, 1999), who also speaks of "the Good" and thereby makes clear his debt to Plato.

13. The poet is Shakespeare in *King Henry V*.

14. As noted above, this is an instance where the Hongs do not capitalize "the eternal," but I have chosen to write it as "the Eternal," given its clear identification with God.

person's actual life. Thus, repentance is necessary. The human task is not simply understood as a triumphant ethical achievement. To achieve selfhood, a person must first confront the problem of guilt, which Climacus has described as the "decisive" expression of the religious life. After this opening prayer, most of the book relentlessly and in concrete detail describes the ways in which this failure occurs. However, already in the introduction, Kierkegaard makes clear that the purpose of the discourse is to remind the listener of guilt. (It is a reminder and not new information since it is presumed that there is already some awareness of guilt.)

The consciousness of guilt makes it possible for a person to hear the voice of "two guides" who constantly call to a person: remorse and repentance (UDVS, 13–16).[15] Remorse calls for a person to turn back and rightly understand the wrong of the past; repentance calls the person to change and move forward toward the Good in the future. Kierkegaard claims that these two guides "belong to the Eternal in a human being" (UDVS, 15). They therefore are not subject to the proverbial claim that "there is a time for everything" (Ecclesiastes 3:1–8) but are always appropriate and necessary. These guides make confession to God possible. Why do we confess? Not to change God, who is unchangeable, but to change ourselves (UDVS, 22).

*Purity of Heart* takes as its text yet another verse from Kierkegaard's favorite book of the Bible, James 4:8, "Keep near to God, then he will keep near to you. Cleanse your hands, you sinners, and purify your hearts, you double-minded." The argument is that it is only if we will the Good and will the Good in truth that we can truly "will one thing" and avoid being double-minded (UDVS, 24). Everything other than the Good that a person wills turns out, in the end, to be a multiplicity and not "one thing," leading to a divided self.

Paradoxically, one way that a person can go wrong is by recognizing the importance of a unified self. Such a person, in the grip of a "diabolical wisdom" (UDVS, 31–32), sees that most people are too lethargic to will anything with enthusiasm and have any definite character at all. This person thus decides to will one thing "whether it is good or evil" (UDVS, 32). The kind of person pictured here is someone who desires "greatness" even if this greatness comes at the cost of morality. There are certainly people who are attracted to greatness in this sense, and they may indeed think of themselves as single-mindedly pursuing one great goal, whether that be wealth, glory

15. The Hongs translate the Danish *Fortrydelsen* as "regret," but I prefer Steere's choice of "remorse."

(perhaps athletic fame or military renown), or just being known as someone who "changed the world" and thereby acquired world-historical significance.

Kierkegaard thinks that this self-understanding is a form of self-deception. The person who wills greatness even if this requires moral compromise will not have a truly unified self. Such a person cannot succeed for two reasons. First, evil is never just "one thing" but always a multiplicity. Second, and perhaps even more important, a person who wills evil cannot help but be divided, because a person cannot help but will the Good as well.

Kierkegaard here lines up on the side of Plato and Aristotle, over against David Hume and his followers, over the question whether what is objectively valuable has motivational power just because of its value. Hume and his followers assume that it is only our desires that motivate our actions. Those who follow the great Greek philosophers think, with Iris Murdoch, that the Good itself has a kind of magnetic power.[16] Kierkegaard believes that the Good has this power, because God has created us with an intrinsic attraction to the Good. We are constituted in such a way that we cannot help but be drawn to the Good. We are motivationally pulled not just by what we believe to be good but by the Good itself. "A person, despite all his defiance, does not have the power to tear himself away completely from the Good, because it is the stronger" (UDVS, 33). A rebel against the Good thus always has a kind of "fifth column" (a kind of treasonous power) within his own self and cannot be fully committed to his own rebellion (UDVS, 30–31).

One might think that Kierkegaard would have been on the side of Hume in this dispute, since Kierkegaard is a great defender of the importance of the passions and rejects the idea that merely knowing what is right or good is sufficient to motivate a person to act rightly. Rather, he says the person must desire the Good if the Good is to shape his or her behavior. So how can the Good have motivational power in itself for him? The answer to this puzzle lies in Kierkegaard's understanding of God's creational activity in humans. It is true that our actions stem from passions and never solely from the intellect. However, it is also true that God has instilled a longing for the Good into our nature. We are hardwired, so to speak, to want the Good. Of course, this is not a causal deterministic wiring. It is all too easy for humans to do what is wrong. However, when we do what is wrong, it is hard for us to be "single-minded" because of the built-in attraction for the Good. This is why, when we do manage to muster real passion for evil, we first must convince ourselves that it is not evil but good, often through self-deception.

16. See Iris Murdoch, *Metaphysics as a Guide to Morals* (New York: Penguin, 1993).

## The Reward Disease

One of the ways that a person can fail to will the Good in truth is to will the Good for the sake of a reward. This error was already discussed in chapter 4, since Climacus, in his description of the religious life, also gives an acute description of the person who would gladly commit to an "eternal happiness" if he could be assured that this commitment is one that will pay off.[17] Kierkegaard is not suggesting that the person who wills the Good does so in a purely disinterested, passionless manner. There is a legitimate reward for willing the Good, the "reward that God has eternally joined together with the Good" (UDVS, 37). However, this reward is not an external reward that is contingently attached to the Good, but a reward that is gained when one loves the Good and is united to the Good and thereby gains what one loves. Such a lover of the Good is rewarded in the same way that a man who loves music is rewarded by being able to play and hear music. Such a lover of music is quite different from the musician who sees music as a means to become rich or famous.

External or worldly rewards are quite different from this kind of internal reward. If one wills the Good for the sake of such things as being honored by humans, or becoming wealthy, then "the Good is one thing; the reward is something else" (UDVS, 37). One cannot therefore be willing just one thing when one wills the Good for the sake of a worldly reward.

Perhaps fortunately, Kierkegaard thinks that the world is not very friendly to the Good, so the idea of gaining such rewards by a commitment to the Good is dubious. One is more likely to be disliked or even hated if one truly wills the Good. (This theme becomes much more pronounced in Kierkegaard's later writings on Christian spirituality.) However, even if one were fortunate enough to gain riches or fame by doing good, one would not truly be getting these things as a *reward* for the Good, since one would not really be committed to the Good at all. A person who is good only when there is a reward of this type for being good is not truly willing the Good. Such a person is double-minded, to use the apostle's language. I wish to conclude this section of the chapter by giving a fictional illustration of this "reward disease."

There is a powerful fictional treatment of this condition in the movie *Amadeus*. The film revolves around two historical figures, the great musician Wolfgang Amadeus Mozart and another musician of the time, Antonio

17. See chapter 4, pp. 70–73.

Salieri, though it is likely that both characters are highly fictionalized.[18] The film begins with Salieri in an institution, who tells his life story to a priest in the course of making his confession. As a young person in Italy, Salieri desperately wanted to become a musician, but it seemed impossible; his family had other plans for him. Salieri prays to God to have his dream come true. He promises to live a devout life if God will grant him his wish, and, much to his surprise, in a way that seems almost miraculous, it does. He becomes court musician to the emperor in Vienna, Joseph II.

Mozart is portrayed in the film as a childish person, always hard up for money and looking for sex with beautiful women. However, Mozart is endowed with a genius that allows him to produce sublime works. Poor Salieri cannot understand this. He claims to have served God faithfully, but God has endowed Mozart, a "vulgar child," with true genius, while giving Salieri just enough ability to be the only person who truly recognizes that genius. It seems completely unjust to him, and his envy and jealousy lead him to seek Mozart's death. Salieri's case against God is told in such a convincing way that the priest hearing his confession becomes undone.

However, does this fictional Salieri have a case? Has God dealt him a raw hand? Salieri says that he has been a faithful servant of God and the Good, but he complains bitterly that God has not rewarded him for his service but instead lavished his gifts on someone who has no concern for the Good at all. Kierkegaard's verdict on the fictional Salieri would be that he has no legitimate grievance against God at all. (And this is not just because Mozart was Kierkegaard's favorite composer.) Salieri has not truly served God at all, but only himself. In his own mind, he has made a deal with God, but it is a deal grounded in his own desires. Salieri is infected by the reward disease. He is a double-minded person who has never truly willed one thing.

## Willing the Good out of Fear of Punishment

A second form of double-mindedness that Kierkegaard describes involves willing the Good out of fear of punishment. Popular forms of religion, in-

18. The 1984 film, directed by Miloš Forman, won many Oscars. Most historians view the film's version of the story as fiction. The premise of the film is that Salieri is so jealous of Mozart that he brought about his death, but there is no historical evidence for this. In my discussion of the film, I treat "Mozart" and "Salieri" as fictional characters.

cluding Christianity, often focus on fear of hell (or some other punishment) as a motivation for the Good. However, Kierkegaard rejects this as a form of willing the Good and claims that such a view confuses "the sickness and the medicine" (UDVS, 46). The reason this is the case is that Kierkegaard does not accept the view of God that holds he is an angry or vengeful ruler, who punishes those who transgress his laws in a retributive way. God is love and wants only the Good for everyone, even those who are rebelling against the Good. His punishments are chastenings that are intended to change people, not to inflict suffering on them because they deserve it. If God "punishes" someone, the punishment is not the sickness but the medicine. If someone wants to avoid only the medicine, then that person fails to understand what is genuinely for his own good. Such a person does not really want to be healthy, but only to be free from the medicine.

If someone seeks the Good out of fear of punishment, then such a person *"is continually doing what he does not really will*, or what he has no pleasure in doing" (UDVS, 50). A person who really understood his own good would actually welcome God's chastening and not fear it (UDVS, 55).[19] Fear can be a valuable and important instrument for a person's upbuilding. However, one must learn to fear what really ought to be feared and not to fear that which should not be feared. Kierkegaard says that it is good for a person to have a sense of shame; it is a "rescuing attendant" that serves the cause of "sanctification and true freedom" (UDVS, 52). However, what is helpful is not simply "seeming" to be good so as to win the approval of others. Rather, a person should be ashamed of merely seeming to be good, ashamed of failing to will the Good in truth.

Shame is for Kierkegaard a relational quality, something that one has "before others" (UDVS, 53). In order to have the right sense of shame before another, Kierkegaard says it is crucial to value the judgment of the right kind of person. One wants the approval of those who care about the Good because one wants to be good. To make sure that one is not attempting to gain some worldly advantage from someone's approval, Kierkegaard suggests that one picture oneself wanting the approval of someone who has died. A deceased person is transfigured and perfected, someone whose judgment cannot be corrupted (UDVS, 54).

Ultimately, the judgment that matters most is not human judgment, but the judgment of God. God cannot be deceived, and so merely seeming

---

19. Kierkegaard actually goes so far as to say that the person who wills the Good *"even hopes for punishment"* (UDVS, 55), but this seems extreme to me.

to be good to win approval cannot succeed. Both God's approval and God's chastening have as their end connecting us to the Good, and they cannot be had as things that are external to that end.

## Conclusion: Living *Coram Deo*

Kierkegaard spends much of *Purity of Heart* contrasting two kinds of persons who live different lives. He distinguishes the "active person," who lives what one might call a normal life, doing such things as working and raising a family, from the "sufferer." The sufferers are people who, through no fault of their own, are prevented from engaging in these normal activities. Such people are not able to engage in the "give and take" of life; they cannot be part of reciprocal relationships in which they give as much as they receive, but rather are "objects of sympathy and compassion" (UDVS, 110). Of course, most human lives are a mixture of these two qualities. Most people are perhaps active at times and sufferers at other times, but Kierkegaard tries to make the two types of life clear by contrasting the active person with an "essential sufferer" (UDVS, 118), someone who has never had any chance for worldly happiness, even as a child. Kierkegaard thinks that it is very beneficial for those who are *not* unfortunate in this way to contemplate with sympathy those who suffer.

He argues again for a kind of equality between the two. Both persons can "achieve the highest," the active person through courage, and the sufferer through the virtue of patience.[20] The sufferers cannot achieve anything in a worldly sense, but they still can offer us heroic examples of those who accept the life God has given them. Such a person can will the Good and therefore will one thing by willing to endure with patience the suffering that is his or her lot (UDVS, 113). This is not, I think, a claim that humans should always accept suffering and not try to avoid or ameliorate suffering. Rather, it is a recognition that sometimes suffering is unavoidable no matter what one does. One might think that there is no virtue in accepting what cannot be changed, but Kierkegaard argues that this is not the case. Just as a poor person can have the virtue of thrift even if the person has little opportunity to exercise it, so a sufferer can freely accept what cannot be changed. A person who wants to will one thing, "whether he was *one who acts* or *one who suffers,*

---

20. One of the last of *Upbuilding Discourses*, "Against Cowardliness" (EUD, 347), focuses on courage, and I have already looked at two discourses that focus on patience.

*. . . must will to do everything for the Good* or *he must will to suffer everything for the Good*" (UDVS, 120).

The active person can will the Good in the midst of daily life: "You are not asked to withdraw from life, from an honorable occupation, from a happy domestic life" (UDVS, 137). Kierkegaard goes on to describe what this might look like for work and family life. Both the sufferer and the active person can live as "a single individual" (UDVS, 135). Everyone knows that this phrase is deeply important to Kierkegaard, but what does it mean? Essentially, it means that one lives one's life *coram Deo* (before God), conscious of being individually accountable to God for the whole of one's own life (UDVS, 127). Obviously, a married person is also accountable to a spouse, and an employee to an employer. However, Kierkegaard insists that even in such relationships there is also an accountability to God for how one treats one's spouse and how one relates to one's employer.

Kierkegaard illustrates what it means to live one's life "before God" through a theatrical illustration, in which a church service is compared to a theater performance. Many people who go to church think of the preacher as a performer and see themselves as critics, dissecting the quality and beauty of the sermon. On this view, the preacher is like an actor, and the congregation is made up of spectators. Kierkegaard argues that we ought to view things differently. "The speaker is the prompter; there are no spectators" (UDVS, 124). Those who make up the congregation are really the actors, and each person in the congregation "performs" before God himself, who is the only audience. For Kierkegaard, this illustration does not merely describe how a person should view a worship service in church, but how life as a whole should be viewed.

As we saw in chapter 1, for Kierkegaard, the self is a "relation that relates itself to itself by relating itself to another" (SUD, 13). Although there are many "others" a person can relate to, we are intended to become a self in relation to God. Socratic spirituality in its richest forms is essentially a spirituality in which the "other" is recognized to be God, and God is understood as having an absolute claim on a person's life.

What makes this spirituality attractive and not fearful is that the God to whom I must relate is a God of love who desires only my good. Human persons can and do fail to achieve this relation to God; they may break with God or rebel against God. If they do this, they cut themselves off from their own happiness and good. However, nothing they do can change God's love for them. God's love is unconditional and unchangeable.

It seems likely that in this conviction that God's love is unconditional, Kierkegaard is drawing implicitly on Christian doctrines. Certainly, this is a view that Kierkegaard himself derived from his reading of the Christian Scriptures. However, it does not seem impossible that a "Socratic saint," who thinks of God as unconditionally good and tries to live accordingly, would affirm something like this as well. Since *Purity of Heart* contains no discussion of original sin or Christ's atonement, it still can be read as exemplifying Socratic spirituality.

# CHAPTER 6

# Christian Spirituality (1):
# Upbuilding Christian Spirituality

We have seen that for Kierkegaard humans are spiritual by virtue of the fact that they must become the selves they are to be, through a process that is always carried out in relation to an "other" that defines the self. In a healthy human self, the "other" that defines the self must be God. The Socratic spirituality I have spent the last three chapters discussing defines the self over against God understood as creator, the one to whom humans are accountable. Christian spirituality is also a spirituality in which humans must live "before God." However, God is now understood in and through the God-man, Jesus of Nazareth. Christian spirituality is not merely a spirituality of immanence or "recollection," in which God is known through our natural capacities. Rather, God is now known through an historical figure. For Kierkegaard, this means that Christianity is a religion of "transcendence." The term here is not used ontologically, although Kierkegaard certainly believes that God is transcendent. Rather, the term is being used epistemically. Our knowledge of God in Christ requires a revelation that transcends our natural cognitive capacities.

In this chapter and the following two, I shall explore this distinctively Christian spirituality. When God is known through Christ, the human problem is understood in a new way: not merely as guilt, but as sin, a revealed Christian concept. Christianity intensifies the problem of guilt but then offers a radical solution. The forgiveness of sins is offered to us through Christ's atonement. This forgiveness is completely due to God's grace and cannot be earned or merited. It is achieved through faith and not by works. Nevertheless, for Kierkegaard, genuine faith must express itself in a striving. Thus, Kierkegaard, without rejecting the Lutheran claim that salvation cannot be earned, puts new emphasis on the claim of the apostle James that faith without works is dead. Christian faith is not merely assent to propositions. The genuine believer must be a follower of Christ (UDVS, 217–29).

One of the first places in which Kierkegaard spells out what this means is in the discourse "What Meaning and What Joy There Are in the Thought of Following Christ," the first discourse in part 3 of UDVS. The Danish term used for "follower" here is *Efterfølger* and literally means "after-follower." Kierkegaard takes this very literally. He describes Christ as the one who has "walked the road before us" (UDVS, 219, 223), and our task is to follow along after him on the same road, which is the road of suffering.

Christ thus plays two significantly different roles in the life of the Christian. He is both the Redeemer and the "Pattern" (Danish *Forbilledet*).[1] The entry point into the Christian life is the consciousness of sin. If one asks why someone would accept Christianity, the answer given is a "Lutheran-like" one: only the consciousness of sin can motivate becoming a Christian (PC, 67).[2] Nevertheless, the person who accepts Christ as savior and thus takes refuge in Christ's atonement for sin thereby incurs an enormous debt of gratitude to Christ. Just as Socratic spirituality sees humans as accountable to God because of our debt to God as the creator, so Christian spirituality sees believers as accountable to Christ because of the enormous debt they owe to Christ as the Redeemer.

---

1. The Hongs translate *Forbilledet* as "the prototype." In the *OED*, this rendering at first seems correct, since the first definition begins "the first or primary type of something," from which copies or imitations are made. However, part of the meaning is that these later copies may be "improved forms" of the original, and this makes the translation dubious, since followers of Christ will always recognize the gap between Christ's example and their own lives. This is even more obvious from the third definition given: "A trial model or preliminary version." I believe this third meaning has become the dominant meaning in contemporary culture; today companies release prototypes for products that are assumed to be preliminary and in need of revision. I thus prefer Walter Lowrie's choice of "the Pattern," with an initial capital to show that this refers to Christ and Christ alone. The word could also perhaps be translated as "Exemplar" or "Model."

2. Strictly speaking, this book is pseudonymous and is attributed to Anti-Climacus, and so the voice is not Kierkegaard's. However, as I argued in chapter 1, Anti-Climacus is a different kind of pseudonym in Kierkegaard's writings. He is created because he embodies a lofty type of Christian faith that Kierkegaard aspires to but does not feel he is entitled to present personally. However, there is no doubt that Kierkegaard does not disagree with what Anti-Climacus says; he just feels personally inadequate to say it in his own voice.

There is a kind of dialectical succession or rhythm between the two roles Christ plays as the Pattern and as the Redeemer in the life of the Christian. Even the consciousness of sin is derived from knowledge of Christ. Even without the incarnation and the example Christ provides of a perfect human life, we humans can still recognize our guilt. However, when we see Christ as the Pattern, we can realize how far from the ideal our lives are, and guilt-consciousness can be transformed into sin-consciousness. The difference between guilt-consciousness and sin-consciousness is simply that those who recognize themselves as guilty still believe that they have the power to change and eliminate the moral gap between their actuality and the ideal. Sin-consciousness includes an understanding that this is impossible through our own unaided efforts. In his mature writings, Kierkegaard consistently maintains that we can come to know ourselves as sinners only through a revelation from God and that this revelation comes through Christ. Only God, for whom all things are possible, can heal "the moral gap" in a person who is a sinner.

When a person accepts God's gracious forgiveness through Christ, the natural and fitting response is love for Christ and gratitude. Jesus says that those who obey his commands are the ones who "abide in his love" (John 15:10) and that those who want to be his friends must keep his commands (John 15:14). So those who know Christ as the Redeemer will want to be his followers and devote themselves to him as the Pattern. However, when believers attempt to follow Christ, they fail, and they must again have recourse to Christ as the Redeemer. Upon receiving God's forgiveness, the rhythm repeats itself. For the believer, Christ must always be both Pattern and Redeemer.

It is true that most of the emphasis in Kierkegaard's Christian writings falls on Christ as the Pattern, the one whom believers must follow. The reason for this emphasis is that Kierkegaard knows his Lutheran readers already understand and believe that Christ is the Redeemer. The danger is that Christ's forgiveness will be taken for granted. The forgiveness of sins is understood simply as a propositional doctrine, something that one can assent to and then ignore. In looking at Socratic spirituality in chapter 4, I tried to show how for Kierkegaard, even in Socratic spirituality, it is not enough to believe intellectually that God exists and is the creator. Rather, one must try to live one's life in a way that *shows* that God is the creator. Recognizing God as God requires giving up control and resigning every finite good that impedes a relation to the Eternal. This requires suffering and ultimately leads to guilt. In a similar way, Christian spirituality demands that Christian doctrines be embodied in one's life.[3] Faith is not merely an intellectual act of assent. One shows that one believes by living as if one believed.

When one lives a truly Christian life, one must break with worldly ways of thinking and acting. Christian spirituality can never be seen simply as a refinement or development of natural human virtues. Christian existence is rooted in the actions of the God who is three in one; it incorporates human striving, but it is something that cannot be accomplished merely through human striving. As we shall see, this requires a kind of "inverse" perspective, in which the worldview of the "natural person" is turned upside down.

From the very beginning, this view of Christian spirituality includes a polemic against the idea of "Christendom." Christendom can be described in various ways, but it is perhaps best understood as the idea that a human society or culture can become so deeply Christian that a person who grows up within that society becomes a Christian simply by the process of enculturation and formation that the society offers. As Christendom sees things, people in a "Christian" country, such as Denmark is supposed to be, naturally become Christians by growing up and absorbing the values of their society. Christendom believes in what William James called the "once-born" type of religiousness.[4] Kierkegaard, however, steadfastly holds to the biblical teaching that to become a Christian, "you must be born again" (John 3:7).

Although there is a basic consistency to Kierkegaard's view of Christian spirituality, there are differences between his earlier and later Christian writings. In earlier works, such as the "Christian discourses" that form the last part of *Upbuilding Discourses in Various Spirits*, as well as in the book with the title *Christian Discourses*, the polemic against Christendom is certainly present but is less strident. In these works, Kierkegaard addresses the ordinary Christian, and he seems to assume some willingness on the part of his readers to respond to his appeals. I would characterize these works as Christian "upbuilding discourses." Their aim is to help readers develop

3. There are places in Kierkegaard's writings where he uses the term "doctrine" to mean "purely intellectual doctrine." This leads him in a few places to say that "Christianity is not a doctrine." However, even in one of those places in the authorship, he attaches a footnote making clear that he is not at all denying that Christianity includes doctrines, but merely wishes to claim that those doctrines are not really believed in a Christian manner unless they express themselves in the lives of the believers (CUP 1:379–80).

4. See William James, *The Varieties of Religious Experience* (New York: Penguin, 1985), 80, 82. The source of this terminology—"once-born" and "twice-born"—appears to be Francis W. Newman, *The Soul: Her Sorrows and Her Aspirations* (London: J. Chapman, 1849), 111–12.

the Christian emotions and ways of thinking and acting that will help them make progress toward becoming genuine followers of Christ.

However, in some later writings, such as *For Self-Examination, Judge for Yourself!*, and *Practice in Christianity*, the polemic against Christendom becomes more strident, though Kierkegaard never breaks openly with the church until the public attack he makes on the church at the end of his life, in 1854 and 1855. One can also see this stronger tone appearing in sections of *Works of Love*, although I would argue that this book as a whole is more closely related to the earlier Christian writings. The seeds of the open attack on the state church can certainly be seen in works such as *Practice in Christianity*, but there is still a sharp difference in both content and tone between the later works of the authorship and the newspaper and magazine articles Kierkegaard published in the last two years of his life. Therefore, in discussing Kierkegaard's view of Christian spirituality, I shall for the most part postpone looking at that open attack until chapter 8, though the subject will come up in chapter 7 as well. The open attack calls for separate consideration, because it combines genuine insights already present in the earlier writings, with troubling notes of misogyny and even downright misanthropy.

In this chapter, I shall focus on the earlier Christian writings that have an upbuilding character, works that we might consider as coming from the middle of Kierkegaard's total authorship. I shall focus mainly on the last part of *Upbuilding Discourses in Various Spirits* and then parts 1 and 4 from *Christian Discourses*. Kierkegaard wrote many of these sermon-like discourses at a time when he was still seriously considering becoming a pastor, a course that he eventually decided against.

## The Gospel of Sufferings

Part 3 of *Upbuilding Discourses in Various Spirits* is entitled *The Gospel of Sufferings: Christian Discourses*. We have, of course, already seen the importance of suffering to the religious life even in Socratic spirituality. However, in Christian spirituality, suffering not only takes on greater significance; it changes its character. Socratic spirituality accepts the sufferings of life as things that one must endure as coming from God's hand. However, the suffering in Socratic spirituality is mainly what Kierkegaard calls ordinary human suffering, the kind of suffering that every human life must encounter to a greater or lesser degree, such as illness, grief over loved ones, financial distress, and death.

The mark of Christian suffering is its voluntary character. Christian suffering is not masochistic. In fact, Kierkegaard constantly stresses that Christian suffering is something that leads to joy (or should lead to joy). It is not an embrace of suffering for its own sake, or even something that is endured simply for the sake of improving one's own character, though, as we shall see below, Kierkegaard thinks suffering does have this beneficial result. Kierkegaard is not afraid to say that Christian suffering will be rewarded, both with joy in this life and with eternal happiness after death.[5] So what is Christian suffering? It is the suffering that results when a person takes a stand for a good cause, for the sake of Christ, when the person foresees that the actions taken will lead to opposition, persecution, or even, in some cases, martyrdom.

Kierkegaard acknowledges that it is not easy to believe that this kind of suffering leads to joy. Humanly speaking, it seems foolish to embrace suffering when one could easily avoid it. The rewards that the suffering is supposed to lead to are far from obvious, whether they be joy that one is supposed to experience now or eternal happiness that one will gain after death. It is just for this reason that this kind of suffering is something that stems from faith. For Kierkegaard, genuine faith always involves risk. If a dictator rigs an election, then it takes no faith to believe that the dictator will win. It is a sure thing. Faith, however, is a response to uncertainty, a commitment to a cause when it is not certain that the cause will be triumphant. So for Kierkegaard, the idea that the "heavy suffering" one undergoes as a Christian is actually beneficial is far from a certainty; it is something that must be *believed* (UDVS, 235).[6]

The burden of suffering that the Christian must be prepared to carry is heavy, but Kierkegaard insists that for the true Christian it is light. The reason for this is that the "cross" that the Christian must take up and bear is actually light in comparison with the burden of sin that is removed when one becomes a follower of Christ: "*The one who takes away the consciousness of sin and gives the consciousness of forgiveness instead*—he indeed takes away the heavy burden and gives the light one in its place" (UDVS, 246).

5. See UDVS, 228–29, where Kierkegaard agrees with Saint Paul that if there is no life after death, the Christian would be deceived and foolish.

6. It is important to realize that Danish, unlike English, has only one noun, *Tro*, that can be translated as "faith" or "belief." The same Danish word is also used as a verb. In English, the word "faith" cannot be used as a verb, so one must use "believe" to talk about faith as an action. In Danish, when people say that they believe something, they are really saying that they "faith" it.

The voluntary embrace of suffering is neither easy nor natural. Kierkegaard goes so far as to say that "it can never occur to the natural man to wish for suffering" (UDVS, 250). To will to suffer requires that "the most profound change" must take place in a person (UDVS, 250). For this to occur, a person "must first be gripped by and then be willing to learn from the only one who went out into the world with the purpose of willing to suffer" (UDVS, 250). That one is of course Christ.

Does Kierkegaard here overstate the differences between the Christian and what we might call the noble pagan? There are, after all, pagans who have shown themselves willing to face suffering and even death for the sake of noble causes. And even the Christian surely does not will suffering for the sake of suffering, as I have affirmed above. So there is at least a formal parallel between the Christian and the noble pagan, in that both willingly embrace suffering as a necessary means for achieving a good end.

Despite this parallel, I agree with Kierkegaard that there is something distinctive about Christian suffering. The distinctiveness lies in the nature of the end the suffering makes possible. The Christian does not accept suffering as a regrettable but necessary means to some end, such as saving the life of a friend or, on a grander scale, saving one's country from defeat, as is the case for the noble pagan. In such cases, the necessity of the suffering still seems contingent; it is necessary given the circumstances.

One might think Christian suffering is also contingent; it is necessary, but only necessary given the reality of sin. However, if sin is a universal human condition,[7] as Christians affirm, and if sin is the ground of suffering, then suffering would still be something that everyone must expect to face, not something that is made necessary by unusual and unfortunate circumstances. From a Christian point of view, sin is certainly tragic, but it is clearly not unusual.

However, Kierkegaard actually denies that suffering is made necessary only by sin; rather, suffering is in some way necessary for finite humans to achieve perfection. His argument for this claim is scriptural. Jesus, although he was sinless, "learned obedience from what he suffered" (Hebrews 5:8). The obedience of Christ does not stem from his divine will as the second person of the Trinity, always perfectly attuned to the will of the Father.[8] Rather, Jesus learned obedience as a human because he had to choose between doing what

---

7. Except, of course, for Jesus, and Mary for some Christians.
8. See UDVS, 263, "the eternal harmony of his will with his Father's will is indeed not obedience."

he himself wished to do and doing what the Father willed. In the Garden of Gethsemane, Jesus prayed, "If it is possible, Father, let this cup pass from me, yet not my will be done but yours" (UDVS, 255).[9]

Perhaps what lies behind Kierkegaard's claim is this: a finite human being, with many needs and desires, has a will that does not naturally and inevitably coincide with the will of God. This was true even for Jesus, who was fully human even while being divine. Thus, even for Jesus, the possibility of a conflict between what he desired and doing the will of God was present. Jesus became perfect only through the suffering of self-denial. What Jesus was facing was something no human could naturally desire: a painful and torturous death. To obey the Father and fulfill his mission, he therefore, as genuinely human, had to deny himself, giving up doing what he himself wished to do, and align his will with the will of the Father. Even Jesus as a human being had to learn obedience (UDVS, 255).

Kierkegaard generalizes from this lesson. It is through suffering that one learns that God is God and how we must relate to God. When one "learns obedience in the school of sufferings," then one learns "to let God be master, to let God rule" (UDVS, 257). The fear of the Lord may be the beginning of wisdom, but Kierkegaard claims that learning obedience through suffering "is the consummation of wisdom" (UDVS, 258).

The whole of this discourse is entitled "The Joy of It: That the School of Sufferings Educates for Eternity." It is only through obedience to God that we humans discover what eternity really is. If it is true that even "the pure one" had to learn obedience through suffering, "how much more then for the sinful human being" (UDVS, 263). The discourse concludes by affirming that obedience cannot exist without suffering, faith cannot exist without obedience, and eternity cannot be possessed without faith (UDVS, 263).

## A Spiritual Response to the Problem of Evil

Several of the other discourses in the *Gospel of Sufferings* are noteworthy, but I want to give at least one other discourse special attention. In "A Person Always Suffers as Guilty," Kierkegaard argues that no one other than Christ can legitimately claim to suffer as someone who is purely innocent, and that this thought is one that is comforting and upbuilding. This discourse is one of the few places in Kierkegaard's authorship that directly addresses what is usually

9. The scriptural passage quoted can be found in Matthew 26:39 and Luke 22:42.

called the problem of evil, as well as the problem that doubt, which often arises out of the problem of evil, poses for the Christian life. However, contrary to what one might think from the title, the discourse does *not* attempt to say that human suffering should be viewed as a punishment for guilt.

The problem of evil is not addressed in this discourse in the way philosophers commonly do, as an epistemic challenge to the reasonableness of belief in God. Rather, for Kierkegaard, the problem is a spiritual problem, and the solution is spiritual as well.

It becomes evident as one reads this discourse that Kierkegaard's view of the problem of evil is similar to the perspective that is today usually called "skeptical theism." This label is, however, very misleading when applied to Kierkegaard (and also when applied to such contemporary philosophers as myself).[10] The view is not grounded in anything that resembles skepticism, and it is not based on generic theism but on specifically Christian convictions.

The problem of evil is, of course, bound up with questions about why there is evil in a world created by a God who is both completely good and also totally powerful. The doubter raises questions, as David Hume does in his *Dialogues concerning Natural Religion*: "Epicurus's old questions are yet unanswered. Is he [God] willing to prevent evil, but not able? Then he is impotent. Is he able, but not willing? Then he is malevolent. Is he both able and willing? Whence then is evil?"[11] Some philosophers and theologians have responded to such questions by trying to provide a theodicy, an explanation of why God allows evil. Typically, theodicies attempt to explain and justify evil in the world by showing how allowing evil leads to a greater good or how eliminating evil would lead to eliminating some great good. As one might expect, such theodicies are the subject of much debate in philosophy.

The person who holds the position usually called (misleadingly) skeptical theism does not attempt a theodicy. Instead, skeptical theists respond to "Epicurus's old questions" by honestly admitting that they do not know why God allows evil. Skeptical theists respond from a place of humility, recognizing their own cognitive limitations. Rather, the problem is answered in something like the following way:

---

10. For brief statements of my own views, see C. Stephen Evans, *Why Christian Faith Still Makes Sense* (Grand Rapids: Baker Academic, 2015), 67–73; and C. Stephen Evans, *Why Believe? Reason and Mystery as Pointers to God* (Grand Rapids: Eerdmans, 1996), 95–104.

11. David Hume, *Dialogues concerning Natural Religion*, ed. Norman Kemp Smith (Indianapolis: Bobbs-Merrill, 1947), 182.

I have reason to believe in God and reason to believe that God is good. Just because I do not know why God allows evil does not imply that God does not have good reasons for doing so. After all, God is omniscient; his knowledge and wisdom are without limits. I, on the other hand, am a finite creature, an animal on the third planet from the sun. Why should I think that if God had a reason for allowing evil, I would know that reason or even be able to understand it if I did? If I do have reasons to believe in God and believe in his goodness, then I should trust him, even when I fail to understand why God acts as he does.

These words are my own and not Kierkegaard's, but it is clear that his view is very similar to the one I have just constructed. Kierkegaard says clearly that "faith's eternal happiness is that God is love. This does not mean that faith understands how God's rule over a person is love" (UDVS, 273). Faith believes that God is love, but it recognizes that it is not always possible to understand how God's providential rule is loving. "We are not . . . required to be able to understand the rule of God's love, but we certainly are required to be able to believe, and believing, to understand that he is love" (UDVS, 268). Kierkegaard insists that God can be loved even if God and God's ways are not understood: "If God is love, then he is also love in everything, love in what you can understand and love in what you cannot understand, love in the dark riddle that lasts a day or in the dark riddle that lasts seventy years" (UDVS, 268).

But why believe that God is love? Kierkegaard's answer is to point to Christ. Christ is the only person who has ever lived before God without guilt. However, Christ is also a person who has suffered in the most agonizing ways, both physically and mentally. On the cross, even Christ experienced the world, as we sometimes do, as a world in which he has been forsaken by God. Yet Christ affirms that God is love, and Christ as God shows that love by suffering with us humans and suffering for us humans. When we are "at Christ's side," we learn that there is only one person who suffered before God as innocent (UDVS, 272).

Why is this important? For Kierkegaard, it is because it teaches us humility. In the end, the "problem of evil" is a spiritual problem, a problem that cannot be solved by theodicy or endless philosophical argument. Rather, the person who doubts God on the basis of evil wants to put God on trial: the doubter "wants to make God the defendant, to make him the one from whom something is required. But along this road God's love will never be found" (UDVS, 273).

What entitles a person to put God on trial in this way? Kierkegaard sees such doubt as the product of "presumptuousness" and arrogance (UDVS, 273). It is the manifestation of a spiritual flaw. Why should we think that if God has reasons to permit evil, we would necessarily know them or understand them? Just a recognition of our finitude and creaturely limits ought to make it obvious that nothing about the goodness of God is implied by my honest admission that I do not always understand God's ways. However, when there is a "struggle of faith" (UDVS, 273), if humility does not stem simply from this awareness of finitude, then "the consciousness of guilt comes to rescue as the relief, as the last reinforcement" (UDVS, 273). The consciousness of guilt teaches the person to doubt himself, rather than God. It teaches him that he has no standing to put God on trial. "If doubt is to have the least show of a foundation, it must have innocence to appeal to, . . . innocence *before God*" (UDVS, 274). However, this is just what all but Christ lack.

For Kierkegaard, one must maintain faith that God is love in order for human life to have any meaning at all. It is only if God exists and is love that every human life is meaningful, because God's existence means that every human "has a task," whether that task be action or the patient endurance of suffering (UDVS, 277). Every human being has the task of becoming the self God intends that person to be. There is then hope for every human being; the task is one that can lead to eternal life. No human life is intrinsically meaningless or wasted. For Kierkegaard, to despair of God's love would also be to despair of the significance of human life. To give up faith in God's love is not merely to break faith with God, but also to break faith with humanity. To doubt that God is love is essentially to give up a belief in the value of human life.

## Christian Spirituality Encounters the World

As noted above, I shall not give an extensive treatment of all the discourses in part 3 of *Upbuilding Discourses in Various Spirits*. Discourse 5, "That It Is Not the Road That Is Hard but That Hardship Is the Road," reiterates and deepens the theme that suffering is not merely an accidental element of human life, but something that plays an essential role in our becoming who we should become. Discourse 6, "That the Happiness of Eternity Still Outweighs Even the Heaviest Temporal Suffering," is based on 2 Corinthians 4:17 and reassures hearers that "the eternal weight of glory" is incommensurable with any temporal sufferings.

However, I shall linger a little longer over discourse 7: "That Bold Confidence Is Able in Suffering to Take Power from the World and Has the Power to Change Scorn into Honor, Downfall into Victory." This discourse focuses on the necessity for someone who is a true Christian to be willing to confess Christ before the world, when this is required (UDVS, 322). This discourse takes as its starting point Acts 5:41: "Then they [the apostles] went away from the council, joyful because they had been deemed worthy to be scorned for the sake of Christ's name." The treatment Kierkegaard here gives to this passage is noteworthy because it is strikingly different from the treatment given to the same passage by Johannes Climacus in *Concluding Unscientific Postscript*, in the course of his exposition of the role of suffering in what he calls Religiousness A. These differences give us a clear picture of some of the differences between Socratic spirituality and Christian spirituality.

In *Postscript*, Climacus mentions that "one does indeed read in the New Testament that the apostles when they were flogged went away joyful, thanking God that it was granted them to suffer something for the sake of Christ" (CUP 1:452). Climacus does affirm that this was virtuous of the apostles, but he nonetheless says that "the suffering spoken of in that passage is not religious suffering, of which there is on the whole very little mention in the New Testament" (CUP 1:453). For Climacus, genuine religious suffering has nothing to do with persecution or external opposition one might incur as a result of acting for a righteous cause. Instead, true religious suffering is simply the inward "dying to self" that is required of every person who relates properly to God. This passage seems to me to be one of the places in which the pseudonym Climacus has views that diverge from his creator Kierkegaard. I find it hard to believe that in 1846 Kierkegaard would have said this in his own voice, given what he says in *Upbuilding Discourses in Various Spirits*, published less than a year later after *Postscript*.

As I have repeatedly said, both Socratic spirituality and Christian spirituality are attempts to live life "before God," but in Christian spirituality, God is known in history, in Jesus of Nazareth, who is God incarnate. Christ provides the "criterion," or measuring stick, of true selfhood, and Christ's life shows that a genuine commitment to loving God and obeying God essentially involves the possibility of a collision with a sinful world that is in rebellion against God's rule. Christ is the one who "went ahead" and thereby suffered a painful and violent death, after living a life of poverty and concern for others. Kierkegaard believes that all those who have faith in Christ are called to be followers and thus must be prepared to suffer opposition from the world, just as Christ did. We live in a world in which "the good

123

must suffer in the world for the sake of the truth, when the righteous has no reward, indeed, is rewarded with scorn and persecution" (UDVS, 329). So far from it being the case that the suffering of the apostles is not genuine religious suffering, it is now said that such suffering is an exemplary case of Christian suffering.

What Kierkegaard wants to claim about the suffering of the apostles is that it is a form of victory. It is not, of course, worldly victory. He does not claim that the apostles, or those who would emulate them, will always be miraculously delivered from persecution or death. It is not a victory over suffering, but a victory won through suffering. What has happened is that the apostles have shown that what humans think about them, or even what humans do to them, is of no consequence in comparison with the judgment of God. Spirituality is a form of accountability, but it is accountability to God, as revealed through Christ, that completely swamps accountability to humans. This is clear from Acts 4:19, when Peter and John tell the Sanhedrin that their obedience to God must take precedence over obedience to human authority. Kierkegaard notes that the apostles do not respond with anger or even judgment of those who have punished them; their joy simply shows that their hearts are so set on following Christ and being judged faithful by God that worldly goods and rewards are, in comparison, of no consequence (UDVS, 335).

Even in these earlier Christian spiritual writings of Kierkegaard, there is already a criticism of Christendom, sometimes implied and subtle, sometimes more explicit and less subtle. One can see this from this discourse. Kierkegaard anticipates that some of his "hearers" will respond by saying that what was true in the days of the apostles is no longer true. After all, the apostles lived in a pagan world, while Kierkegaard's contemporaries live in a Christian country, in which a person who confesses Christ will never face opposition or persecution for being a person of faith. Kierkegaard thinks this is false; no human society or culture is so Christian that it is not part of the "world." The believer in Christendom may not face persecution for a verbal confession of faith, but the person who genuinely tries to follow Christ and live as Christ lived can still expect, at the very least, to be mocked as foolish and naïve. One "confesses" Christ in such a world not by verbal proclamation, but by living as a follower of Christ, and such a confession is really a kind of "judgment" on Christendom (UDVS, 323).

As we shall see, Kierkegaard's polemic against Christendom becomes increasingly strident in his later writings. Nevertheless, at least until the very last years when Kierkegaard openly attacks the church, he worries about whether this kind of "judgment" on his part is genuinely Christian, or rather whether it might reflect a hypocritical sense of superiority and even lack of love.[12]

## The Concerns or Worries of the Pagans

In *Christian Discourses*, published in 1848, about a year later than *The Gospel of Suffering* (part 3 of *Upbuilding Discourses in Various Spirits*), the polemic against Christendom becomes more evident, especially in sections 1 and 3 of the later work. Still, Kierkegaard's worry that his own critique is possibly hypocritical and judgmental is still present. This leads Kierkegaard to develop his criticism of Christendom in a manner that is somewhat gentle and even reflects, as Kierkegaard himself remarks in one place, a humorous tone.[13] This can be clearly seen in the first part of *Christian Discourses*, *The Worries of the Pagans*.[14]

In this part of the book, Kierkegaard deals with seven "pagan worries": poverty (CD, 13), abundance (CD, 23), lowliness (CD, 37), loftiness (CD, 48), presumptuousness (CD, 60), self-torment (CD, 70), and "indecisiveness, vacillation, and disconsolateness" (CD, 81). The starting point for the seven discourses can be found in the words of Jesus in the Sermon on the Mount, when Jesus tells his hearers first to "consider the birds of the air" and then to "consider the lilies of the field" (Matthew 6:24–38). Kierkegaard treats these seven worries in a virtually formulaic manner. In his account, the bird and the lily (Kierkegaard makes them singular, befitting his emphasis on "the single individual") become our "teachers," helping us learn how the bird and

12. One can see this worry in the passages in UDVS, 325–26.
13. For Kierkegaard's admission that he is intentionally employing humor, see CD, 12, where he says that these discourses, "with the aid of the lily and the bird, . . . [do] not forget first and foremost to relax into a smile."
14. The Danish term (*Bekymringer*) translated as "worries" above is translated by the Hongs as "cares," and thus the title becomes *The Cares of the Pagans*. Walter Lowrie had earlier translated the title as *The Anxieties of the Heathen*. I think Lowrie's translation is closer to the Danish, since the Danish word is stronger than the English term "cares" suggests. Nevertheless, I understand why the Hongs avoid "anxieties," since the Danish word in question is very different from *Angest*, translated as "anxiety" in *The Concept of Anxiety*. I have chosen, therefore, to alter the Hong translations by substituting "worry" and "worries" for "care" and "cares." One could also translate the Danish terms by "concerns." "Care" would be acceptable if one thought of it only in the sense of "the cares of life" and not as referring simply to whatever one cares about.

the lily are different from the pagan, and both similar to and different from the Christian. By employing these teachers, Kierkegaard avoids any personal judgment of anyone: "The lily and the bird are slipped in to prevent judging, because the lily and the bird judge no one" (CD, 10).

The first discourse on the "worry of poverty" illustrates this beautifully. Kierkegaard begins by describing the bird and asking what the bird lives on. (The lily is left for other discourses.) The answer is that the bird lives on the "*daily bread, this heavenly food*" (CD, 13). The daily bread is "just exactly enough but not one bit more: it is the little that poverty needs" (CD, 13). (It is clear that the bird and the lily as Kierkegaard describes them are poetic creations; he is not making biological generalizations about the actual food of wild animals and plants.) If one judged the bird by its external circumstances, one would say the bird is poor, but the bird "is not in poverty because it does not have the worry of poverty" (CD, 14; translation modified).

Pagans are not like the bird in this matter. According to Jesus, they worry and ask about what they will eat or drink. The Christian is like the bird in that the Christian also lacks this worry that the pagan has. This is not true because the Christian is necessarily rich and has no temporal needs, though Kierkegaard acknowledges that there might be rich Christians. To avoid confusion, Kierkegaard focuses on the case of a poor Christian. Such a Christian lacks the worry or concern of poverty because the Christian "resembles the bird" in living on "the daily bread" (CD, 14). In this way, the Christian, like the bird, "is poor and yet not poor" (CD, 14). He is poor judged by external circumstances, but not poor because he lacks worry or concern about his poverty.

There is, however, also an important difference between the Christian and the bird. The Christian receives the daily bread by praying for daily bread and thus receives it from the hand of God (CD, 14–15). For the Christian, how the bread is received is much more important than the bread, but this is not the case for the bird. A human being is different from the bird by virtue of an inability to live "on bread alone." A human being, unlike the bird, has an eternal destiny as a spiritual being. The Christian "does indeed pray for the daily bread and gives thanks for it, something the bird does not do. But to pray and give thanks are more important to him than meat or drink" (CD, 16). A human being's spiritual life here on earth points to an "eternal life" that is "certainly beyond all comparison with food and drink."

The Christian's task is to live without the cares or concerns of poverty, regardless of how poor the Christian may be. The pagan, by contrast, is controlled by these concerns or worries. The pagan, according to Kierkegaard, "lives in order to *slave*" (CD, 21). The problem is not that one must work for a living, but that one is so wrapped up in worries about making a living that one has lost oneself, "ceased to be a human being." Such a person has literally "lost his soul" (CD, 21).

One might object here that Kierkegaard does not realize that we do not have full control over our emotions. As someone who has often lain awake in bed at night full of worry, I can understand doubting that a person can really avoid worry and anxiety about such things. Kierkegaard knows that the task is hard and that we cannot simply control our emotions by a simple act of will. He says that achieving such a state of being free from worry is "a difficult walk." I cannot just tell myself to stop worrying and thereby make it happen all at once. However, he insists that we are not helpless victims of our emotions. We must be able to live without this kind of concern because we are commanded to do so by Christ, and Kierkegaard obviously agrees with Kant that what we ought to do we must be able to do (CD, 20–21). The key to making progress is continually to focus on the fact that we live our lives "before God." We see once more that accountability to God is a gift, a blessing. A person may not be able to avoid poverty, but a person can make progress toward avoiding worry about poverty by continually reminding himself of God's providential care. Trust in God's fatherly care displaces worry about poverty.

Kierkegaard's primary aim here is to help his listeners deepen their spiritual lives and thereby eliminate a worry or concern that dehumanizes them. There is no overt denunciation of Christendom as a society obsessed with making and accumulating money, something one does find in Kierkegaard's final writings. Rather, Kierkegaard asks his hearers to learn from the bird and the lily, leaving it to the hearers to decide whether they and others in their society are more like the true Christian or the pagan. The critique of Christendom is present but subtle and implied.

As I said above, each of the discourses has the same formulaic structure. The formula works like this: first there is a delineation of a worry or concern that the pagan has but that the bird or lily does not have. The Christian is then described as someone who also lacks this worry, but the Christian lacks this worry for a reason different from that of the bird and the lily. The bird and lily simply obey the will of God spontaneously and immediately, while the Christian must constantly choose to obey God's will (CD, 38). This is grounded in an ontological difference. The bird and the lily simply are what they are; they are not spirit. Humans, because they are spiritual, are beings who must become what they are. If they lack the worries of the pagans, it is because they have eliminated them, not because they never had them, which is what is true of the bird and the lily.

The Christian has replaced the emotions of worry or concern that the pagan has by other emotions that stem from the Christian's ability to live spiritually before God, emotions connected to love, hope, faith, and humility. Since these are Christian discourses, living spiritually is now understood and interpreted in terms of living before Christ—following him and imitating his earthly life.

Of course, there are some differences between the discourses. The concern or worry of presumptuousness, for example, is different from the concerns of poverty and abundance, lowliness and eminence. Poverty, abundance, lowliness, and eminence are all in themselves neutral or innocent; one can be a Christian in any of these states. Presumptuousness, however, is intrinsically evil, and thus this is a worry or concern that is inseparable from a vice. The only way to avoid the concern is to avoid being presumptuous (CD, 60).

Because of the formulaic structure, I shall not try to exposit all the forms of worry. Together they provide a compelling picture of the development of Christian spirituality through the displacement of a set of negative emotions with positive emotions that take root in a person who is beginning to follow Christ, and they are all worth reading and pondering. I shall, however, say something about discourse 3, "The Concern of Lowliness," because it seems to provide an especially clear picture of some of the fundamental features of Christian spiritual life.

Kierkegaard begins by noting that birds do not have the distinction of being "eminent or lowly" (CD, 37). (Again, this is a poetic description, and Kierkegaard's account would not be damaged if it turned out that in some species of birds the flock has an "alpha bird.") The bird then does not worry about his status in the flock. One bird may be in front of another as the flock flies, and one may be to the left or the right, but none is recognized by other birds as eminent or lofty. Human beings in our natural state are very unlike the bird in this respect. We are acutely conscious of our place in the pecking order, whether the setting be a high school, a workplace, an athletic team, or just a group of friends. The pagan, whether in ancient Greece or modern Christendom, cares very much about where he stands in relation to others.

Unlike the bird, the Christian is aware of the distinction between lowly and eminent. If he is lowly, "he knows, and he knows that others know the same about him, that he is a lowly human being, and he knows what this means" (CD, 39). However, people who allow themselves to be defined solely by how others view them never discover who they really are (CD, 39–40). They can never really be themselves, because their self is constantly a function of "the others." The Christian is freed from this trap, but not by being completely autonomous and self-defined. "The lowly Christian is himself *before God*" (CD, 40). However, no one can achieve this status immediately or spontaneously, as the bird does. "The bird *is* what it is. . . . [I]f one is a Christian, one must *have become* that" (CD, 41). Becoming a Christian is not something grounded in God's work as creator but stems from God's work in Christ as Redeemer. "As a *human being* he [the Christian] was created in *God's image (Billede)*, but as a *Christian* he has God as the *Pattern (Forbillede)*" (CD, 41; translation modified). So the Christian does not exist merely before God, but before Christ, who is God in human form and is the Pattern that defines the ideal for humans to strive for.

Once again, there is an implied though subtle critique of Christendom here, since the heart of Christendom is the assumption that in a Christian country, one becomes a Christian not through conversion and repentance, but simply through enculturation. This emphasis on being a Christian as something one must become is hammered home in one of the discourses in part 3 of *Christian Discourses*: "We Are Closer to Salvation Now—Than When We Became Believers." In this discourse, Kierkegaard does not argue that one must have a "moment of conversion," a particular time in which one responded to a preacher's invitation or prayed to God for salvation. He says that "it is not important whether it was at twelve o'clock noon and the like" (CD, 217). However, it is important that one have a consciousness of what one was like before becoming committed to Christ. In order for it to be true that a person is "now" closer to salvation than when the person became a believer, there must be a time in which a person's life changed, a "then" that can be distinguished from "now," regardless of whether this change happened in a moment or over a longer period of time (CD, 216). I do not think that this means a person must remember a time when he or she lived a wanton or dissolute life, since many are brought up in Christian homes and perhaps cannot remember a time when they did not think of themselves as Christians. Since becoming a Christian is a process, such a person can still be aware of and remember worldly desires and practices that the person has transcended or perhaps still needs to transcend. All of us can be aware of aspects of ourselves that needed to change or that still need to change.

In making this claim, Kierkegaard does not mean that salvation is a human achievement, something a human can achieve through work. It is not the case that "*we come closer to salvation* but that *salvation comes closer to us"* (CD, 221). Still, in order for this to happen, there must have been a real change in our lives, the change from unbelief to being a believer.

## Is Christian Spirituality Objectionably Egoistic?

I shall mostly pass over the discourses in part 2 of *Christian Discourses*, since much of the material recapitulates themes we have already discussed in *Upbuilding Discourses in Various Spirits*, such as the ways in which suffering and hardship can benefit us spiritually. However, one of them is very helpful in responding to a common criticism of Kierkegaard, which is that his philosophy is infected with a kind of egoism, because his focus is on self-development rather than social transformation. Kierkegaard does offer an ethic and a spirituality that focus on "soul-making." Thinkers who see the human task as that of transforming human society find this objectionable. John Dewey is a perfect example of this kind of thinker. Dewey, while not mentioning Kierkegaard, offers a scathing attack on this sort of ethic: "All the theories which put conversion 'of the eye of the soul' in the place of a conversion of natural and social objects that modifies goods actually experienced, are a retreat and escape from existence."[15] Some critics go so far as to allege that not only is it the case that Kierkegaard advocates excessively egoistic views in ethics, but that this reflects a deep self-centeredness in Kierkegaard himself. H. J. Paton, for example, complains that "if ever a person was self-centered it was Kierkegaard; he hardly ever thinks of anyone but himself."[16]

It is easy to see why Kierkegaard should be criticized in this way. Kierkegaard himself emphasizes that "his category" is the category of "the individual" (*hiin Enkelte*). The Hongs often translate this as "the single individual," and it has even been translated as "the solitary individual." The latter translation is definitely misleading. Kierkegaard's term *hiin* is an obsolete spelling of *hin*, which is simply the equivalent of the English demonstrative "that." Thus, a better translation would be "*that* individual," with a kind of emphasis on the "that." The term does refer to a particular individual, but it does not suggest that this individual is isolated or solitary.

15. John Dewey, *The Quest for Certainty* (New York: G. P. Putnam's Sons, 1929), 275.
16. H. J. Paton, *The Modern Predicament* (London: Allen and Unwin; New York: Macmillan, 1955), 120. Paton's comment here just seems mistaken and reflects a superficial knowledge of Kierkegaard's life and relations to others.

Perhaps partly because of a misunderstanding of what Kierkegaard means by "that individual," and partly for other reasons, Kierkegaard is frequently criticized for ignoring or minimizing the importance of relations to others. There may be some justice in this criticism, since Kierkegaard really never develops anything that looks like social or political theory. However, the claim that Kierkegaard's ethics and spirituality are completely egoistic and unconcerned about others is unwarranted. It is just not true that Kierkegaard's concern to help individuals develop spiritually shows a lamentable lack of concern for the character of society.

It is true that Kierkegaard believes, as did Socrates, that in the end a person's character is the most important thing about him or her. The worst thing that can happen to a person is to become spiritually and morally corrupt. Kierkegaard often affirms that "only sin is a human being's corruption" (CD, 123). The best thing that a person can achieve, the highest good, is to be in relation to a supremely good and loving God, and to achieve such a relationship, a person must be someone who loves the good. However, when Kierkegaard makes these claims about the importance of character, he is not saying that people should care *only* about developing their *own* moral character. Nor does he mean to imply that in caring about character one ceases to care about anything else. In fact, just the opposite is true. The character I must seek to develop is a character in which I practice self-denial and continually seek to put the well-being of others ahead of my own.

Were one to criticize Kierkegaard for his excessive concern for the well-being of others and lack of concern for a person's own good, it would be closer to being justified. Although in *Works of Love* Kierkegaard does say that self-love is legitimate and should not be identified with selfishness, his emphasis seems always to be on the need for a person to deny his or her own needs and well-being for the sake of others. There are passages in which Kierkegaard distinguishes self-denial from what might be called self-hatred, but he could still say more than he does about the nature and value of proper self-love.[17] So Kierkegaard, if anything, needs to say more about self-care. On his view, the character that a person must develop if the person lives before Christ is anything but egoistic, and the claim that his soul-making account of spirituality is a kind of refined egoism is false.

This is very evident in "The Joy of It: That the Poorer You Become the Richer You Are Able to Make Others." The major theme of the discourse is

17. John Lippitt gives an excellent treatment of this issue in his book *Kierkegaard and the Problem of Self-Love* (Cambridge: Cambridge University Press, 2013).

that there is an immense difference between material, worldly goods and spiritual goods (CD, 115–16). It is of the essence of a worldly, material good that if I possess something, then someone else does not possess that thing. If I own a beautiful piece of land or a splendid sports car, or even a beautiful piece of art, then no one else owns that object. Of course, others may own things just as nice or even nicer. Nevertheless, since these goods are always finite and therefore in limited supply, the world of such goods is a world of competition. What I have someone else does not have, and what someone else has I do not have.

This is not the case with "the goods of the spirit." The very concept of "the goods of the spirit" is "communication" (CD, 116). There is something "merciful" about such goods, and this is true in more than one way. First of all, if I have faith or hope or love, this in no way deprives anyone else of faith or hope or love. These are goods that every person can possess, and thus if one person has them, no one else is deprived. In fact, the others may be inspired by the recognition that such goods are real possibilities for humans. Second, the goods themselves manifest themselves in actions that are directed toward the good of others. "If a person has *hope*, eternity's hope beyond all measure, he has not thereby in the slightest way taken anything away from anybody—on the contrary, he has thereby worked for all" (CD, 117).

Kierkegaard emphasizes the "humanity of spiritual goods," which is contrasted with the inhumanity of worldly goods. Genuine humanity is, he says, "human likeness" or "equality," and spiritual goods always reflect this equality (CD, 117). Even if a person appears to be focusing on himself in developing these spiritual goods, he is always "communicating," for it is part of the essence of such goods that "their possession is communication" (CD, 117).

Nor is it the case that Kierkegaard believes that a concern for others exhausts itself in a concern for the spiritual status of others. It is true that Kierkegaard believes that the most important goods a person can possess are spiritual, and thus the greatest thing one person can do for another is to help the person learn to love God. Since a God-relation is possible for anyone, a person's existence is not necessarily meaningless or wasted, even if that person suffers grinding poverty or debilitating illness, for the person's faith in God in such situations may still be rewarded in eternity as well as making earthly life meaningful. However, it does not follow from this that those seeking spiritual goods should be indifferent to earthly or material needs.

This is evident from one of the "Deliberations in the Form of Discourses" that makes up Kierkegaard's *Works of Love*, a work that forms an important part of Kierkegaard's Christian writings. The Christian character of *Works of Love* can be seen in the Trinitarian prayer with which the book begins. Discourse 7 in part 2 is entitled "Mercifulness, a Work of Love Even If It Can Give Nothing and Is Able to Do Nothing." The discourse makes an important distinction between the virtue of mercifulness and what might be called material generosity, the trait of those who practice philanthropy. As Kierkegaard uses the term, material generosity is a trait possessed by those who have abundant material goods and is basically a willingness to share of this abundance.[18] So, at least as Kierkegaard is using the term, material generosity is a virtue that those who are poor cannot possess.

However, there is another virtue that is deeper than material generosity, and Kierkegaard calls it mercifulness. Mercifulness, as Kierkegaard describes it, could be defined as a willingness to do whatever it is possible for a person to do to help others, regardless of the material circumstances of the one who is the helper. Someone who is very poor can thus be merciful even if that person cannot be philanthropic because of a lack of material goods to share.

This discourse is also sometimes criticized as an example of Kierkegaard's indifference to the material conditions of life. The reason for this is that in the discourse, Kierkegaard argues that in the world material generosity is overvalued, while mercifulness is undervalued. Material generosity is indeed a good thing, or at least it usually is, but it is a violation of Kierkegaard's egalitarianism to believe that the highest virtues are ones that only those with wealth can attain. There is much that a poor person can do for others, even if the person is too poor to contribute to the alleviation of anyone's poverty. Even in a case in which a rich person has shown indifference to the plight of the poor, the poor might mercifully offer forgiveness to this person.

Mercifulness is more significant than material generosity for several reasons. First, it is a virtue anyone can possess. Second, it is a virtue that stems from a genuine concern for the well-being of others, often in the form of compassion. The philanthropist, on the other hand, in some cases may simply be making a display of wealth and seeking to acquire a prominent status in the community. Even a large gift from a very wealthy philanthropist may be far less costly to the giver than the merciful gift of time that a poor person might offer another.

18. The Danish term *Gavmildhed* is translated by the Hongs as "generosity," but this does not seem quite right. In the discourse, it is clear that it is not possible for those who are poor to have *Gavmildhed*. However, it seems evident that those who are poor can be generous through giving time, attention, and affection, even if they cannot be financially generous. I think it is clear that Kierkegaard has in mind here the stance of someone who is a philanthropist, a type of person who must have some wealth.

Kierkegaard certainly distinguishes material generosity and mercifulness and argues that the latter is more significant. However, despite this,
he is not saying that material help to another is unimportant, but the very
reverse. He takes for granted that the person who has the quality of mercifulness will also be materially generous, when it is possible for the merciful
person to exercise generosity. It is true that a person who has mercifulness
may have nothing material to give others. However, Kierkegaard insists that
when mercifulness is present, "it is self-evident that if the merciful person
has something to give he gives it more than willingly" (WL, 317; translation
modified). What he wants to emphasize is that a person can be merciful
even when "external conditions" prevent the person from being materially
generous (WL, 316). Nevertheless, far from seeing spiritual goods as isolated
from material actions, Kierkegaard takes it as obvious that a good such as
mercifulness will express itself as material generosity when circumstances
allow. Thus, the concern one should have for others is for the whole person
and is not limited to the spiritual well-being of the other.

## Discourses at the Communion on Fridays

Parts 3 and 4 of *Christian Discourses* have a very different tone from each
other. I have already noted that in part 3, the critique of Christendom becomes more explicit, and these discourses thus have a more polemical tone.
One can see that from the very title of the first one: "Watch Your Step When
You Go to the House of the Lord." This polemical character becomes still
stronger and more explicit in Kierkegaard's later writings, *Judge for Yourself!*, *For Self-Examination*, and *Practice in Christianity*. Since I will discuss
these writings in the next two chapters, I will here omit any further look at
part 3 of *Christian Discourses* and move directly to a consideration of one
of my favorite parts of Kierkegaard's authorship: the seven "Discourses at
the Communion on Fridays" that form the concluding section of *Christian
Discourses*.

Kierkegaard was well aware of the contrast between parts 3 and 4 and
worried about including part 3 in the book.[19] However, Kierkegaard ultimately justified publishing the two parts together by comparing part 3 to
Jesus's cleansing of the temple, which in the Synoptic Gospels precedes the

---

19. For Kierkegaard's misgivings on this score, see the supplement the Hongs provide from
Kierkegaard's *Papirer* on pp. 399 and 402–3 in CD. See also the historical introduction to CD.

Last Supper with the disciples. Thus, parts 3 and 4 provide, in turn, "a temple-cleansing celebration—and then the quiet and most intimate of all worship services—the Communion service on Fridays" (CD, 402). Besides the seven communion discourses in *Christian Discourses*, Kierkegaard published five others, three in 1849 and two in 1851. Sylvia Walsh has retranslated all of these, plus a discourse from *Practice in Christianity*, and published them as *Discourses at the Communion on Fridays*.[20] The discourse from *Practice in Christianity*, while not called by Kierkegaard a communion discourse, was actually delivered by Kierkegaard at a communion service in the Church of Our Lady in Copenhagen, as were a few of the others.[21]

The great importance of the communion discourses in Kierkegaard's authorship is evident for several reasons. One of the most important is that it is clear that Kierkegaard himself saw these discourses as in some way the culmination of his authorship, the point where he could finally "rest." The preface that he wrote for the last two of the discourses, published in 1851, makes this clear: "A gradually advancing author-activity that began with *Either/Or* seeks here its decisive point of rest at the foot of the altar" (DCF, 125). There are other reasons to give them special attention also. One is that, although Kierkegaard often mentions the atonement of Christ and its significance in his writings, the communion discourses offer the only extended treatment of how Kierkegaard understood Christ's atonement. These discourses also include some explicit attention to the role played by the Holy Spirit in the life of the believer, a theme that Kierkegaard does not discuss often.[22]

I began this chapter with an account of the twofold role that Christ plays in Kierkegaard's Christian spiritual writings: Christ is both Pattern or Exemplar and Redeemer. Most of the emphasis in these writings is on Christ as the Pattern, since that is the element that Kierkegaard believes is most underemphasized in Christendom, especially in Denmark. However, that does not imply that Christ's role as the Redeemer is any less important, and the communion discourses make this clear. As we shall see, these discourses also have much to say about the role of the Holy Spirit in the Christian life.

20. Søren Kierkegaard, *Discourses at the Communion on Fridays*, trans. Sylvia Walsh (Bloomington: Indiana University Press, 2011). Hereafter and in the sigla as DCF.

21. See Sylvia Walsh's discussion in the introduction to DCF.

22. I believe the reason Kierkegaard does not frequently address the role of the Spirit has to do with the misuse of the idea of "Spirit" in the philosophy of Hegel and his followers. Hegel often speaks of God as "Spirit" and generally uses the Christian doctrine to reject a view of God as a transcendent being. Instead, God's existence as Spirit means that God exists only as embodied in human communities.

The first of the communion discourses takes as its text Luke 22:15: "I have longed with all my heart to eat this Passover with you before I suffer." Although the text is about Christ's longing to eat with his disciples, Kierkegaard, who always wants to read Scripture so that it has direct relevance for a person's life, focuses on the longing for communion on the part of a worshiper. He assumes that the one who comes to communion is someone who feels a "stirring" within that is a "heartfelt longing" for communion (CD, 253). Such a longing is not something that a human can generate; it is a gift of God, a "prompting of the Spirit" within, and Kierkegaard makes it plain that he is here referring to the Holy Spirit (CD, 253–54). Although this longing is God's work and God's gift, the person who receives the gift has a responsibility to accept the gift and use it properly, in which case it becomes a blessing in a deeper way (CD, 254).

Why is it good to long for communion? Kierkegaard tries to make this evident by describing the thoughts of the person who will take communion. To begin, this person is someone who recognizes the "uncertainty of all things" (CD, 257; translation modified). "The wisest person who ever lived and the most limited person who ever lived get equally far when it is a matter of guaranteeing the next moment" (CD, 256). The only real certainty in the midst of this earthly uncertainty is death, which is equally certain "for the old and the infant born yesterday," and also something that is "equally certain at every moment" (CD, 257). The natural response to this is a desire for a connection to a God who is eternal and unchangeable, and God makes this possible through Christ, our "one friend, one trustworthy friend in heaven and on earth" (CD, 258). Christ was not only faithful *unto* death, but also faithful *in death* (CD, 258). It is thus wholly natural to long for fellowship with God through Christ.

When a person focuses on Christ's passion, the seriousness of sin becomes more evident. Christ was the Holy One who came to redeem humans, but "when he walked here upon earth," he experienced great opposition from sinners, so that "his whole life was sheer suffering of mind and spirit through belonging to the fallen human race" (CD, 259). If someone pictures himself living at the time, Kierkegaard says a person dare not believe he would have behaved any better or any differently than Christ's historical contemporaries. The magnitude of my sin is made plain to me by the enormity of Christ's suffering on my behalf.

However, the proper response to this sense of sin is a still more intensified longing for communion with Christ. I must realize that Christ "has atoned for my sin also, has atoned for my every slightest actual sin, but also for the one that may lurk most deeply in my soul without my being aware of it and that possibly would yet burst out if I am led into the most terrible decision" (CD, 260).

Kierkegaard affirms that this longing for God should increase every time a person takes communion. Normally, what one longs for is something one does not have. However, when one takes communion, the longing for God is actually satisfied "because in the longing itself the eternal *is*, just as God *is* in the longing that is *for* him" (CD, 260). The Christ we receive in communion is really present, living and not dead (CD, 261). Kierkegaard does not speak of the resurrection frequently in his writings, because he wants to emphasize the fact that we must follow Christ as he lived on earth, as a lowly person who suffered. Nevertheless, in the communion discourses, the reality of the resurrection is constantly presupposed, because Christ is not merely *remembered* in the meal but is actually present as a living person.

The second discourse is based on Matthew 11:28: "Come here to me, all who labor and are burdened, and I will give you rest." This is one of Kierkegaard's favorite passages and forms the basis for the first part of *Practice in Christianity* as well. Anyone who has worshiped at the Church of Our Lady in Copenhagen would be reminded of this passage by the famous statue, by Bertel Thorvaldsen, of Christ with hands extended, which stands at the front of the church with the inscription "Come unto Me" carved below the statue. Since I will discuss *Practice in Christianity* in the next chapter, I shall here pass over this discourse, except to note that Kierkegaard understands the matter of laboring and being burdened in a distinctive way. On his view, the invitation is not just directed to a certain group of people, those who are poor and therefore "labor and are burdened." Rather, there is a kind of obligation implied in the invitation (CD, 264). Everyone whom Christ invites to communion must work to understand his or her brokenness and need of communion. We must strive to become those who "labor and are burdened." Only those who have seen their need of repentance and repented will "find rest for their souls" (CD, 264–65).

I shall also be brief in my discussion of the third discourse, based on John 10:27: "My sheep hear my voice, and I know them, and they follow me." Kierkegaard assumes here that the communion service is carried out properly, with an ordained priest who delivers the prescribed words of institution, words that are "said accurately as handed down from the Fathers" (CD, 271). Nevertheless, the follower of Christ does not merely hear the priest but hears Christ himself speaking (CD, 271). It is Christ who says, "Come here, all who labor and are burdened," and it is Christ who says, "This is my body"

(CD, 271). Those who do not hear Christ speak are not genuine followers of Christ. Those who are followers recognize that Christ is really present in the service, which is not merely a memorial but a meal that Christ himself hosts.

Discourse 4 is a profound meditation on the suffering of Christ in his passion, based on a section of 1 Corinthians 11:23: "the Lord Jesus, on the night when he was betrayed." Once more the emphasis in the discourse is on the immediacy of the event. Christ's suffering, unlike the suffering of other "glorious ones who met an innocent death," is not simply a long-past event (CD, 278). "His [Christ's] innocent suffering is not past even though the cup of suffering is empty; is not bygone even though it is past, is not an event finished and done with although it was eighteen hundred years ago, would not become that if it were eighteen thousand years ago" (CD, 278).

The reason this is so is that all of us humans are responsible for the death of Christ. It is not an event to be blamed on Pilate or the Sanhedrin, the Romans or Jewish leaders.[23] Christ had to die for all our sins, and so all of us humans are "accomplices" to his betrayal and crucifixion (CD, 278). For Kierkegaard, this fact should not cause us to recoil in fear and anxiety, as we respond to our guilt. Rather, the fact that Christ died for me, even when I am one of his betrayers, "moves me irresistibly" toward him, taking advantage of "his sacrifice of Atonement for the sin of the world" (CD, 280).

Discourse 5 is rooted in 2 Timothy 2:12–13: "If we deny him, he will also deny us; if we are faithless, he still remains faithful; he cannot deny himself." Here Kierkegaard confronts the "terrifying thought" that a follower of Christ might deny him, might fall away (CD, 283). What is remarkable about this discourse is the serene confidence Kierkegaard here expresses that God is the one who holds on to the believer, regardless of the weakness of the believer. Although, as a product of Lutheran Denmark, Kierkegaard hardly ever has a good word to say for Calvinism, he here sounds like a good Reformed theologian. God is faithful to us and always will be faithful, even if we are faithless. God's love and favor toward us are unconditional, based on his own nature, and not conditional on our own behavior. Even when we speak about "God testing us," our speech is really "second-rate"

23. Kierkegaard has been criticized by Peter Tudvad for anti-Semitism, and there are certainly anti-Semitic elements in his writings. However, it is noteworthy here that Kierkegaard rejects a common ground for anti-Semitism in this period, the charge that the Jewish people have a special responsibility for Jesus's death. See George Connell, *Kierkegaard and the Paradox of Religious Diversity* (Grand Rapids: Eerdmans, 2016), 26–66 and especially 51–59, for a good discussion of Kierkegaard's relation to Judaism, which includes an account of the anti-Semitism.

and "half-true," for in reality God is always "holding on to us" (CD, 286). Rather than agonizing about whether we are really faithful, we should take comfort in God's faithfulness to us. In fact, Kierkegaard says that we should not "ask God to apply a test to our faithfulness," for we cannot pass such a test (CD, 286). "*Fundamentally*, we are faithless and . . . at every moment . . . *fundamentally* it is you who are holding on to us" (CD, 286). In a clear allusion to the Thorvaldsen statue in the front of the church, Kierkegaard says that Christ stretches out his arms to us because he cannot deny his own nature, which is one of unconditional and unmerited love. Anyone who is worried that Kierkegaard's emphasis on following Christ leads to some kind of human merit or works righteousness should read this discourse.

Discourse 6 is based on 1 John 3:20: "even if our hearts condemn us, God is greater than our hearts." The major theme of this discourse is that God's greatness is seen most clearly in God's "forgiving, in showing mercy" (CD, 290). The discourse emphasizes a common theme in Kierkegaard's spiritual writings: the inverse character of our relation to God. God's ontological status is so much greater than that of humans that no direct comparisons are possible. "You do not reach the possibility of comparison by the ladder of direct likeness: great, greater, greatest; it is possible only inversely. Neither does a human being come closer to God by lifting up his head higher and higher, but inversely by casting himself down ever more deeply in worship" (CD, 292). Thus, real union with God is made possible when we come to God repentantly with a broken heart that condemns itself (CD, 292). That heart does not, however, have the last word. God, whose mercy is beyond all comparison with human mercy, does not condemn us, and "God is greater than our hearts."

The seventh and last communion discourse from *Christian Discourses* takes as its text Luke 24:51: "And it happened, as he blessed them, he was parted from them." Kierkegaard begins with a criticism of what might be called a superstitious view of God's blessing, in which God's blessing is valuable because it leads to some successful outcome on some human project. For Kierkegaard, God's blessing is not an instrumental good: "No, the blessing is the good in itself; it is the one thing needful, is infinitely more glorious and blessed than all success" (CD, 297). By praying for God's blessing, a person "dedicates himself and his undertaking to serving God—regardless of whether or not it, humanly speaking, succeeds or progresses" (CD, 297).

In coming to communion, the worshiper is seeking God's blessing and, just as in Luke 24:51, hopes to receive that blessing directly from Christ, who blessed his disciples. What blessing does the person hope to receive?

It is again Christ himself who is the blessing. Kierkegaard clearly asserts that Christ blesses us by way of being an atonement for our sins. When we come to the communion, we have nothing to offer: "you are capable of less than nothing" (CD, 298). Although Kierkegaard does not elaborate on the theme in the manner of a systematic theologian, it is clear that he accepts the traditional orthodox picture of Christ as someone who offers himself as a sacrifice on our behalf: "Satisfaction is made there [at the communion table]—but by someone else; the sacrifice is offered—but by someone else; the Atonement is accomplished—by the Redeemer" (CD, 298–99). It is true that Christ is for Kierkegaard the Pattern, the one who has "gone on before" and whom we must follow. However, we can hope to follow that Pattern only if he is also for us the Redeemer who atones for sin.

## Conclusion: Kierkegaard and the Church

Kierkegaard's *Discourses at the Communion on Fridays* provides a deep and rich portrait of Christian spirituality. One lesson to be learned from the discourses is that Kierkegaard sees Christian spirituality as something gained and deepened through participation in the worship practices of the church. It is true that Kierkegaard thinks it is God who is the ultimate source of the spiritual goods the person gains through Christian worship, and it is also true that for Kierkegaard, the worshiper stands as an individual before God even when participating in corporate worship. However, Kierkegaard clearly thinks that God "builds up" those who would be his friends by participation in the worship life of the church, particularly through the sacrament of communion. He sees this as a sacrament instituted by Christ himself, one that was faithfully transmitted to later generations from "the Fathers" of the church.

Kierkegaard's stormy and dramatic attack on the state church[24] in the last few months of his life can easily lead to overlooking the fact that he was, for virtually his entire life, a faithful and committed participant in the life of the church. Christian spirituality can certainly be cultivated through private prayer and meditation on Scripture, and later I will discuss Kierkegaard's view of how Scripture should be read. However, there is no doubt that Kierkegaard, at least until the final months of his life, thinks life in the church is a vital source of genuine Christian spirituality.

24. This attack is discussed at some length in chapter 8 of this book, pp. 186–95.

# CHAPTER 7

# Christian Spirituality (2): *Practice in Christianity*

In this chapter and the next, I shall continue my exploration of Kierkegaard's Christian spiritual writings, looking selectively at some themes from *Practice in Christianity* in this chapter and *For Self-Examination* and *Judge for Yourself!* in the next chapter.[1] *Practice in Christianity* was published in 1850, a year earlier than *For Self-Examination*. The authorship of the book is attributed to a pseudonym, Anti-Climacus, also the named author of *The Sickness unto Death*. I discussed Anti-Climacus briefly in the first two chapters, and I will say something about him again below.

I noted at the beginning of the previous chapter that these later writings of Kierkegaard all have a more strident and polemical tone than the earlier *Christian Discourses*. The critique of Christendom is less subtle and more hard-hitting. However, it would be a mistake to think that Kierkegaard changed his view of genuine Christian spirituality in any essential way. What changed was his attitude toward the actual Christianity of the established church. Most of the themes in the later writings had already appeared in Kierkegaard's earlier pseudonymous works, and the criticisms of Christendom were already present in these earlier works, albeit in a milder tone. Nevertheless, the change of tone in the later works is evident, a change that becomes very pronounced in *Judge for Yourself!*, where Kierkegaard plainly

---

1. There are a number of other works from about this same period that could be discussed, most of which are collected in the volume *Without Authority* in the Princeton edition of Kierkegaard's Writings edited by the Hongs. Although some of these writings are very valuable, I have chosen not to discuss them in this work, for a number of reasons, the most significant being that I wanted to keep this book to a reasonable length.

asserts that Christendom is a falsification of genuine Christianity, which has really ceased to exist. That theme is also central to the newspaper and magazine articles of the very last period of Kierkegaard's life, in 1854 and 1855. I will refer to these last, shorter writings as "the attack literature." One of the great issues in Kierkegaard interpretation is how to read the attack literature and how to understand its relation to Kierkegaard's main authorship. I will give a fuller account of this in the following chapter, but I need to say something about it here, to clarify how I am reading such books as *Practice in Christianity* and *For Self-Examination*.

## Practice in Christianity's Relation to Kierkegaard's Later Attack on the Church

Kierkegaard considered publishing *Practice in Christianity* under his own name, just as he did for *The Sickness unto Death*, but both were finally attributed to Anti-Climacus. I discussed *The Sickness unto Death* extensively in chapters 2 and 3 and there explained that the pseudonym was adopted because Kierkegaard felt that the "ideality" of the Christian life called for in the book was far higher than the ideality exemplified in his own life. Since Kierkegaard believed that a person who affirms some existential truth must relate that truth to his own life, he decided that the book must be pseudonymous. In that way, he could view what was said as being said *to* him rather than as coming *from* him. Legally and causally, the book did of course come from him as the responsible author, but he believed he needed a pseudonymous author to represent a pure and strict form of Christianity.

The pseudonymity of *Practice in Christianity* has exactly the same status, for the same reasons. Kierkegaard's own name does appear as "editor," and he also adds an "Editor's Preface" in which he makes all this clear. In his own voice, in the preface, he affirms the necessity that the requirements of Christianity "should not be scaled down" (PC, 7; translation modified). Rather, upon being reminded of those requirements, the individual should respond with "personal admission and confession" (PC, 7). What is said in the book he regards "as spoken to me alone—so that I might learn not only to resort to *grace* but to resort to it in relation to the use of *grace*" (PC, 7).

In 1855, shortly before his death, and in the midst of his open attack on the state church and "Christendom," Kierkegaard wrote that if *Practice in Christianity* were coming out now, he would not have used the pseudonym but would have published the book under his own name (PC, xvi). However, the reason he would have published the book under his own name is almost the opposite of the original reason for the pseudonym. Originally, the pseudonym was used to make possible a viewpoint that is higher and stricter than the one Kierkegaard thought he could himself adopt. However, in 1855 he claims that the pseudonym is too mild, not strict enough. In the "Moral" to part 1 of *Practice in Christianity*, Anti-Climacus offers encouragement for a reader who might find the requirements of Christianity too daunting. He describes Christianity as something so "terrifying and appalling" (PC, 67) that he questions why anyone would want to become a Christian, and he answers the question in this way: "only the consciousness of sin can force one, if I dare to put it this way (from the other side grace is the force), into this horror. And at the very same moment the essentially Christian transforms itself into and is sheer leniency, grace, love, and mercy" (PC, 67). The fact that Anti-Climacus wants to describe Christianity as something that at least appears to be a "horror" does give one pause, but I think it is reasonable to emphasize that this is just the way Christianity *appears* to the worldly mind. It is what I like to call "perspectival language."

This "Moral" enables Anti-Climacus to describe Christianity as something that could actually be lived by ordinary human beings. When asked to summarize what the book means, Anti-Climacus said we must all recognize our sinfulness and need for grace. "And then nothing further; then, as for the rest, let him do his work and rejoice in it, love his wife and rejoice in her, joyfully bring up his children, love his fellow human beings, rejoice in life. If anything more is required of him, God will surely let him understand and in that case will also help him further" (PC, 67). Thus, Anti-Climacus affirms the validity of the way Kierkegaard himself reads the book in the editor's preface.

Later, during the attack on the church, Kierkegaard clearly became uncomfortable with this "leniency" and wanted to affirm that anyone who cannot embody the strict Christian ideals should honestly admit that he is not a Christian at all. The dialectical balance between Christ as the Redeemer and Christ as the Pattern (discussed in chapter 6) is lost. To be sure, even in the final writings of the attack period, Kierkegaard never says that a human being can earn God's favor or merit God's forgiveness. He does not embrace a doctrine of "works righteousness." However, he does come very close to implying that a person who does not follow Christ's way strictly is not entitled to hope for God's grace and mercy.

Furthermore, his understanding of what it means to follow Christ becomes dubious. He casts doubt, for example, on whether a true Christian should get married. The Christian life looks less like a fulfillment of our created human nature and more like an annihilation of that nature. These late writings give some support to critics of Kierkegaard who have argued that his overall vision of Christian spirituality is distorted, even inhumane, and was so from the beginning. In what follows, I shall at several points consider Kierkegaard's attack on Christendom, but something must be said about it here, because how one views that later literature has a great impact on how one reads the earlier works.

How one evaluates Kierkegaard's account of Christian spirituality requires one to make a judgment about the stance present in the attack writings. One must ask whether the spirituality present in these writings is fully healthy and authentically Christian. The answer I myself give, and which I will defend at more length in chapter 8, is that it is not fully healthy and authentically Christian, though it still embodies insights that Christians need to hear. That answer leads to a second question: Do the unhealthy elements in the late writings show that Kierkegaard's understanding of Christian spirituality was flawed from the beginning?

My own answer to this second question is no. There are critics who want to write off Kierkegaard's whole perspective as inhumane because the late writings embody some themes that are already present in some form in the Christian writings I will discuss in this chapter.[2] I agree with those critics that there is some continuity in the authorship. I am also prepared to admit that, at times in these late writings (not the writings of the "attack period" but those written between 1849 and 1851), Kierkegaard begins to *emphasize* and highlight the dark and strenuous elements of Christian life. I shall voice some critical reservations about Kierkegaard's views on such themes as the role of persecution and suffering in the Christian life. However, I believe that he is emphasizing these themes consciously as a "corrective." That is, he is not rejecting the dialectic of Christ as the Redeemer as well as the Pattern and not substituting works for grace. Rather, he believes that Christendom is putting forth what Bonhoeffer will later call "cheap grace," taking grace in vain. A church that suffers from this problem needs to hear anew the call to discipleship. There is a kind of critical attack on the state of the church in *Practice in Christianity*, but that attack is made from the point of view of genuine Christian faith itself. The notion of corrective does not mean that

2. For an influential example of those who read Kierkegaard as this "inhuman" thinker, see Joakim Garff, *Søren Kierkegaard: A Biography*, trans. Bruce Kirmmse (Princeton: Princeton University Press, 2005).

everything Kierkegaard says in the later writings must be fully endorsed, but it does, I think, mean that he is at this point still writing as a Christian, holding to the dialectic of Christ as the Redeemer and the Pattern.

There is indeed a tradition of using the concept of "corrective" to try to justify the later attack literature itself, and there is evidence that Kierkegaard himself thought in these terms about his attack literature.[3] Even if this is so, however, I will argue in chapter 8 that viewing the attack writings as a corrective does not fully justify them, precisely because their one-sided character gives critics an excuse to evade the challenge they need to hear.

In any case, I want to clearly affirm that I believe that *Practice in Christianity*, *For Self-Examination*, and *Judge for Yourself!* need to be read for what they say, and not primarily as preparation for the later attack literature. I believe that when they are read for their own sake, they have much to offer the person who is seeking a deeper form of Christian spirituality, even if they also contain some elements one may wish to raise questions about. I am personally grateful that Kierkegaard *did* include the editor's preface to *Practice in Christianity*, and I am also grateful that Anti-Climacus provided the "Moral" in which he tells us how to read his book and use it in our lives.

## Part 1 of *Practice in Christianity*: The Invitation and the Obstacle

The three parts of *Practice in Christianity* all focus on the difficulties of being a Christian. Anti-Climacus tries to argue that genuine Christianity cannot be identified with the "hidden inwardness" described in some of Kierkegaard's earlier pseudonymous works. Rather, genuine Christian faith requires a militant stance that defines itself over against the "world," even if "the world" is the world of Christendom, in which everyone is assumed to be a Christian.

Each of the three parts begins with a scriptural passage, and part 1 takes as its text the invitation Christ offers in Matthew 11:28: "Come here to me, all you who labor and are burdened, and I will give you rest."[4] This passage, which Kierkegaard had written about before (see chapter 6), was carved at the front of the Church of Our Lady, the cathedral in Copenhagen, and thus was familiar to many Danish Christians. In the first part of the first section of the book, Anti-Climacus emphasizes the amazing power of this invita-

3. See, for example, Kierkegaard's conversation with Emil Boesen on his deathbed, which I will discuss in more detail in chapter 8.
4. This is the Hong English translation of the Danish text of Kierkegaard's day.

tion. Humanly, we would expect the person who is laboring and burdened to ask for help, but Christ offers his help unconditionally and to all without being asked. Christ's invitation shows God's infinite mercy and grace. It is an invitation precisely for those who labor and are burdened with guilt, and so one should not think that our relapses disqualify us from being those who are invited:

> Do not despair over every relapse, which the God of patience has the patience to forgive and under which a sinner certainly should have the patience to humble himself. No, fear nothing and do not despair; he who says "Come here" is with you on the way; from him there is help and forgiveness on the way of conversion that leads to him, and with him is rest. (PC, 19)

However, having stressed the open and unconditional character of this amazing offer, Anti-Climacus then turns, in the remainder of part 1, to the "halt." He wants to help us understand why, rather than seeing vast crowds of people who accepted Jesus's invitation at the time he gave it, the majority of people were repelled by the invitation, and that remains true for later generations as well. The reason this is so is that the Christ who makes the invitation must be understood as "the specific historical person he was eighteen hundred years ago" and not "the person one has come to know something about incidentally from . . . world history" (PC, 23).

This quote may sound contradictory. Anti-Climacus wants us to understand Christ as the actual historical figure he was, but he does not want us to try to understand Christ from "world history." There is no contradiction here, if one understands the actual historical Christ as the figure presented to us through Scripture. The reference to "world history" is a reference to what one might come to know about Christ through some objective, neutral method that is supposed to give objective certainty about Jesus's divinity. However, Kierkegaard does not think one can come to know Christ as the God-man through objective historical inquiry, whether that be historical inquiry into the biblical documents themselves or reflection on the "world-historical results" of Christ's life. (The latter was a popular form of apologetics in the nineteenth century.) Christ understood as the incarnation of God in human form is the "paradox, the object of faith" (PC, 25). No set of facts about Christ's life, such as his miracles, could prove he was divine, and no set of facts about how Christ has transformed human history can show that Christ was divine either. One cannot learn that Christ is the God-man through secular or "profane history," but only through "sacred history," history as seen through the eyes of faith (PC, 25n). If one could prove or demonstrate the divinity of Christ through objective evidence, then the riskiness of faith would be abolished. To commit to Christ would be to commit to a sure thing. If that were the case, perhaps there would be hordes who would respond to the invitation. However, the Christ to whom one must commit oneself looks just like an ordinary human being, even if he does offer "signs" that point to something more (PC, 41). Anti-Climacus believes, as did his pseudonymous predecessor Johannes Climacus, that even the best possible historical evidence would never be sufficient to show that an individual human was God.[5]

We have seen that for Kierkegaard spirituality is always relational and that authentic spirituality (even Socratic spirituality) involves a relation to God in which one lives "before God." Christian spirituality in turn understands living before God as living before Christ as a contemporary of Christ. Christian spirituality is all about the imitation of Christ, and Kierkegaard perhaps stresses this theme more than any other Protestant thinker. Of course, what this means turns on how one understands Christ and how one understands what it means to live contemporaneously with Christ. It thus matters greatly that the Christ who issues the invitation is the figure who lived in poverty and had a handful of followers who were themselves poor and powerless. It is not the Christ who lives in glory at the right hand of the Father who issues the invitation. According to Kierkegaard, faith believes that Christ is in glory, but we do not come to know Christ in that form, but through sacred history in the form of a lowly servant who died a cruel and painful death.

Even though Christ lived his human life at a particular time, if he is God, then he is the "Absolute," and this means that the one who relates to Christ must not think of Christ's life simply as a collection of facts about the past. "In relation to the absolute, there is only one time, the present; for the person who is not contemporary with the absolute, it does not exist at all" (PC, 63). It thus makes no difference whether one was an historical contemporary of Christ or one lived centuries later, just as it does not really matter what secular historical scholars (or at least those who proceed with secular methodologies and who do not look at the testimony through the eyes of faith) conclude about what really happened. What is important for Anti-Climacus is the biblical testimony; regardless of what scholars may say, a person may in faith believe that testimony and choose to become a follower of Christ.

5. See PF, chapters 4 and 5, and CUP 1:29–49, for Climacus's arguments on this point.

Anti-Climacus tries to show the true difficulty of following Christ by a series of vignettes of historical contemporaries of Christ who rejected faith. These people, as eyewitness contemporaries, certainly did not lack for historical evidence, but the "signs and wonders" that Jesus did simply made him more repellent in their eyes. Anti-Climacus describes a sensible first-century businessman, clergyman, and philosopher, among others, all of whom make it clear that becoming a follower of Christ is something that seems foolish and even crazy. (Although the people are described as first-century figures, it does seem evident that they are remarkably like figures from Kierkegaard's own time!) The reaction of a "sensible man" is typical. "What has he [Jesus] done about his future? Nothing. Does he have a permanent job? No. What are his prospects? None. To mention only this simple matter, how will he pass the time when he becomes old, the long winter evenings—with what will he fill them—he cannot even play cards" (PC, 43). The decision of this man is easy: "To join him—no thanks, thank God I certainly have not gone crazy yet" (PC, 44).

The genuine contemporary must either imaginatively put himself into Christ's own time or else imaginatively place Christ in his own time. Despite the initial attractiveness of the invitation, Christ will attract only followers who realize that "*sin is a human being's corruption*" (PC, 61). If one does not realize that one is a sinner and that sin is *the* human problem, then the healing that Christ offers requires a cost that is too great to pay.

## Part 2 of *Practice in Christianity*:
## Blessed Is the One Who Is Not Offended

Part 2 of *Practice in Christianity* gives a deeper account of the "halt" discussed in part 1, by focusing explicitly on the concept of "offense." Few Christian theologians or sermons focus on the idea of offense, but for Anti-Climacus (and for Kierkegaard), offense is a central category for Christian faith. "The possibility of offense is the crossroad, or it is like standing at the crossroad. From the possibility of offense, one turns either to offense or to faith, but one never comes to faith except from the possibility of offense" (PC, 81). Kierkegaard had already discussed faith and offense as the only possible responses to the paradox of God's incarnation in human form in *Philosophical Fragments* (PF, 49–54). However, the discussion there was brief and short on concrete descriptions of offense, as was befitting in a book from the non-Christian pseudonym Johannes Climacus. Anti-Climacus provides both a conceptual taxonomy of forms of offense and very vivid accounts of offense that illustrate the various forms.

Although Anti-Climacus certainly holds that the possibility of offense is essentially linked to faith, one should note that it is only the *possibility* of offense for which this is true. Careless readers sometimes confuse Kierkegaard's claim here about the importance of the possibility of offense with a radically different view, in which the person of faith must actually be offended to experience faith, which would make offense part of faith. However, faith and offense are opposite passions that mutually exclude each other.[6] The person who has faith must reject offense, and the person who is offended has rejected faith.

Why does faith in Christ always encounter the possibility of offense? Anti-Climacus discusses three different aspects of Christ's life that pose this possibility. The first is one that is not grounded in Christ's nature as one who is both divine and human, but simply in the fact that he lived as "the single individual" who came into conflict with "the established order" (PC, 85). This kind of offense is not unique to Christ but could arise from any person who stands against the accepted practices and views of a human society about how life should be lived and who, implicitly or explicitly, encourages others to follow his example. Perhaps Socrates could serve as a non-Christian example of this.

Anti-Climacus has in mind here something like the Hegelian view that *Sittlichkeit*, the laws and customs of a particular society, is the highest authority for an individual. For Kierkegaard, such a view is a form of idolatry; it is essentially a denial of God's authority by deifying the existing human order of things. Anti-Climacus uses the example of Christ's collision with the Pharisees and scribes as an example of this: "The established order, however, at that time insisted and always insists on being the objective, higher than each and every individual, than subjectivity" (PC, 86). For Anti-Climacus, offense in this case and every case is never purely intellectual in origin. The person who becomes a follower of someone who challenges the established

---

6. There is a parallel here with another confusion. Popular accounts of Kierkegaard sometimes claim that for Kierkegaard doubt is an element in faith. However, faith and doubt, like faith and offense, are opposites that exclude each other for Kierkegaard. Faith and doubt are contrasting ways of responding to the uncertainty that is endemic to the human condition for Kierkegaard. This uncertainty is, like the possibility of offense, something that faith presupposes. See my article "Kierkegaard on Faith, Doubt, and Uncertainty," in *The Theological Virtues*, ed. David Eckel, Boston University Studies in Philosophy, Religion, and Public Life (Dordrecht: Springer, forthcoming).

order can expect that establishment to come down hard on him, just as the established order came down hard on Christ. What is offensive about such a person is partly that following such a person means that one must give up desires for comfort and worldly success and accept the possibility of suffering.

The other two grounds of offense that Christ raises are linked to his essential character as the God-man. Anti-Climacus describes these as the "offense of loftiness" (PC, 100) and the "offense of lowliness" (PC, 102). In the former, Christ offends people because, though he is obviously a human, he speaks and acts as though he were divine, with divine authority. In the latter kind of offense, Christ is offensive because, although he claims to be divine, he does not manifest the qualities humans would expect from a divine being but lives as a poor and lowly individual.

Anti-Climacus illustrates the offense of loftiness by a careful look at the passages from Matthew 11 and Luke 7, in which John the Baptist sends some of his followers to find out whether Jesus is really the Messiah. Jesus does not give John's disciples a direct answer. Anti-Climacus quotes Jesus's response from Matthew 11:4–6: "Go and tell John the things you hear and see: the blind see and the lame walk, the lepers are cleansed and the deaf hear, the dead are raised up, and the good news is preached to the poor, and blessed is he who is not *offended* at me" (PC, 94). The answer of Jesus may seem strange to those who are used to apologetic arguments. Jesus seems to point to the evidence that supports his claim to be the expected one, but rather than finishing with a triumphant assertion that he has proved his case, he ends with a blessing upon those who have seen the evidence yet will not be offended by him.

For Kierkegaard, one cannot prove or demonstrate that Jesus (or any human) was God. The signs that are given that point to divinity (such as miracles, Jesus's own teachings, and his work) cannot prove such a staggering claim. If faith could be proved or demonstrated, then for Kierkegaard it would not be faith. Jesus's answer makes this clear: "He [Christ] himself makes it clear that in relation to him there can be no question of any demonstration, that we do not come to him by means of demonstrations, that there is no *direct* transition to becoming a Christian" (PC, 96). To understand this, Anti-Climacus asks us to imagine that some actual person we know, someone who appears to be a "lowly human being," nevertheless claimed to be God. Even if this person appeared to perform miracles, it would not be easy to believe such a thing, and neither was it easy for Christ's historical contemporaries. To claim to believe in Christ as the God-man without realizing the true meaning of what one believes is a misunderstanding and an illusion. The offense of loftiness for Kierkegaard chiefly stands as a barrier to the claim that faith in Christ can be secured by some kind of rational proof.

The offense of lowliness stems from the same qualities of Christ as both divine and human, but the emphasis is different. In the offense of loftiness, the lowliness of Christ is obvious, and what seems impossible is that such a person should be divine. In the offense of lowliness, those who believe in Christ as divine find their faith tested by the fact that the one whom they accept as God is a "lowly, poor, suffering, and finally powerless human being" (PC, 102). It is in fact Jesus's own disciples who illustrate this form of offense, and Jesus himself predicts that this will happen: "This night you will all *be offended* at me" (Mark 14:27). The disciples could believe that Jesus was divine, but they balked at believing that a divine being could suffer and die. Although the disciples later acquired faith, on the night of Jesus's death, they were all offended.

For Kierkegaard, the possibility of offense marks a kind of boundary for human reason, in which "all human understanding must come to a halt in one way or another" (PC, 105). Ultimately, however, the offense is not purely intellectual in character. It stems also from the way in which a person recoils from becoming a follower of the God who appears as a lowly human being. It would be different if Christ spoke to us from heaven as triumphant and glorious. The Christian believes that Christ is risen and is triumphant and glorious, but the Christ we come to know through Scripture is the one who is lowly and powerless, who conquers by suffering and dying. Christ's followers must take the same road.

The requirement that one only comes to know Christ through faith is not due to some kind of withholding of evidence on the part of God. It is not that Christ does not tell us plainly about his divinity or manifest it through mighty acts. The problem is that the one who tells us directly that he is God and does the miracles still appears to be an ordinary human being. Thus, even "direct communication" on the part of Christ still involves a kind of indirectness (PC, 135). Not even Christ himself can remove the possibility of offense. Part of the suffering of Christ is that he knows that what he must do in order to be the Savior of the world also necessarily creates the possibility that some will be offended by him.

## Part 3 of *Practice in Christianity*:
## "From on High He Will Draw All to Himself"

Part 3 of *Practice in Christianity* consists of seven sections (as did part 2), all of which are sermon-like reflections on John 12:32: "And I, when I am lifted up from the earth, will draw all to myself." The first of these seven was an address actually delivered by Kierkegaard in the Cathedral Church (Church of Our Mother) on Friday, September 1, 1848. Anti-Climacus, conforming to the conventions of pseudonymity, actually adds a footnote telling the reader this, mentioning that he has included it "with the consent of Magister Kierkegaard" (PC, 151n). In the same footnote, Anti-Climacus says that, in order to make the beginning fit with the ending, he has composed the seventh of the discourses in the "same, more lenient tone" and thus in those two has "relinquished part of what is characteristic of me" (PC, 151n).

The first discourse, which was actually delivered by Kierkegaard at a communion service, affirms that Christ, who is now ascended and reigns on high, does indeed draw people to himself. Indeed, the people who have come to receive communion are obviously people who are drawn to Christ. However, it is one thing to be drawn to Christ and another to be *"wholly drawn"* to him, and the discourse ends with a prayer that those who are to receive communion should be wholly drawn in just this way. Though the discourse may show a more lenient tone than some of those that follow, it by no means takes a complacent view of the Christian life.

Indeed, even in this first discourse, the major point made is that although Christ draws all to himself, he does not *entice* anyone. In fact, in order to draw people to himself, there is much that must be removed, and the painfulness of this process is such that Christ can be said to thrust people away even as he draws them (PC, 153). To entice someone is to draw someone to oneself under false pretenses, but Christ cannot and will not do this. If one is drawn to Christ only as the risen and victorious Christ, one does not really love Christ. Someone who loves Christ only "in his loftiness" is confused; such a person "does not know Christ and therefore does not love him either" (PC, 154). Christ was the truth, but if one loves the truth only when it has conquered, "when it is in possession of and is surrounded by power and glory and honor," but cannot love the truth "when it was struggling, . . . to the Jews an offense, to the Greeks foolishness," then that person does not really love the truth at all (PC, 154). So even though Christ is now "on high," the means whereby he draws people to himself is the consciousness of sin, and he calls them to *"the way,"* the life of self-denial that Jesus himself followed.

Despite the more "lenient" tone of the first discourse, it captures the main theme of all the remaining discourses, which return again and again to the challenge of being drawn to a Christ who spoke these words when he was in a lowly and abased state. The second discourse echoes the distinction between being drawn to Christ and being enticed, by way of a play on words with the Danish terms for "draw" (*drage*) and "deceive" (*bedrage*). Christ does want to draw us to himself, but if he is not to deceive us, it must be his true self we are drawn to. Otherwise, the drawing would be a form of seduction, in which one gets something different from what was promised. Furthermore, the process by which we are drawn to Christ must be a process in which our own selfhood is preserved and deepened, rather than undermined.

A human self as a spiritual being is free, and thus a self cannot be drawn in the way a magnet draws iron (PC, 159). Rather, we are drawn by being presented with a choice. Only in that way can we be drawn in such a manner that we become more ourselves through the drawing process (PC, 159). It is, I think, important that even in the Anti-Climacus writings, Kierkegaard views the process of becoming a Christian as one that is a fulfillment of our created human nature. (As we shall see, there are questions about whether this is still the case for Kierkegaard's very late writings, in which he attacks the church.) Anti-Climacus says plainly that "Christ also first and foremost wants to help every human being to become a self" (PC, 160).

Even though Christ is now ascended and on high and indeed is drawing all to himself, the fact that he initially says these words from his abased and humbled state shows that the choice given to humans is genuine. A Christ who spoke only from glory as a glorified and powerful figure would be a Christ who could seductively entice us. However, when the Christ who speaks does so as a lowly human, then the choice is preserved. Anti-Climacus imagines an historical contemporary who sarcastically responds to Christ's prediction. When Christ says "when I am lifted up," the contemporary adds a skeptical dash: "yes—when!" If we really are drawn to Christ, it will be to the abased one that we will be drawn: "You are not going to escape the abasement, for if these words remind you of the loftiness, the speaker reminds you of the abasement. You cannot choose one of the two without becoming guilty of an untruth, whereby you only deceive yourself, not him, and you defraud yourself out of the truth, which he is" (PC, 166).

Discourse 3 zeroes in on what it means to be a contemporary of Christ: the theme is that the Christian life ought to be marked by voluntary suffering, a suffering for the name of Christ and Christ's cause that one could easily avoid. However, the one who really loves Christ will not wish to avoid such suffering. Anti-Climacus tries to provide some psychological understanding of this by an illustration. Imagine, he says, a man who "has gone through indescribably much in his life," because he has had to stand alone, endure poverty, scorn, and mockery (PC, 172). Then imagine that the man's life takes a radically different turn, "his cause is victorious and he is the one admired by all" (PC, 172). Imagine further that the man then falls in love with a girl whom he did not know in his time of suffering. Although the woman is obviously completely innocent of the suffering and could have done nothing to prevent it, Anti-Climacus thinks that in this case the woman, if she is truly in love, will almost feel a sense of guilt that she did not go through the man's sufferings with him. She will almost feel ashamed that she has only shared in the man's glory. The point of the story is clear. Even if it is not the case that every Christian will experience persecution, the one who truly loves Christ ought to be someone who welcomes the opportunity to suffer with Christ and identify with Christ in his suffering.

This theme is deepened by a long passage, clearly autobiographical, in which a young child, who is completely ignorant of Christianity, is shown pictures of various human heroes, such as William Tell and Napoleon. A picture of the crucified Christ is mixed in among these pictures, much to the child's initial shock and surprise.[7] The child will not immediately understand why this picture of someone suffering and dying was included. The child will only be more baffled and confused when he is told that the person being crucified was the most loving person who ever lived (PC, 175). Anti-Climacus says that the adult who explains all this to the child "stands there as an accuser who accuses himself and the whole human race" (PC, 176).

If the child is then told that the one who was killed in this painful and humiliating way later rose from the dead, ascended, and entered into glory, Anti-Climacus says that the impression made by the story of suffering will be so overwhelming that the child, at least initially, "will not feel like hearing about the glory that followed" (PC, 177).[8] The effect on the child will be overwhelming, so much so that the child "would completely forget the other pictures showed him" (PC, 177). Initially, the child perhaps would be angry

7. The whole story is found in PC, 174–78. Many commentators assume that this story draws on a memory from Kierkegaard's own childhood, in which he was shown such a set of pictures by his father.

8. This is one of the passages that sounds autobiographical to me, because the reaction described may be distinctive to Kierkegaard himself. I think most children who heard this story would be very glad to hear that the suffering one was vindicated.

with the ones who killed the man crucified, would want to strike at them and get even. However, when the child became older, he would see things differently: "He no longer wishes to strike them, because, he said, I am not like him, the abased one, who did not strike, even when he was struck. No, now he wished only one thing, to suffer approximately as he suffered in this world" (PC, 178).

This is, says Anti-Climacus, the kind of impact the story of Jesus had on the apostles and the early Christians, many of whom did become martyrs. Even if we are far from that status, the story may still move us to become Christians in truth. The mark of genuine Christianity is not simply to bear patiently the unavoidable sufferings of life, though the Christian does do that as well. The distinctive mark of Christianity is voluntary suffering:

> To suffer in a way akin to Christ's suffering is not to put up patiently with the inescapable, but it is to suffer evil at the hands of people because as a Christian or in being a Christian one wills and endeavors to do the good; thus one could avoid this suffering by giving up willing the good. (PC, 173)

Thus, the person who is really drawn to Christ and is moved by love for Christ's suffering will welcome the chance to suffer for Christ's sake.

## Is Kierkegaard's View of Christian Suffering Healthy?

At this point, I want to pause in my account of what is going on in *Practice in Christianity* to reflect critically on what Anti-Climacus is saying. What should we say about this kind of spirituality, which places such an emphasis on suffering? The first thing to affirm is that Kierkegaard has solid grounding in the New Testament for his claim that the Christian life is one that must include a willingness to suffer for the sake of Christ. Jesus says to his followers in Matthew 5:11 that they are blessed "when people insult you, persecute and falsely say all kinds of evil against you because of me." Those who are thus persecuted should "rejoice and be glad, because great is your reward in heaven." Similarly, in John 15:30, Jesus tells his followers to expect persecution: "If they persecuted me, they will persecute you also."

Christian spirituality not only expects and accepts persecution but sees it as something beneficial to the Christian life. Paul speaks in Romans 8:17 of the Christian as one who shares in the sufferings of Christ "in order that we may also share in his glory." In Philippians 3:10, Paul even speaks of "the fellowship of sharing in his [Christ's] sufferings" as a way to "attain to the resurrection of the dead." So, for the Christian, suffering for Christ is not simply something to be expected and endured, but something to be welcomed. In the context of nineteenth-century Christendom, in which Christianity had virtually become identified with being a nice person who lives a comfortable and successful life, Kierkegaard's emphasis on the place of suffering in the Christian life must be recognized as salutary. Furthermore, it is a theme we still need to hear, especially in prosperous Western countries.

However, I do think there is something about the way Kierkegaard makes his claims that provides some cause for worry that he sometimes talks about suffering in an unhealthy way. What I mean is this: Kierkegaard increasingly describes Christian suffering as something that is absolutely necessary for genuine Christian living, in such a manner that a person whose life goes well in worldly terms has good reason to believe he or she is spiritually failing. It almost appears that the Christian ought to be someone who seeks out persecution and suffering. In *Practice in Christianity*, this is only a kind of undertone, but it becomes explicit and strident in the latest "attack on Christendom" writings and surely is part of the basis for the claim Kierkegaard makes in *Judge for Yourself!*—that genuine Christianity in Denmark has ceased to exist.

What is worrying about this is that it seems to imply that genuine Christianity simply cannot be combined with what one might call a normal human life, in which one marries, raises a family, seeks to make a living, and enjoys some of the features of human life. In the attack writings, Kierkegaard expresses hostility to marriage, especially for the clergy. Near the end of his life, a big part of his disdain for Bishop Mynster, who had been Kierkegaard's father's pastor, seems to have been that Mynster had lived a long, happy, and comfortable life.

It must be noted that although the New Testament certainly does teach that suffering is to be expected and must be welcomed, it never teaches that the Christian should seek out persecution or suffering. To be fair, Kierkegaard never says that either, partly because he worries that a person who did that would be helping to make offenders guilty because of their persecuting acts. Kierkegaard actually wrote an essay late in his life on whether it is right for a person to allow himself to be executed for the truth, which focuses on just this issue (WA, 55–89).[9] The fact that Kierkegaard is worrying about this question shows how strongly he is tempted by the idea that one must be persecuted to be an authentic Christian (PC, 115).

9. This essay was published under a pseudonym, "H. H."

When one looks at the New Testament as a whole, it seems that the theme of expecting and welcoming persecution and suffering is balanced with a hope that this is something the Christian may be able to avoid. The First Epistle of Peter provides an excellent illustration of this. On the one hand, Peter is obviously writing to churches that are experiencing persecution. Peter's message about this is very similar to that of Paul. Persecuted believers should "rejoice that you participate in the suffering of Christ, so that you may be overjoyed when his glory is revealed" (1 Peter 4:13). Nevertheless, Peter still hopes and prays that those to whom he writes can avoid such sufferings, and he urges them to do all they can to do so. In 1 Peter 2:12, he tells his readers "to live such good lives among the pagans that, though they accuse you of doing wrong, they may see your good deeds and glorify God on the day he visits us." In 1 Peter 3:10, he quotes from the Old Testament and urges his readers to seek a good life by doing good deeds: "Whoever would love life and see good days must keep his tongue from evil and lips from deceitful speech." Peter is not, of course, saying that Christians will avoid suffering; after all, he is writing to those who are experiencing persecution. Nonetheless, he seems to think that there is at least the possibility that godly living, even in a pagan culture, might in some cases lead to a better human life. Much of his writing recommends that, to avoid unnecessary suffering, one should conform, to a degree, with what is recognized as good even in the pagan culture. Wives should be submissive to their husbands, and slaves should respect their masters, for example (1 Peter 2:18 and 3:1–2). Even the pagan kings should be honored, so long as this does not come at the expense of devotion to Christ (1 Peter 2:17). If avoiding persecution seems a goal that is conceivably attainable and worth seeking even in a pagan society, it surely seems possible that someone who seeks to "follow the good" and who lives in the midst of Christendom might not always be persecuted for standing up for what is right. In Christendom, most people will have been taught Christian principles and at least nominally accept them. It does not follow from this that they will not resent and attack the person who lives to a high standard and thereby reveals their own hypocrisy. Suffering and persecution are certainly *possible* in Christendom. However, it does not seem correct that persecution in such a society will be inevitable.

Paul often views the Christian life through the lens of the idea of an individual calling, and he specifically connects the idea that each person has a calling from God with the actual situations people find themselves in: "Each one should retain the place in life that the Lord assigned to him and in which God has called him. This is the rule I lay down in all the churches"

(1 Corinthians 7:15). One part of what Paul seems to presuppose here is that ordinary human life must go on, even as the Christian awaits the return of Christ. People who are married should stay married if possible, even if they are married to unbelievers. The idea of an individual calling naturally suggests that not everyone will be called to endure the same situations. Perhaps some will be called to martyrdom, while others will live out their lives quietly, supporting themselves and the church through their work, raising families, and attempting to get along with pagan neighbors.

The notion of calling is actually central to Kierkegaard's own thinking. As we saw in looking at *The Sickness unto Death*, each person is called to become the self God wills for that person to be. At the time Kierkegaard published *Practice in Christianity*, the "Moral" provided by Anti-Climacus makes this clear: "Each individual in quiet inwardness before God is to humble himself under what it means in the strictest sense to be a Christian" (PC, 67). This ideal surely must embody a willingness to suffer for the cause of Christ, and none of my worries about Kierkegaard's views here should be taken as softening this requirement. Kierkegaard is right that the person who is *willing* to suffer and ultimately die for Christ provides the ideal for all of us. However, this does not mean that every Christian will suffer persecution. Anti-Climacus says that, of the person who honestly admits the requirement, "if anything more is required of him, God will surely let him understand and in that case will also help him further" (PC, 67).

Anti-Climacus surely gets things right here, but it is troubling that, at the end of his life, Kierkegaard himself says that if he were to publish the book at that time under his own name, he would have withdrawn "the thrice-repeated Moral" (PC, xvii). At this point, Kierkegaard's account of Christian spirituality begins to acquire an unhealthy, inhumane tone. It is a tone that is unambiguously expressed in the attack literature I shall discuss in the next chapter.

If we connect the suffering of the Christian life with the notion of calling, we can, I think, also bring together the "voluntary suffering" that Kierkegaard wants to emphasize with the more ordinary human suffering as well. Anti-Climacus does say that the Christian bears ordinary sufferings patiently, but he does not seem to view this kind of suffering as having much spiritual significance. However, if both the voluntary and involuntary suffering a Christian experiences are understood as part of a divine calling, then both may provide opportunities for spiritual growth and upbuilding. In both cases, the believer may be called to accept and endure what is painful as something that comes from God's hand, and which God ultimately intends for good.

## Judging Christendom: A Militant Church versus a "Triumphant" Church

Kierkegaard's view of the normativity of Christian suffering is tightly linked to his critical judgment of Christendom. In discourse 5 from part 3 of *Practice in Christianity*, this becomes a major theme. Here Anti-Climacus implicitly responds to the criticism I just made of his view that threatens to make Christianity into something that destroys rather than fulfills humanity. He affirms that "neither Christianity nor Christ is cruel" (PC, 196). What seems like cruelty "comes from the Christian's having to live in this world and having to express in the environment of this world what it is to be a Christian" (PC, 196). What grounds this claim is a pretty harsh judgment of the so-called Christians of Denmark. If someone really steps out and seeks to follow Christ, this person will inevitably suffer, and the more unselfish and better the person is, the more the person will suffer (PC, 197). Christendom only tolerates a "hidden inwardness," and anyone who actually tries to express Christianity in life will be attacked (PC, 216–17).

I believe that some of this reflects Kierkegaard's own personal experience during the so-called *Corsair* affair, in which Kierkegaard attacked a scandalous satirical newspaper. As a result, he was himself victimized by the newspaper and suffered terribly from the nasty cartoons and caricatures. Furthermore, even though many of Copenhagen's leading citizens thought that the *Corsair* was morally dubious, no one came to Kierkegaard's aid. From this period on, Kierkegaard became lonely and embittered, losing his ability to walk freely around the town and converse with common people.

The heart of Kierkegaard's critique of Christendom (which is here expressed through Anti-Climacus) is the claim that Christendom sees itself as a kind of "church triumphant." The gospel has won, and Christ's message has permeated every aspect of Danish society and produced a genuinely Christian culture. On this view, becoming acculturated and socialized as a Dane was the same thing as becoming a Christian. The "new nature" that is supposed to be acquired by being born again has become identified with ordinary human nature. If this is true, then it makes perfect sense that the kind of suffering and persecution Christians had to endure when paganism was dominant would no longer be necessary or even possible.

Kierkegaard vehemently denies that anything like this victory has happened or can happen short of Christ's return. On his view, the church prior to the return of Christ can never be a church triumphant but must always be a church militant. It will never be the case that people will acquire the

Christian virtues of faith, hope, and love simply by being socialized in a particular society. No human society can perfectly or even approximately actualize the kingdom of God. To become a Christian, people in every age and society must recognize their sinfulness, repent, and turn to God in faith. The very idea of Christendom is a disaster from Kierkegaard's point of view.

I agree completely with this critique. Nevertheless, I do not agree that Kierkegaard's uncharitable characterization of his contemporaries follows from this, despite his own bitter experiences. First, it seems impossible that Kierkegaard could have made an accurate judgment of the minds and hearts of all his contemporaries. How could he possibly know what he claims in *Judge for Yourself!*, which is that New Testament Christianity has ceased to exist and that there are no Christians? At the very least, there is a great tension between the harsh judgment that none of his contemporaries are genuinely Christian and the claim Kierkegaard himself makes in *Works of Love*, which is that each of us has an obligation to interpret the acts of others in the most charitable way possible (WL, 280–99).

It is also important to realize that there are many societies that fall in between a pagan society that might offer violent opposition to anyone who makes a Christian confession, on the one hand, and the kind of "Christian society" that Christendom imagines itself to be, on the other. Kierkegaard is quite right that no society can be identified with the kingdom of God, just as he is right to insist that the church must always define itself in opposition to worldly values and practices. However, the fact that Christendom makes false claims does not mean that Christianity might not in some ways make a real difference to a society, as the witness of the church is heard and even heeded by some. Kierkegaard himself admits that this is the case in *Works of Love*, where he notes that the abolition of slavery and serfdom and the recognition that women are persons and not property are the results of Christianity (WL, 38–39). A society that is far from being genuinely Christian might still be one that reflects some Christian values.

Think for example of Martin Luther King Jr. and the American civil rights movement. King's commitment to equality for African Americans was clearly rooted in his own Christian faith. Kierkegaard might well respond that the example supports his own case. After all, King spent time in jail, was beaten, and ultimately murdered, as were numerous others who fought for racial equality, many of whom were motivated by Christian faith. This is true, and it does back up the claim that the Christian must be willing to endure suffering and persecution for the sake of doing what is right. Nevertheless, it is also important to remember the gains that the sacrifices of King and others made possible. In the end, most Americans were persuaded that segregation and denial of human rights to black people were wrong. I think the example shows that even in a society that is very far from perfect, at times someone who does what is right can succeed and be honored, as was the case for some of King's associates.

My conclusion is that Kierkegaard was quite right to denounce the idea of Christendom if this is understood as the identification of a human society with the kingdom of God. He was also right to remind us of the New Testament claim that the one who follows Christ must be willing to suffer with Christ. Furthermore, he was right to say that such suffering is still possible in a society that thinks of itself as Christian. However, it is a mistake to claim that suffering and persecution will be the inevitable fate of all true Christians, and so anyone who fails to experience this fate thereby manifests a spiritual flaw. Perhaps, however, it is true that those of us who have not had to endure persecution or severe suffering should reflect on our lives and ask ourselves whether we ought to be taking bolder and more courageous stands as Christ followers. Such self-reflection would surely be something that a Kierkegaardian spirituality would regard as beneficial.

# CHAPTER 8

# Christian Spirituality (3):
## *For Self-Examination* and *Judge for Yourself!*

In this penultimate chapter, I shall continue a close examination of Kierkegaard's later Christian spiritual writings, focusing mainly on *For Self-Examination* and *Judge for Yourself!* I will also return to the subject of the "attack writings" of 1854–55, looking at both similarities and differences between the attack literature and the two books I will focus on in this chapter, as well as the writings examined in the previous two chapters, where Kierkegaard's mature account of Christian spirituality can be found.

For *Self-Examination* was published by Kierkegaard in 1851, just after the publication of *On My Work as an Author* and *Two Discourses at the Communion on Fridays*. Kierkegaard had intended to publish *Judge for Yourself!* as a kind of sequel to *For Self-Examination*. However, he worried about the polemical tone of the second book and ultimately withheld it from publication altogether. Kierkegaard's brother, Peder Christian Kierkegaard, finally published the book in 1876, long after Søren had died.

### *For Self-Examination*

*For Self-Examination* has as its subtitle *Recommended to the Present Age*, which Kierkegaard also used for *Judge for Yourself!* It is clear that these books are aimed squarely at Kierkegaard's contemporaries, and the focus is on the concept of Christendom. They do not intend to give balanced, comprehensive accounts of the Christian life but intend to describe contemporary ailments and prescribe remedies for those ailments. Despite the topical character, *For Self-Examination* contains deep insights that remain timely and relevant today. Even though it is often claimed we live in a "post-Christian age" today, perhaps some of the maladies of Christendom are still present even if Christendom in Kierkegaard's sense is mostly a thing of the past.

The book contains three sections. I will devote most of my attention to the first section, "What Is Required in Order to Look at Oneself with True Blessing in the Mirror of the Word?" (For brevity I will refer to this discourse as "The Mirror of the Word.") In this section, Kierkegaard (and here we have no pseudonym to worry about) gives an existential account of how Christians should read the Bible if they want to gain spiritual benefit from such reading. Since Bible reading is one of the most common Christian spiritual practices, this discourse gives a helpful account of a practical strategy for developing Christian spirituality. After looking in some detail at this discourse, I will also briefly discuss parts 2 and 3, "Christ Is the Way" and "It Is the Spirit Who Gives Life."

## Reading the Bible as a Mirror

"The Mirror of the Word" is based on a text from James 1:22–27, which focuses on being a doer of the Word and not merely a hearer. (I have already noted that James was Kierkegaard's favorite book of the Bible.) James here says that a man who is only a hearer is like a man who looks at his face in a mirror but then goes away and forgets what he looks like. So Kierkegaard interprets James as saying that the Bible can function like a mirror, in which people can come to see themselves as they really are. God's word is a gift, but God does not force humans to read it or act according to it (FSE, 13). Kierkegaard wants to describe how the word of God can function as a mirror so that the person who gains genuine self-understanding from it will also know how Scripture can guide the person's actions.

The discourse begins with a kind of introduction, in which Kierkegaard provides a context by critically examining contemporary Danish society. It begins with the claim that "times are different" and "different times have different requirements" (FSE, 15). The discourse accepts (at least for the sake of the discussion) the common view (in Lutheran Denmark) that the Christianity of the Middle Ages had been one that viewed salvation as coming through works: "There was a time when the Gospel, *grace*, was changed into a new Law" (FSE, 15). Martin Luther responded to this by "restoring faith to its rights" (FSE, 16). Luther himself was a man of faith whose life "expressed works," but he insisted that salvation was in no way due to human merit.

Kierkegaard makes no criticism of Luther at this point, but he does pointedly criticize the use made of Luther's view by his contemporaries. There is, Kierkegaard says, "a secular mentality that no doubt wants to have the name of being Christian but wants to become Christian as cheaply as possible" (FSE, 16). This mentality basically reads Luther as providing a rationalization for a life devoted to selfish pleasure, a stance Kierkegaard illustrates by quoting a German proverb: "Who loves not women, wine, and song; he is a fool his whole life long" (FSE, 16). Kierkegaard affirms that true Christianity may be foolishness according to this way of thinking, because its requirement is this: "Your life should express works as strenuously as possible; then one thing more is required—that you humble yourself and confess: But my being saved is nevertheless grace" (FSE, 17).

Kierkegaard insists that his protest against the way Christendom takes Christianity in vain is made "without authority" and that he is not judging any individual (FSE, 17). But he nonetheless argues that his view is actually a sound Lutheran view, because Luther himself had insisted that "faith is a restless thing," something that demands expression in works (FSE, 17–18). Kierkegaard goes on to compare a person whose faith involves only "inward deepening," which is the category he would apply to himself, with someone who is a genuine "witness to the truth," a description that suggests a connection to the martyr, since the New Testament term for a martyr is the term for a witness. The honest person who compares his own life to the life of such a witness will himself think that it is a "flagrant wrong" to think that the two of them will be "equally blessed" (FSE, 23). Lutheran doctrine may be fine, but because of human cunning, "the Apostle James must be drawn forward a little" to prevent "faith and grace as the only redemption and salvation from being taken totally in vain, from becoming a camouflage for a refined worldliness" (FSE, 24).

## Looking in the Mirror and Not at the Mirror

So what are the things that must be done if the Bible is to become a mirror that enables us "to look at ourselves with true blessing"? Kierkegaard says that there are basically two things that are necessary. The first requirement is *"that you must not look at the mirror, observe the mirror, but must see yourself in the mirror"* (FSE, 25). The main idea here is that one must not think of the word of God primarily as an object to be studied, but as a tool to be used. Scholarly inquiry about the Scriptures has its place and even its value; I will discuss Kierkegaard's view of this below. However, Kierkegaard insists that when we want to read Scripture for spiritual growth, we must not think of the Bible as an object of scholarly investigation, but as the means whereby God speaks to us.

Given Kierkegaard's basic view of spirituality as "living before God," a relational state in which one is accountable to God, it is easy to see why the Bible must not be read as an object of scholarly study when one is reading it as a spiritual practice. To live before God, one must be in communication with God, listening to God's voice and addressing God in prayer. For Kierkegaard, the primary means whereby a Christian hears God speak is through Scripture. It is indeed God's word to us. Kierkegaard certainly does not rule out the possibility that God can speak to an individual through a personal experience that is independent of Scripture, but as a Christian writer, he subordinates such experiences to the word Christians get from Scripture. That word is not to be identified with the outcome of a scholarly investigation. Such a view would compromise God's freedom to speak to those who want to love him and obey him.

Kierkegaard's worry is that scholarly study can easily become an end in itself, rather than a means to hearing God speak. The scholarly enterprise is "enormously complicated" (FSE, 25). Even before we begin the process of interpretation, there are many questions: "Which books are authentic? Are they really by the apostles, and are the apostles really trustworthy?" (FSE, 25). When one begins the process of interpretation, things only get worse: "As for ways of reading, there are thirty thousand different ways" (FSE, 25). Kierkegaard hints that all this scholarly industry may not always be in good faith. (Yet, as I shall presently show, he accepts the value of honest scholarship.) Rather, we humans can sometimes use scholarship as a kind of defense mechanism, in that "we tell each other that we are perfectly willing to do God's will if we could only find out what it is" (FSE, 26). (Kierkegaard might well see contemporary ethical theory as an analogue to this in Socratic spirituality, in which we humans substitute objective inquiry about ethical questions for ethical actions, again telling ourselves we would be perfectly willing to seek the good and the right if only we could complete the arduous scholarly task of discovering what they are. On this view, scholarly work on ethics substitutes for ethical action.)

To help us understand what it would mean to really value God's word, Kierkegaard then presents an extended analogy that compares someone reading the word of God with a man who is reading a letter he has received from his beloved. To make the analogy close, Kierkegaard assumes that the letter from the beloved is written in a foreign language that the man does not understand. The man must therefore obtain a dictionary and work very hard to translate the letter (FSE, 26–27). We could even make Kierkegaard's analogy still more realistic and assume that the man also needs to consult grammar books for that foreign language, since it is hard to translate if one has only a dictionary. The man regards all this laborious work, these "scholarly preliminaries," as a "necessary evil" that he must do before he can read the letter (FSE, 27). He is impatient to finish all this work, because all he really wants to do is read the letter. As long as he is toiling away on the preliminaries, he is not really reading in the sense in which a lover wants to read a missive from a beloved.

Some readers of Kierkegaard have taken this analogy as a kind of attack on biblical scholarship, but this is clearly not the case. Biblical scholars who are not interested in reading Scripture as communication from God are perfectly free to go about their work, and Kierkegaard is not making any objection to the validity or value of such work. Presumably, this kind of scholarly work will have whatever intrinsic and extrinsic value other work on ancient texts would have. Nor is Kierkegaard denying that the Bible must be read in its historical context. The analogy makes it clear that there are "preliminaries" that must be carried out before one can read the Scriptures. After all, they were written in other languages and in a different culture. Without some historical understanding, the Bible could not even be translated properly. The practice of reading that Kierkegaard is recommending does not assume that anyone can simply pick up any scriptural text and understand what God is saying through that text without any knowledge of the historical or cultural or theological context. (However, as we shall see, Kierkegaard certainly thinks that some texts should be clear to just about anyone.)

The scholarly preliminaries are necessary for reading God's word, though they do not count as reading God's word. Kierkegaard simply wants to make a distinction between the scholarly preliminaries and the practice of reading Scripture to hear what God is saying. "When you are reading God's Word in a scholarly way, with a dictionary, etc., then you are not reading God's Word" (FSE, 28–29). In just the same way, the lover who is toiling away with a dictionary would say that it is not until he is finished with the toilsome work that he can really read the letter from the beloved.

To be sure, there are many passages in the Bible that are obscure and difficult to understand. Certainly, some of them make no sense without some guidance from a scholar. Kierkegaard knows that this is the case. He imagines someone who objects to his view of how one should read the Bible: "There are so many obscure passages in the Bible, whole books that are practically riddles" (FSE, 29). Kierkegaard accepts that there are such obscure passages. His answer is that a person is not responsible for dealing with the obscure passages but should focus attention on the passages that are easy to understand:

> When you are reading God's Word, it is not the obscure passages that bind you but what you understand, and with that you are to comply at once. If you understood only one single passage in all of Holy Scripture, well, then you must do that first of all, but you do not first have to sit down and ponder the obscure passages. God's Word is given in order that you shall act according to it, not that you shall practice interpreting obscure passages. (FSE, 29)

The analogy of the love letter is used to support this stance. If the love letter contained a request, a "wish" from the beloved, the lover who reads the letter will try to comply at once with that wish, and if there are passages he does not understand, those can be left for later. If the lovers later meet, the lover can say with a good conscience that he has done his best to comply with what he has understood. If, however, he had not complied with the wish he did understand, but simply spent his time speculating about the passages he did not understand, he could hardly claim to be a devoted lover.

In a similar way, Kierkegaard claims that Christians who are lovers of Christ should focus their efforts on living in accordance with scriptural teachings that are easy to understand. He lists a number of such passages:

> "Give all your goods to the poor."
> "If anyone strikes you on the right cheek, turn the left."
> "If anyone takes your coat, let him have your cloak also."
> "Rejoice always."
> "Count it sheer joy when you meet various temptations." (FSE, 34)

Kierkegaard claims that all of these are "just as easy to understand as the remark 'The weather is fine today'" (FSE, 34).

Someone might well object that these passages are not so obvious and straightforward as Kierkegaard seems to imply. The command to "give all your goods to the poor" was given to the rich young ruler, a particular individual, and no such command is presented as a universal duty anywhere in Scripture. Similarly, in the Sermon on the Mount, when Jesus says to turn the other cheek, Jesus is clearly teaching a stance of nonviolence, but it is not obvious that this means that one should never use force to protect a child or some other innocent person *from* violent harm.

Objections such as these make a legitimate point, which is this: Not all deliberation and reflection about what Scripture means is simply a means of evading the vital task of obeying God's word. Kierkegaard is surely right to remind us that Scripture is given primarily to allow us to become more spiritually mature and to live in accordance with God's word. And he is also right to remind us that a concern for interpretation and understanding can become an end in itself, divorced from the true purpose of God's word. Amusingly, he compares the biblical scholarly industry to a napkin a boy puts under his pants when he is going to get a whipping (FSE, 35). Biblical scholars shove in between us and action "one layer after another, interpretation and scholarly research" (FSE, 35). However, it is not right to say or imply that honest inquiry about the text is always of this nature. I do not think Kierkegaard believes this is the case either. His own example of the "toil" that translation requires shows that some scholarly work on the Bible can inform and deepen our obedience. Such work might be a necessary evil, but even if it is, it is still necessary.

Kierkegaard draws one more lesson from the analogy of the letter to the lover that seems less defensible to me. He claims, plausibly enough, that the lover who reads the letter will want to be alone when he reads the letter. Similarly, he says that the person who reads God's word should also want to be "alone with Holy Scripture" (FSE, 31). Of course, one can understand why a lover would want to be alone when reading a letter from the beloved. However, the analogy between the love letter and Scripture may fail at just this point. A romantic love relation is one shared between only two people, and third parties are usually unwelcome. However, the one who loves God does not have an exclusive relation to God in this way. The Christian is a member of Christ's body, the church, and ideally all members of the church should want to read God's word for blessing. Perhaps Kierkegaard thinks that when people read alone, they are more likely to be honest with themselves. That may often be the case, but it also seems possible that at times, reading with others could be beneficial, since the others might well challenge our tendency to deceive ourselves and help us see ourselves in the mirror as we are.

Kierkegaard rightly stresses the idea that humans are accountable to God as individuals. Each of us must give an account, and we cannot excuse our unfaithfulness by putting the responsibility on others. His emphasis on "the individual" highlights this well. However, as much as I would like to defend

Kierkegaard's view of community, I believe that his understanding of Christian community is at best one-sided. He always seems to see relations to other humans as ones that will distort or drown out God's voice, and he does not recognize often enough that God might speak to us through other humans.

Indeed, Anti-Climacus in *Practice in Christianity* goes so far as to say that "the congregation" does not really exist in time but "belongs first in eternity, where it is at rest" (PC, 223). Anti-Climacus rightly says that "everyone is an individual before God" and must as an individual "give an accounting on judgment day" (PC, 223). However, it does not follow from this that individuals who are "struggling jointly" (as Anti-Climacus says true Christians are doing) cannot be a means of grace to each other in time. I conclude that, although reading the Scriptures alone is certainly a helpful and beneficial practice, it is not right to claim that this is an essential element of reading for spiritual blessing.

In fact, such a view would contradict the fact that God's word is also heard in corporate worship, both in the reading of Scripture and in the sermon. Kierkegaard himself both participated in corporate worship and supported this practice for almost his whole life, until the attack on the church at the very end. (As already noted, the attack literature raises special issues, some already discussed, and will be treated again in this chapter.)

Perhaps Kierkegaard's emphasis on reading alone is partly motivated by the distinction he wants to draw between the objective study of the Bible and reading the Bible as God's word. He may think of the former as a communal enterprise, since that is the nature of scholarly work, but sees spiritual reading as something an individual can do. However, even if scholarly study of the Bible is communal in nature, it does not follow that all communal reading of the Bible is scholarly study. Besides the reading and hearing of the word in corporate worship, there are many small groups of Christians who come together to read and study the Scriptures, not with a view to do historical scholarship or any other kind, but to grow together as disciples of Christ. I do not think Kierkegaard ever enjoyed this kind of "small-group experience," but if he had, I think his understanding of the Christian life would have been richer.

## The Second Requirement: Applying Scripture to One's Own Life

We have looked at the first requirement Kierkegaard describes: that we use the mirror to look at our own lives, rather than simply examining the mirror itself as an object of scholarship. The second requirement is that when we read God's word, we must always seek to apply it to our own individual lives: "*You must remember to say to yourself incessantly: It is I to whom it is speaking; it is I about whom it is speaking*" (FSE, 35).

Kierkegaard illustrates his point with a brilliant account of the Old Testament narrative (from 2 Samuel 11 and 12) about King David and Bathsheba. The story is a familiar one. David desires Bathsheba and arranges to have her husband killed so that he can have her. Nathan the prophet comes to David and tells David a story about a very rich man with large herds who took and slaughtered a lamb that a poor man kept as a pet, "almost like a child in his home." In the biblical story, David becomes angry when he hears about the rich man's actions and says that the rich man deserves to die. At that point, Nathan changes the character of the story by telling David, "You are the man" (2 Samuel 12:7).

Kierkegaard alters the biblical narrative a little to make it fit his own cultural situation. On his telling, David is a great poet, a cultural connoisseur, and Nathan is described as another cultured man. In this version, David recognizes the story as a poetic creation, and his initial response is to assess it aesthetically, giving an evaluation of the "charming little work" (FSE, 38). When Nathan tells David, "You are the man," then everything is transformed: "this was the transition to the subjective" (FSE, 38).

Objectively, David already had the requisite moral knowledge to make a correct judgment about his case. He already "was well aware beforehand how abominable it is to have a woman's husband killed in order to marry her," and he himself, as a great poet, could have described the situation brilliantly (FSE, 39). None of this objective knowledge had any impact on David's behavior until the prophet's words led him to think about what he had done from his own personal perspective as a moral agent. Without the transition to "the subjective," one cannot hear God speak. One way of blocking oneself from hearing God's word is to transform that word into something "objective, impersonal, a doctrine" (FSE, 39).

Kierkegaard here is not opposing subjectivity to objective truth. Nathan's story would make no sense if one claimed that it was not objectively true that David's actions were really morally wrong. Rather, when Kierkegaard speaks about a "doctrine," he here means a kind of objective proposition that we are supposed to assent to intellectually, and perhaps debate and ponder, but never apply to our own lives.

His semantic usage here may be eccentric. One can justifiably claim that for the fathers of the church, Christian doctrines were never conceived as objective propositions that merely call for intellectual assent. Rather, one only really believes Christian doctrines if they make an impact on one's life. To accept Jesus as Lord is not simply to think of the proposition "Jesus is Lord" as true, but to build one's life around Jesus. Nevertheless, Kierkegaard thinks that this is what "doctrines" have come to mean in Christendom. For Christendom, it is important to believe the right propositions, but to seek to apply them to one's own life is seen as personal vanity (FSE, 36). Kierkegaard protests against this by stressing the importance of the subjective. Assenting to correct objective propositions does not by itself shape a person's life spiritually. It is only when the doctrines are applied to one's own life that they have genuine value. The remedy for all of this detached objectivity is that when we read God's word, we are to tell ourselves what Nathan told David: "You are the man." Or, updating to contemporary nonsexist language: "You are the person."

Some have objected to Kierkegaard here by arguing that this simply cannot be correct as a universal injunction. For example, when Jesus says, "I and the Father are one," we surely are not to tell ourselves: "This passage is about you." Moreover, there are long passages of history in the Old Testament that clearly describe people who lived a long time ago and whose situation differs radically from our own. Such an objection, however, stems from a very literal and uncharitable reading of Kierkegaard. He surely does not mean that each and every sentence in the Bible must be read as about the reader. Rather, what he is urging is that whenever we read the Scriptures, we must always seek to hear what God is saying through that Scripture to us and think about what that message implies for who we are and how we are to live. We are not literally to think of every sentence of Scripture as referring to ourselves, but we are always to seek to hear what Scripture means for us and our lives.

## The Urgency of Prompt Obedience

In the last section of the "Mirror of the Word," Kierkegaard stresses the need to transform the self-understanding gained through the mirror into action. An effective tool for the person who wants to resist such transformation is procrastination. When they hear God's word, few people will have the temerity to self-consciously defy God. Not many will acknowledge that God is calling for them to live in a certain way and then simply say they choose to disobey. What is far more common is delay. I tell myself, "Certainly, I want to live as God commands, but right now . . ." The situation can be compared to a teenager whose parents have asked her to clean up her room. The teenager does not usually say, "I refuse to do that," but rather, "Okay, but not right now."

The remedy for this self-deception is for the Christian to begin on the task right away. We should have a healthy suspicion of promises and assurances we make about the future. Rather than say, "I will never forget," a person ought to seek to promptly remember (FSE, 44). Big promises and assurances are an excellent tool for deceiving ourselves; beginning the task right away is earnest money that our commitments are genuine. Kierkegaard illustrates the principle beautifully with a story of a man addicted to gambling. If the man makes a solemn vow to stop gambling but takes no actual steps toward this end, he is likely to fail. Kierkegaard imagines the man saying to himself something like this: "I solemnly vow that I will nevermore have anything to do with gambling, never—tonight will be the last time" (FSE, 45). Such a person is fooling himself. However, the man who says to himself, "Well, now, you may gamble every blessed day all the rest of your life—but tonight you are going to leave it alone," may be saved, if the man truly is able to do what he says (FSE, 45).

Kierkegaard ends this section of the "Mirror of the Word" with an extended picture of an ordinary woman who embodies what it means to read the Scripture so as to gain true blessing. The woman who exemplifies this characteristic does so by practicing silence. The woman in this example is married, unfortunately reflecting stereotypical assumptions about male and female roles that seem to most people today to be sexist. Women are described in terms of their role as the ones who transform a house into a home, and Kierkegaard affirms the idea that women ought to be silent in church. However, what (partially) redeems the stereotyping is this: Kierkegaard is not describing the woman's role as one that applies only to *women*. Rather, he is holding up the woman he describes as a model that *men* ought to emulate. All those who want to read God's word with blessing must cultivate silence. I think the defensible point he is trying to make is that all of us, if we are to hear God's word, must be "quick to listen" and "slow to speak" (James 1:19). A temptation for anyone who has been given the gift of hearing God's word is to become prideful, the kind of person who sees himself or herself as a spiritual expert whose main task is to lecture others. The discipline of silence helps us understand that what we need to gain from hearing God's word is to be transformed ourselves. The silence we all need to practice has nothing to do with gender stereotyping.

## Christ Is the Way

The second discourse from *For Self-Examination* is entitled "Christ Is the Way" and is designed as a sermon to be preached on Ascension Sunday. The ostensible text is the account of the ascension from Acts 1:1–12, but the real text is John 14:6, in which Jesus affirms that he is the way, the truth, and the life. Kierkegaard takes Jesus to be literally teaching that his life is the way to eternal life, and thus the discourse is an extended reflection on what it means to be an imitator of Christ, a person who follows along the way Christ led. The Danish term here translated as "imitator" (*Efterfølger*) literally means an "after-follower," someone who "follows after."

Kierkegaard stresses that "the way" that we must follow to imitate Christ is a "narrow" way, echoing Matthew 7:14. The Danish word translated as "narrow" here (*trang*) suggests "difficult" or even "burdensome," and it is clearly these meanings that are at the forefront of Kierkegaard's understanding of what it means to follow Christ, to be an imitator. Christ's life is "narrow" in this sense of being difficult and hard from beginning to end. It begins with "poverty and wretchedness" at his birth (FSE, 58). It continues with the difficulty of temptation, not merely in the desert when tempted by Satan, but with the constant temptation "to take his calling, his task, in vain" (FSE, 59). The story is also a story of suffering, including the enormous suffering involved in knowing from the beginning the terrible suffering he will face at the end of his life (FSE, 59–60). This all culminates on the cross with the cry of dereliction, in which Jesus feels forsaken by God the Father. The way is a way of suffering and self-denial to the very end.

Yet the discourse is for Ascension Sunday, and the assigned text describes how Jesus ascended to heaven as triumphant. Kierkegaard affirms that Christ did ascend into heaven and is now victorious, sitting at the right hand of power (FSE, 65). Kierkegaard does not doubt that the Christian way is one that is victorious and leads to heaven (FSE, 67). However, he insists that in this life, the way is narrow and never becomes easy. In fact, it becomes harder and harder, since the sufferings of the Christian who imitates Christ are voluntary and can easily be avoided if one simply reverts to ordinary human ways of living and does not risk persecution by seeking to live like Jesus and obey Jesus's commands.

At this point in the discourse, there is a jarring transition. So far, Kierkegaard has talked about the Christian life as a life of voluntary suffering but has said very little about the ascension, except to affirm that, like Christ, the one who follows Christ can look forward to a heavenly reward. Suddenly Kierkegaard affirms that the ascension is a teaching that people in his day are doubting. Why do they doubt, and what is the remedy?

Kierkegaard's analysis of this doubt is one that rejects any intellectual account of the problem, and also rejects any intellectual solution to the doubt. The true imitator of Christ, he claims, is a person who has no doubts about the ascension: "But those whose lives are marked by *imitation* have not doubted the Ascension" (FSE, 68). Such people live in a way that is "too strenuous" to "keep company with reasons and doubt" (FSE, 68). All those who are true imitators of Christ are "convinced that their Lord and Master ascended into heaven" (FSE, 69). The basis of their belief is not reasons or arguments; Kierkegaard says that intellectual defenses of the doctrine actually fuel the doubts (FSE, 68). The true ground of faith is need; the imitator of Christ believes in the ascension because he or she must believe: "So it always is with need in a human being; out of the eater comes something to eat; where there is need, it itself produces, as it were, that which it needs" (FSE, 69).

Kierkegaard here seems to walk right into the problem of the Freudian critique of religion as wish fulfillment. How, one might ask, does the fact that the imitator of Christ needs to believe in the ascension in order to continue the struggle justify the belief? The epistemological issues raised here are deep, and I cannot treat them adequately here. I can only say that Kierkegaard rejects the evidentialist picture of human faith, in which faith is seen as a degree of intellectual assent that is proportioned to the evidence for the belief. On my view, and this is one I have defended in other places, Kierkegaard takes a view of religious belief similar to Alvin Plantinga's "Reformed epistemology."[1] On this view, which is a form of epistemological externalism, not all reasonable beliefs are based on evidence. What provides a belief with justification (or warrant, in Plantinga's language) is that the belief is the result of a truth-conducive process. For example, for ordinary human beliefs, processes such as memory and perception give rise to beliefs that, when true, can amount to knowledge. The

1. See my essays "Kierkegaard and Plantinga on Belief in God: Subjectivity as the Ground of Properly Basic Religious Beliefs" and "Externalist Epistemology, Subjectivity, and Christian Knowledge: Plantinga and Kierkegaard," in C. Stephen Evans, *Kierkegaard on Faith and the Self: Collected Essays* (Waco, TX: Baylor University Press, 2006), 169–205. For Plantinga's own work, see *Warranted Christian Belief* (New York: Oxford University Press, 2000).

warrant for the belief does not have to stem from evidence that is internally accessible to the knower, but from the fact that the belief is the product of reliable faculty, one that is working properly and is designed to arrive at truth. As Kierkegaard sees things, God has providentially ordered human life so that our needs drive us to the truth. In this case, our needs do not lead to wish fulfillment that cuts us off from reality, a situation in which we believe what is easier for us to believe. In the case of Christianity, our sense of our sinfulness and need for God's grace and forgiveness actually drive us to believe things we would rather not believe. These beliefs are not the easy way out but rather are difficult to believe because they make our lives more strenuous. However, they bring us closer to the truth about ourselves and human life.

Kierkegaard therefore claims that the solution to doubt is not apologetic arguments, but to live as an authentic Christian, imitating Christ. "When it is for a good cause that you live despised, persecuted, ridiculed, in poverty, then you will find that you do not doubt his [Christ's] Ascension, because you need it" (FSE, 70). Actually, the bar is even lower than this. Kierkegaard claims that the person who has not ventured out that far can deal with doubt by simply humbly admitting that one has "coddled oneself" and that one's life "is not marked as the life of an imitator in the strict sense" (FSE, 70). Such a person will realize that if only he or she were willing to venture out in imitation, doubts would cease. A person who is humble enough to admit this will not presume to doubt.

My own view is that there is much wisdom in Kierkegaard's response at this point, but it is a mistake to claim that *all* doubt is the result of a culpable failing to live as a true Christian. There is, I believe, such a thing as honest doubt that calls for honest reflection. Kierkegaard is surely right to say that doubt can be the result of spiritual flabbiness, and also that the conviction that overcomes doubt can be strengthened by action. Even secular psychologists agree that acting as if some belief is true increases one's confidence that the belief is true. However, even to act as if a belief is true, one must have some reasons to believe that it is true. One would not seek to imitate Christ if one did not already have at least a weak belief that Christ was the way, the Son of God, and the Savior of the world. As Plantinga and Kierkegaard both affirm, that conviction must come from the testimony of God's Spirit, a theme I will discuss in the next section. Nevertheless, the honest person of faith who takes an objection seriously and tries to think it through is not being unfaithful. For God is a God of truth.

## The Spirit Gives Life

The last discourse in *For Self-Examination* is entitled "It Is the Spirit That Gives Life." The discourse reads as a sermon for Pentecost Sunday, and the text is Acts 2:1–12, which recounts the giving of the Holy Spirit to the apostles. This discourse is especially important for an understanding of Kierkegaard's view of Christian spiritual life, since it contains what is probably the most extended treatment of the Holy Spirit found anywhere in Kierkegaard's authorship.

Kierkegaard begins with a discussion of how his contemporaries speak of "spirit." His contemporaries all believe in some kind of spirit, but what they believe in is "the spirit of the age," "the spirit of the world," "the human spirit," or "the spirit of the human race" (FSE, 74). The last of these is a clear reference to the Hegelian concept of Spirit, which Kierkegaard sees as completely embodied in human history. Despite believing in all these "spirits," Kierkegaard hints that few people in his time really believe in the Holy Spirit, and perhaps even fewer believe in "an evil spirit" (FSE, 74). The spirits people believe in are impersonal spirits. A person can speak of such spirits without being personally bound by what is said, because the content of the spirit is vague and indefinite (FSE, 74–75). If one believes both in the Holy Spirit and in the evil spirit, then one must have "earnestness," because "one cannot speak about there being a Holy Spirit and about believing in a Holy Spirit without binding oneself by one's words, and furthermore, not without binding oneself to the Holy Spirit in renunciation of the evil spirit" (FSE, 75).

Kierkegaard here makes it plain that he believes in the reality of the Holy Spirit, and even of Satan. Christian spirituality is a spirituality in which one is bound by the authority of God, in whose presence one lives and to whom one is accountable. He continues to affirm that humans are inherently spiritual creatures, but the kind of spirituality present in Christendom is a counterfeit kind of spirituality, not what God intends for humans. Here is a picture of someone who has this counterfeit kind of spirituality:

> Slack as he is, or disintegrated, doubting in his faith, unstable in all his ways, bending to every breeze of the times, the object of his faith is of the same kind: something flimsy, the spirit of the age; or secularized as he is in all his thoughts and aspirations, the object of his faith is accordingly: the spirit of the world. (FSE, 75)

Once more, we see that for Kierkegaard the decline of Christian faith in the nineteenth century has nothing to do with intellectual issues; it is not the result of scientific discoveries or biblical criticism. Rather, doubts about faith are the result of spiritual weakness.

How does the Spirit give life? It is not life in the natural sense, although Kierkegaard certainly believes that all life is created by God. The life that the Holy Spirit makes possible for the Christian is neither natural life nor any natural human quality of life. The life that the Spirit gives is something that is supernatural in character, something that can come only by way of God's special action.

## What Does It Mean to Die to Selfishness?

What protects the "essentially Christian" from being confused with any natural quality is that the life that the Spirit makes possible requires as "the middle term" a kind of dying (FSE, 76). So "the life-giving in the Spirit is not a *direct* heightening of the natural life in a person in *immediate* continuation from and connection with it" (FSE, 76). As we shall see, the supernatural virtues of faith, hope, and love that the Spirit makes possible are profoundly different from any natural forms of these qualities. It is a new life because "death goes in between," a dying that makes possible a life on the other side of death (FSE, 76).

Kierkegaard certainly believes that actual physical death is the gateway to eternal life, a life after death. However, in this discourse, he is focusing on the new life that the Spirit makes possible during earthly life. Eternal life is not something that one gains only after death, but something that one can acquire in this life. It follows from this that the death that is necessary to gain this new life is not physical death but a kind of dying that one must practice during one's life. Kierkegaard calls this "dying to," because this kind of dying has a kind of intentional object: "You must first die to every merely earthly hope, to every merely human confidence; you must die to your selfishness, or to the world, because it is only through your selfishness that the world has power over you" (FSE, 77).

What does this mean? I do not think it can literally mean that a person who has died to selfishness has extinguished all earthly hopes or has no desires at all. Such a person would simply have ceased to be a human person completely. Rather, a person who has successfully "died to the world" would be someone who would never allow a human desire or hope to block the person from doing God's will. The person's ultimate identity is so bound up with God that he or she would willingly sacrifice any finite good for the sake of the God-relationship.

There is a formal parallel here with Socratic spirituality, which I described in chapter 4 as requiring an "absolute relation to the absolute" that requires a willingness to resign any finite good. The resignation required is dispositional; one must be willing to sacrifice the finite when that is necessary. Similarly, the Christian who dies to the world must be willing to sacrifice any finite good when God calls for such a sacrifice.

There are, of course, significant differences between Socratic spirituality and Christian spirituality. The goal of the resignation is not an abstract ethical absolute, but a concrete relation to Jesus, an actual human person, who gives his followers specific commands: to love all people as their neighbors, even their enemies. Despite the difference in content, there is one additional formal similarity. Both Socratic resignation and Christian "dying to" are tasks for a lifetime. Kierkegaard does not think that short of eternity any human person can finish the task of dying to self once and for all.

Although the task is dispositional and cannot be understood as literally ceasing to have any finite desires or hopes, Kierkegaard is convinced that anyone who is seriously committed to following Christ will actually have to sacrifice things. The goals of the kingdom cannot be achieved simply by following one's natural desires to live a long and happy life, if that life is measured in a worldly way. The Christian may have to sacrifice wealth, social status, and worldly fame and will almost certainly experience opposition and even persecution.[2] Kierkegaard even gives as an illustration a story that recalls his own sacrifice of Regine, the woman to whom he was engaged (FSE, 78–79), though he makes a thin attempt to disguise the story as one "fashioned on those old tales about what a person in former times had undergone in intense suffering" (FSE, 78). In the story, a man has fallen in love, and his love "is the delight of his eye and the desire of his heart" (FSE, 78). Nonetheless, he is commanded to give her up, and although the suffering is dreadful, including the pleas of the young woman, "he must let go of the object" (FSE, 79).

What should we say about this story? If we take Kierkegaard's example as fictional, disregarding his own history, I think he is right to affirm that Christian faith sometimes will require this kind of sacrifice. After all, Christ himself says in Luke 14:26 that anyone who wants to be his follower must "hate his father and mother, his wife and children, his brothers and sisters—yes, even his own life" to be Christ's disciples. Kierkegaard's own understanding

2. Note, however, my critical worries about Kierkegaard's claims about Christian suffering, in chapter 7, pp. 155–58.

of this verse is that Jesus does not mean one must literally hate one's family, but that commitment to Christ may well require acts that one's family will construe as hatred for them. I personally know people whose conversions to Christ resulted in painful breaks with family members who could not accept that their loved one had become a Christian. One friend told me that his father, when he found out that his son had become a Christian, had said, "Why do you hate us?" Furthermore, the martyr, who is willing to sacrifice his or her very life, has always been revered as the exemplar of Christian spirituality. So Kierkegaard's claim that this kind of sacrifice may be required by faith has solid backing.

Nevertheless, though I fully agree that this kind of sacrifice is one that Christian faith can require, both in the past and today, I think it is important to recognize that Kierkegaard's example should not be universalized. Every Christian ought to be willing to give up whatever finite good God requires, but we must not slide from this into the view that this story of the sacrifice of earthly love is universally normative. God himself instituted marriage, and Jesus, of course, did his first miracle at a wedding. As we shall see, in the attack writings of Kierkegaard's very last period, he begins to slide from the view that the Christian must be willing to give up any finite good, toward the view that natural human goods such as marriage must simply be renounced. However, I do not think that this is what he is saying in *For Self-Examination*.

If dying to self is dying to selfishness, then it cannot be understood as the destruction of all finite desires and hopes, because not all such desires and hopes are selfish. Dying to selfishness must be seen as the willingness to sacrifice any such good when that good interferes with one's relation to God. This cannot mean that every Christian must live a celibate life, renouncing family happiness, or that every Christian must literally give away all his or her financial goods.

To be sure, Kierkegaard is right to ask those of us who have had relatively good lives to reflect on our situation and ask ourselves whether we have "coddled ourselves." We ought to ask ourselves whether we should have done more and should do more in the future. It hardly seems truthful for someone to claim that he or she would be willing to give up anything for the sake of Christ if that person has never actually sacrificed a single thing. Kierkegaard often admits his own failures in this regard and recognizes that his own life has been no better than the lives of his contemporaries. What he is urging us to seek is a humble honesty about our own status, and a willingness to consider what more we could do and should do.

## The Gifts of the Spirit

The gifts that the Spirit provides are the traditional theological or supernatural virtues: faith, hope, and love. In each case, Kierkegaard tries to help us see the distinctive character of these virtues when understood in the Christian way. In each case, the Christian version of the virtue requires a kind of death, a renunciation of a human quality that sometimes is confused with the Christian virtue.

Humans tend to describe the quality of human self-confidence as faith. This self-confidence can be bolstered by the human understanding, which thinks through things on the basis of probability. (In the next section, I will examine Kierkegaard's attack on probability as a foundational element in human spirituality.) Genuine Christian faith, however, is not self-confidence, and it is not a view about what will probably happen given a shrewd understanding of how things go on in the world. Since God is the God for whom all things are possible, one really only discovers whether one has faith in God when all human sources of faith have dried up. "It is when all confidence in yourself or in human support, and also in God in an immediate way, is extinct, when every probability is extinct, when it is dark as on a dark night . . . then comes the life-giving Spirit and brings faith" (FSE, 82).

I think that this account of faith must also be understood as dispositional in character. It is not that one can have Christian faith only in the "dark night of the soul," when the truth of Christianity seems impossible and God seems not to be present at all. Surely it is not the case that people have faith only when they are in such extreme circumstances. Rather, what seems right is that genuine Christian faith will persevere, even when one is in such a situation. It exhibits itself in a unique way when human faith fails.

Kierkegaard says something similar about hope "in the strictest Christian sense" (FSE, 82). Genuine Christian hope is "hope against hope," hope when there are no human grounds for hope (FSE, 82–83). Human hope must die for Christian hope to be present. Genuine Christian hope is not the paltry comfort that comes when one believes that there is some probability that the cancer will go into remission, or that one might avoid financial disaster by getting a better-paying job. Of course, in one sense, the Christian hopes for such things as well. Such hopes do not literally cease when one has Christian hope. However, the Christian's ultimate hope does not rest on such things. Genuine Christian hope is hope that can be present even when, humanly speaking, no hope seems possible. I can still hope that my life will be meaningful and that I will have eternal life even if I am dying from cancer or find myself in a financial disaster.

Finally, Kierkegaard affirms, in a section where he briefly alludes to the extended argument he offers in *Works of Love*, that the love that the Spirit brings is not identical to human natural loves, such as friendship and romantic love (WL, 44–60). All such loves are tarnished by selfishness and do not, as they naturally occur, constitute the love of God and neighbor that the Spirit provides. Genuine love of neighbor requires that one love the other as one loves oneself, and this requires the extinction of selfishness. True love of neighbor is not a natural love of what seems loveworthy; it is a willingness to join with God in loving those that one has no benefit from loving (FSE, 84–85).

Kierkegaard is certainly right to insist that selfishness is a huge problem that lurks in the human self, and right to insist that becoming a friend of God requires a transformation that kills off this selfishness. However, it is also worth remembering that the biblical command is to love the neighbor as oneself. Although Kierkegaard sometimes talks about "hating oneself," this language should be taken literally no more than the command to "hate" one's family members. On the contrary, as Kierkegaard himself admits in *Works of Love*, there is a healthy form of self-love, and one way of failing to be the self God wants one to be consists in failing to love oneself in the proper way: "Whoever has any knowledge of people will certainly admit that just as he has often wished to be able to move them to relinquish self-love, he has also had to wish that it were possible to teach them to love themselves" (WL, 23).[3] A person who loves the neighbor as himself wills the good of both himself and the neighbor.[4] Kierkegaard clearly says that neighbor love transforms but does not abolish forms of natural love, such as marriage and friendship.[5] Christian love requires the "death" of all natural loves in this sense: they too must be things that one is willing to renounce, if necessary, for the sake of love of God.[6] However, in loving the stranger and the enemy, one is certainly

3. In this passage, Kierkegaard goes on to describe a variety of ways people fail to love themselves properly, including people who waste their gifts and talents, people who suffer from depression, and those who simply despair of their own worth.

4. See John Lippitt, *Kierkegaard and the Problem of Self-Love* (Cambridge: Cambridge University Press, 2013), for an excellent treatment of the nature of self-love and its legitimacy in Kierkegaard.

5. See my *Kierkegaard's Ethic of Love* (Oxford: Oxford University Press, 2004), 203–22, for a defense of the claim that love of the neighbor perfects but does not abolish natural forms of love.

6. Interestingly, C. S. Lewis, at the end of *The Four Loves*, when discussing charity, also claims that all of our natural loves must die to be resurrected and preserved in eternity. The following passage is crucial: "The very name of nature implies the transitory. Natural loves can

not to cease loving one's family and friends, and Kierkegaard resolutely opposes the idea that "dissimilarities" can or should be abolished.[7]

### *Judge for Yourself!* and the Task of Becoming Sober

*Judge for Yourself!* has a subtitle, *For Self-Examination Recommended to the Present Age*, which both links it to *For Self-Examination* and makes it clear that Kierkegaard thinks the message, like the one in *For Self-Examination*, is one his contemporaries especially needed to hear. The essay has two sections: "Becoming Sober" and "Christ as the Pattern, or No One Can Serve Two Masters." Since I looked closely at the theme of Christ as the Pattern in the previous two chapters, I will here focus on "Becoming Sober."

This essay is especially valuable in the light it throws on Kierkegaard's view of Christian spirituality because it takes as its major theme what it means to be "filled with the Spirit" and thus is naturally linked to "It Is the Spirit That Gives Life" in *For Self-Examination*. The text for the discourse is taken from Acts 2:12–13. On the day of Pentecost, the apostles are filled with the Holy Spirit, speaking in foreign languages and prophesying. However, despite these supernatural gifts, some of the bystanders mocked the apostles and said, "They are full of sweet wine." It appears that it was easy to confuse being filled with the Holy Spirit with a state of drunkenness! It is interesting that even today, the English language describes forms of alcohol as "spirits."

Kierkegaard uses this text as an occasion to reflect on what it means to be sober and what it means to be intoxicated. He begins by a description of a "callous secular mentality" that prides itself on its serious, sober mind-set. The mentality resembles what is sometimes today called a "positivist" or "empiricist" view that insists on empirical evidence for everything:

---

hope for eternity only in so far as they have allowed themselves to be taken into the eternity of Charity; have at least allowed the process to begin here on earth, before the night comes when no man can work. And the process will always involve a kind of death. There is no escape. In my love for wife or friend the only eternal element is the transforming presence of Love Himself. By that presence, if at all, the other elements may hope, as our physical bodies hope, to be raised from the dead. For this only is holy in them, this only is the Lord" (*The Four Loves* [Orlando: Harcourt, 1988], 136–37).

7. If anything, Kierkegaard is too conservative in assuming that human special relationships are always compatible with neighbor love. See my *Kierkegaard's Ethic of Love*, 215–22. There are forms of human special relationships that can be inherently oppressive and degrading.

I stick to facts. I am neither a fanatic nor a dreamer nor a fool, neither drunk nor crazy. I stick to facts; I take nothing on faith, nothing whatever except what I can touch and feel, and I believe no one, not my own child, not my wife, not my best friend; I believe only what can be demonstrated—because I stick to facts. (JY, 97)

Kierkegaard argues that such a person is, from a spiritual point of view, intoxicated, a person who needs to become sober. Christianity has an entirely different idea for what it means to be sober than the world does.

Of course, the worldly mind does reject a kind of intoxication that Christianity agrees must be avoided. This includes not only literal drunkenness but a "venturing that is foolhardy" (JY, 99). Despite this apparent agreement, the worldly view and the Christian view of intoxication and sobriety are not just different but opposed. What Kierkegaard calls "secularity" and Christianity "have the very opposite views, . . . what the one calls the good the other calls evil, what the one calls love the other calls selfishness, . . . what the one calls being drunk the other calls being sober" (JY, 96).

This does not mean that there is no diversity within the views of the secular viewpoint. Kierkegaard notes that there is a difference between those who use their shrewdness to "coddle themselves completely" and those who appear to be willing to take some risks. The latter sorts of people may appear to the former to be adventuresome, but their venturing is always within a strict limit: "They venture farther out, exert themselves more, do not avoid every danger, but one thing stands firm for them: probability—they never relinquish that" (JY, 99). By contrast with this, the genuine Christian must "relinquish probability," since "the person who never relinquished probability never became involved with God" (JY, 99-100).

This claim that Christian spirituality requires that one "relinquish probability" is difficult to understand and, if one understands it straightforwardly and literally, seems very implausible. As Bishop Joseph Butler famously said, "probability is the great guide of life." It is not clear why a person should want to relinquish probability or even whether this is possible. If I want to drive from Waco to Austin, Texas, it seems reasonable to try to take the route that is probably going to have less traffic and will take less time. If I am deciding which of two medicines to take for a disease, it would be foolish to ignore the fact that one of the drugs has a much higher probability of curing me. When humans make decisions, they constantly factor in their beliefs about the likelihood of success of various options. It just seems straightforwardly irrational to desire some goal G and then pick a means that makes achieving G less likely.

Indeed, a complete elimination of probability seems so impossible and so irrational that I think it would be uncharitable to think that this is what Kierkegaard means by "relinquishing probability." Besides this, there are many passages in Kierkegaard's writings in which he acknowledges the legitimacy of taking into account probability when one is seeking some relative, temporal good. Given a particular end or goal, there is no great virtue in performing an action that is less likely to succeed than another. I therefore do not think Kierkegaard means that the Christian must totally exclude probability from life.

But what does he mean? I think the most plausible answer is that the Christian does not make "probability" the final or ultimate arbiter of life's crucial decisions. The legitimate sphere for probability just is the sphere of choosing between finite temporal and relative goods and deciding how best to achieve those goods. If I am deciding between applying to College X and College Y, two equally desirable schools, and I know that I am much more likely to be accepted at X than at Y, then that is a reason to apply to X. If I am extremely unlikely to achieve a goal, then "cleverness" or "shrewdness," that human faculty that relies on probability, will tell me to pass up that goal, unless the payoff for success is great enough to outweigh the low probability of success. Kierkegaard assumes that the ends or goals of a person who relies only on "probability" are all commensurable. There are no goods that are valued absolutely or unconditionally, and thus any goal is one that can be given up if that is what "shrewdness" seems to dictate. The life of a person who has nothing higher than finite, temporal goals thus is completely determined by probability.

The person who is accountable to God, and especially the person who is accountable to Christ, is in a very different position. To be accountable to God as God is revealed in Christ is to be assigned a task that is absolute or unconditional in nature. My calling as a disciple of Jesus is to take up my cross and follow him, even if this leads to the loss of the worldly temporal goods I desire. The fact that it is *probable* that my actions will lead to what the world would call a disaster (poverty, hardship, suffering, persecution) should make no difference. On this reading, when Kierkegaard says that Christians must "relinquish probability," he means that they must, when they know God has called them to do something or to live in a certain way, obey without hesitation, even though they know that their actions will appear foolish to the world. They may seem "drunk" or "intoxicated" to worldly people, but this spiritual view of life is precisely what it means to "become sober."

Interestingly, Kierkegaard clearly thinks that even when a person does "venture in reliance upon God" and relinquishes probability, the person does not completely abandon rational assessment of the actions. It is true that "it is most likely, humanly speaking, that you will succumb" (JY, 101). You might succeed, despite this, since "everything is possible for God." Still, you ought not to seek what is *impossible*, since in that case "your venturing is presumptuousness" (JY, 101). Clearly, a person must be able to assess the situation rationally to distinguish what is merely improbable from what is impossible.

Why is Kierkegaard so confident that a person who follows God's call will, in all probability, suffer? There are two closely connected reasons, I think. One that I have already discussed at some length is that the call is a call to follow Christ, who is the Pattern, and Christ lived a life of poverty that ended in crucifixion. If we imitate Christ, we must expect to share in Christ's suffering. The second reason is that Kierkegaard has a firm conviction that the world in which humans live is always a sinful world. The world that Christ lived in was a sinful world, and Kierkegaard's own world, a world in which people claim to be Christ's followers, is just as sinful. The latter half of "Becoming Sober" thus consists of a harsh critique of Christendom, though Kierkegaard is always careful to admit that he is no better than his contemporaries.

The Christian view is that to become sober is "*to come so close to oneself in one's understanding, in one's knowing, that all one's understanding becomes action*" (JY, 115). The Christian must be someone who "disdains the world's honor and glory, rank and titles, medals and ribbons" (JY, 138). If a person disdains worldly goods in this way, that person will certainly lose out on some of those worldly goods, and such a life will therefore be costly. Furthermore, Kierkegaard believes that a person who lives this way will be resented by others and suffer persecution as well, and he even hints that his own writings have led some to regard him with resentment, though they have thought it prudent not to express this publicly (JY, 140–41).

Some might explain the lack of persecution of Christians in Denmark in the following way: Christians are not persecuted, because Denmark is a Christian country. Kierkegaard, however, offers a different explanation: Christianity is no longer persecuted, because it has ceased to exist (JY, 141). There simply are no Christians in Denmark, and Kierkegaard unhesitatingly includes himself in this judgment.

It is clear that, with this claim, Kierkegaard has crossed over a line. He is no longer addressing his readers as a Christian speaking to his fellow believers, helping them deepen their faith and deepen their spirituality. Instead, he is accusing them (and himself) of not being Christians at all. Genuine Christians would necessarily be persecuted, and no one in Denmark is living the kind of sacrificial life that would call down persecution upon it. Kierkegaard presents his readers with a stark either/or: "*either* there is an actual renunciation of the things of this world in order, with sacrifice and suffering, to proclaim Christianity . . . *or* one secures the temporal things of this world but then makes the confession that the proclamation is not really Christianity" (JY, 135).

The idea that the Christian requirement to suffer must be understood dispositionally as a willingness to suffer, *if necessary*, to be faithful to God, the view that I argued earlier in this chapter is the best way to understand Christian suffering, is now rejected and even ridiculed by Kierkegaard. The person who claims to be willing to sacrifice everything for the sake of Christianity has no credibility if the person has never been willing to sacrifice anything (JY, 135). The apostles and other early Christians were martyrs, "witnesses to the truth," who transformed the world through their sacrifices. The "capital" accumulated in those early centuries has now been depleted, according to Kierkegaard, and the church can no longer live off these heroic early figures (JY, 130). Only people who live as witnesses to the truth are spiritually sober; all others are intoxicated. It thus turns out that this discourse on how to become sober has the sobering conclusion that there are no sober people in Denmark.

The message of *Judge for Yourself!* is therefore quite close to the attack Kierkegaard makes on Christendom in 1854–55, where Kierkegaard repeatedly and relentlessly claims that Christianity in the New Testament sense has simply ceased to exist (TM, 205). It was clear to Kierkegaard when he finished *Judge for Yourself!* that the book represented a complete break with the church, and this realization was certainly part of the reason Kierkegaard decided not to publish the book. However, in 1854 the situation was changed. Kierkegaard not only broke with the church but openly attacked it. An evaluation of *Judge for Yourself!* and the spirituality it recommends therefore requires a look at the final attack literature from 1854–55.

## The Attack on Christendom

In 1854, Bishop Mynster, who had been the pastor of Kierkegaard's father as well as Kierkegaard himself, died. Though Kierkegaard had become increasingly critical of the Danish church, as we have seen in this chapter and the previous two, as long as Mynster was alive, there was no open break. Rather, Kierkegaard hoped for a kind of honest confession, in which the leaders of the church would admit that the requirements of Christianity had become watered down. At a kind of memorial service in Copenhagen shortly before Mynster's funeral, Hans Lassen Martensen, who had been Kierkegaard's tutor and who soon was to succeed Mynster as the bishop of Zealand, eulogized Mynster as a "witness to the truth," one of the "holy chain of witnesses to the truth that stretches through the ages from the days of the apostles" (NA, 3).[8] The term "witness to the truth" is clearly a reference to the early Christians, including the apostles, who were martyred for their faith. As we have seen, for Kierkegaard these martyrs provide the gold standard for true Christianity.

Bishop Mynster had been in many ways a traditional Christian, defending orthodox doctrine against newer, liberal theological views, and Kierkegaard had taken his side in some disputes. However, as a bishop in the state church, Mynster had lived a long and comfortable life, living in a palace, with plenty of prestige and financial comforts. Rather than living a life of suffering and dying as a martyr, Mynster embodied a cultured and comfortable form of the Christian life, one that saw no tension between Christian existence and worldly prestige and material rewards. Martensen's eulogizing of Mynster as a martyr simply drove Kierkegaard over the edge. Kierkegaard, who for several years had been speaking of "witnesses to the truth" as what Christianity needed but lacked, responded with a newspaper article, "Was Bishop Mynster a 'Witness to the Truth,' One of the 'Authentic Witnesses to the Truth'—Is *This the Truth?*" (NA, 3). With this article, the attack on the church was begun, carried on first in newspaper articles and finally in a periodical Kierkegaard himself founded and financed: *The Moment.*

I shall argue that the attack on Christendom represents a fundamental change in Kierkegaard's thinking and not a change for the better. Kierkegaard's view of spirituality moves from a humanistic stance in which spirituality redeems and ennobles our humanness to a kind of anti-humanism, in which spirituality requires a repudiation and rejection of our created human nature. The attack literature is not subtle in any way. Kierkegaard employs biting wit and sarcasm to attack the state church and its clergy and to argue that Christianity, in the New Testament sense, has simply ceased

8. The Hongs translate the Danish here very literally as "truth-witness," but this sounds very odd in English, though it does not in Danish. So I have here gone back to Lowrie's "witness to the truth," though I provide pagination to the Hong translation.

to exist. As we shall see, it contains some elements of misogyny and down-right misanthropy. As such, it has been used by opponents of Kierkegaard as evidence that Kierkegaard's vision of Christian spirituality is deeply flawed. It is a spirituality that is destructive of human nature, an anti-humanist or even inhuman spirituality. Such writers as Joakim Garff have argued that the objectionable elements in the attack literature are just the outworking of unhealthy themes that are present in Kierkegaard's earlier work as well.[9] I agree with Garff that the attack writings contain these unhealthy elements, but I shall argue that they are in no way required by Kierkegaard's earlier account of spirituality.

At the heart of the attack is the charge that the clergy in the state church are not and cannot be servants of Christ. It is impossible to be a servant of the state and receive a comfortable living, while at the same time proclaiming a faith that requires self-renunciation (TM, 147–48). One might think that Kierkegaard's protest here is simply grounded in opposition to the idea of a state church, a familiar theme among advocates of free churches.[10] That is certainly part of the issue, but I think Kierkegaard's opposition has deeper roots. He sees the state-supported pastors as symptomatic of a more wide-spread problem. It isn't just that pastors are servants of the state, though Kierkegaard does object to that as well. The problem is that it now seems impossible to Kierkegaard for a genuine Christian to take a positive view of any finite good. In *Judge for Yourself!*, Kierkegaard says that the heart of the problem of Christendom is that "we have made the finite and the infinite, the eternal, and the temporal, the highest and the lowest, blend in such a way that it is impossible to say which is which" (JY, 123).

Kierkegaard says it is impossible to determine whether it is the "job, the career, that inspires the theological graduate, or . . . Christianity" (JY, 123). The problem is not found just among pastors, however, but is pervasive in society. If someone aspires to be a professor, is he inspired by "the job, the

9. One can see this at many points in Garff's much-praised *Søren Kierkegaard: A Biography*, trans. Bruce Kirmmse (Princeton: Princeton University Press, 2005).

10. Kierkegaard's view of the state church is complicated. On the one hand, he clearly does attack the idea of a state church, and his writings had a sizable impact on the growth of free churches in Scandinavia. On the other hand, however, Kierkegaard himself resisted any alliance with representatives of free churches, as can be seen by his repudiation of Andreas Gottlob Rudelbach, an advocate of a free church. For Kierkegaard's relation to Rudelbach, see "Historical Introduction," in *The Corsair Affair and Articles Related to the Writings*, trans. and ed. Howard V. Hong and Edna H. Hong (Princeton: Princeton University Press, 1982), xxxvi–xxxviii.

career," or does he really care about scholarship (JY, 123)? Similar questions are raised about the newspaper editor and the popular politician. Does the former really care about his "task" as a journalist, or does he just want lots of subscribers, presumably for a financial reward (JY, 123)? Does the politician who is "at the head of the masses" really love the people, or does he just love being at the head of the masses (JY, 124)?

These are excellent questions, given the complexity of human motives and the duplicity of the human self. It is often unclear what motivates a person, and it may often be the case that someone performs what appears to be an unselfish act for selfish reasons. Kierkegaard himself says of these questions that "no one knows" the answers, but he seems to assume in a cynical way that he does know the answers: people are never genuinely serving the truth if they get some earthly reward. However, it does not follow from the fact that it is difficult or even impossible to discern human motives in such cases that it is impossible for a human person to be doing what is right if there is any kind of earthly reward for the efforts. In the attack on Christendom, Kierkegaard turns suspicion about human motives into a generally negative view of all natural human goods. He argues that if a pastor receives a salary, this means that the pastor is *not* serving Christ and the church, but only himself. True Christianity would "prevent a merging" between "Christianity and a livelihood, Christianity and a career, Christianity and becoming engaged, etc." (TM, 162).

What seems to have happened in the attack literature is that Kierkegaard has slid from the view that the true Christian must be willing to sacrifice any earthly good if called to do so to the much stronger claim that genuine Christianity simply views all earthly goods as things that are inherently spiritually destructive. Kierkegaard, perhaps without fully realizing it, has developed a negative view of creation, seeing the natural world not as something that must be redeemed and transformed, but as something that must be repudiated. Thus, Kierkegaard's attack on pastors who get salaries (especially salaries from the state) is rooted in a deeper view that the Christian life is simply incompatible with ordinary human life.

This is very different from Kierkegaard's earlier writings, which see Christian faith as transforming and healing human nature. As we have seen, in *The Sickness unto Death*, Kierkegaard sees human persons as inherently spiritual and tries to show how the lack of a healthy relation to God produces defective, damaged selves. Christian spirituality here offers healing for sinful selves, a healing that is a restoration of health to human selves. However, in *The Moment*, Kierkegaard begins to see the "human self" and the "spiritual self" as *alternative* ways of existing that one must choose between. The "Christianity of human beings" and the "Christianity of the spiritual person" are two different versions of Christianity, with only the latter being genuine (TM, 183–84). The Christianity of the spiritual person is one in which a person suffers constantly and is totally isolated and alone (TM, 184). The Christianity of human beings is one in which people get married sometimes and live reasonably happy lives, but Kierkegaard now thinks this is not possible for a true Christian. A truly spiritual person who loved a girl "with the passion of his whole soul" would refuse to marry her but would instead "let the girl go in order to love God" (TM, 184).

This, of course, sounds very much like Kierkegaard's own story in which he broke his engagement with Regine, believing he was called by God to do so. However, regardless of whether he was right or wrong in this matter (and he himself at times doubts whether he was right), it cannot be right to universalize this action. However, in *The Moment*, Kierkegaard consistently pours cold water on the whole institution of marriage, affirming that God "recommends" celibacy, holding that the true Christian would choose singleness, at best marrying only because "it is better to marry than to burn" (TM, 247).[11] Kierkegaard also says that a genuine Christian would have to choose singleness because he would not want to have children, children who almost certainly would be damned (TM, 241). Rather than seek to propagate the race, the true Christian would seek to "terminate" his line and not have any children (TM, 240).

Although in Kierkegaard's day, the subject of sexuality was not often publicly addressed, Kierkegaard does touch on this subject in a discussion of childbearing, and he strongly suggests that sexual desire, even within marriage, is just a form of lust. He says that "*Christianly* it is anything but pleasing to God that one engages in begetting children" (TM, 250). The Christian views sexual relationships, even for procreation, in a completely negative way: "*Christianly* it is the highest degree of egotism that because a man and a woman cannot control their lust another being must therefore sigh in this vale of tears and prison for perhaps seventy years and perhaps be eternally lost" (TM, 251). It has to be admitted that this statement implies a low view not just of sexuality but of human existence itself.[12]

11. Kierkegaard here alludes to Paul's words in 1 Corinthians 1:7–9.
12. It might be worth noting here that Kierkegaard developed a strong attachment to Schopenhauer in the latest period of his life, a philosopher whose pessimistic view of nature and human existence seems completely incompatible with Christianity.

Kierkegaard still affirms that God is a God of love, but now God's love seems to be one that requires something that looks like torture: "The truth is: to become a Christian is to become, humanly speaking, unhappy for this life; the proportion is: the more you involve yourself with God and the more he loves you, the more you will become, humanly speaking, unhappy for this life, the more you will come to suffer in this life" (TM, 212). It is simply not possible to be a Christian and live a happy human life in the normal sense (TM, 213). This is a purely otherworldly form of spirituality, one that can view finite earthly life only as something to be endured and finally to escape.

Kierkegaard's very last journal entry, from September 25, 1855, confirms this starkly anti-humanistic view of Christian spirituality. In this entry, Kierkegaard says that the goal of life is to become weary of life: "the destiny of this life is that it be brought to the extremity of life-weariness" (TM, 610).[13] The only people who can be "accepted into eternity" are those who, "brought to this point of life-weariness are able by the help of grace to maintain that it is out of love that God does it" (TM, 611). God does this because God "wants souls who are able to praise, adore, worship, and thank him, the business of angels" (TM, 611). It therefore is logical that, for a human to be able to share eternity with God, the human must "become an angel" (TM, 611). Our created human nature is not something to be redeemed but to be discarded.

This sad repudiation of our created human nature is accompanied by another distasteful theme: a strong element of misogyny. Kierkegaard combines his attack on marriage and his attack on the clergy with an attack on married clergy. He discusses a fictional couple, Fredrik and Juliane. Fredrik is a theological graduate but is having doubts about whether he ought to become a pastor, because he does not really believe Christian doctrines. Juliane, however, convinces Fredrik to go ahead: "Why do you want to trouble yourself with such thoughts; after all, there are 1,000 other pastors just like you; short and sweet, you are a pastor just like the others" (TM, 163). Kierkegaard then adds to this little story a disturbing conclusion. "Juliane plays a large role in procuring clergy for the state," and genuine Christianity should have been "cautious about bringing in Juliane" (TM, 163). It may be true, Kierkegaard says, that it is in the "tender arms" of a wife that a man can become happy by forgetting "the troubles and vexations of the world" (TM, 163–64). The problem is that those same tender arms make a person forget what Christianity is, and the "blather" found in Christendom is "largely

13. This journal entry is included in the Hong volume of *"The Moment" and Late Writings*, and I here cite it from that book.

connected with the way those tender arms have come to intervene a little too much, so that one ought on behalf of Christianity request that the respective owners of those tender arms withdraw a little" (TM, 164). Kierkegaard is here partly blaming the wives of clergy for the distressing state of Christendom. Kierkegaard's attack on the clergy includes other misogynistic elements as well. The "long robes" that priests wear is "feminine attire," and it is symbolic of a "femininity" that is "characteristic of official Christianity," and this femininity is obviously seen as a bad thing by Kierkegaard. Official Christianity is effeminate because it displays "coquetry," the "feminine trait of being willing and yet reluctant" (TM, 109).

Although Kierkegaard claims to be making his case for the "Christianity of the New Testament," he notably fails to say anything about the Old Testament, which, after all, provided the Scriptures for New Testament Christians. This implies at least a faint resemblance to Marcionism, the heretical form of Christianity that dispensed with the Old Testament. In fact, in several places Kierkegaard hurls at Christendom, as an accusation, the claim that the Christianity of his culture is a form of Judaism (TM, 213). In my view, this ignoring of the Old Testament reflects the eclipse of the doctrine of creation in his thinking.

It is in fact dubious that Kierkegaard is even giving a full and balanced picture of New Testament Christianity. After all, Paul says explicitly that "the Lord has commanded that those who preach the gospel should receive their living from the gospel" (1 Corinthians 9:14). As part of his defense of his "rights" as an apostle, Paul also says explicitly that he could have a believing wife if he chose to "as do the other apostles and the Lord's brothers and Cephas" (1 Corinthians 9:5). It is thus hard to argue from the New Testament that Christian workers should not receive material support or that the early Christian "witnesses to the truth" did not marry.

In one passage, Kierkegaard shockingly implies that even the apostles were already selling out Christianity. That three thousand people became Christians on the day of Pentecost shows that something must have gone wrong, since Jesus himself had gotten only eleven followers in three years: "Either the follower is here greater than the Master, or the truth is that the apostle is a bit too hasty in striking a bargain, a bit too hasty about propagation; thus the dubiousness already begins here" (TM, 181). Here it begins to look like the "New Testament Christianity" that Kierkegaard appeals to is his own creation, something that never existed.

Much more could be said, but I think this provides ample evidence for the view that Kierkegaard's attack on Christendom embodies a decisively different view of Christian faith, and a decisively different view of spirituality, from that found in Kierkegaard's earlier writings, even through such late writings as *For Self-Examination*. It is hard to imagine the Kierkegaard who wrote "The Difference between a Genius and an Apostle" (WA, 91–107) daring to criticize the apostles as he does in the attack. In *Works of Love*, although there is a strong argument that Christian neighbor love is not reducible to such natural forms of love as friendship and marriage, there is also a clear view of these forms of love as goods that can be preserved and transformed when neighbor love becomes their foundation. Special relationships are part of the human condition, things to be treasured and transformed, not extinguished. Even Jesus, Kierkegaard notes, as a genuine human being, needed friends.[14]

A few pages ago I offered a reminder of the humanistic character of *The Sickness unto Death*, where faith is seen as the cure for despair, which involves a deformation of our created human nature. The despairing person lacks finitude or infinitude, temporality or eternity, possibility or necessity. In all these descriptions, it is clear that the finite, temporal, earthly elements of human nature are part of what must be redeemed and healed. Though in his earlier writings, as we have seen, Kierkegaard does frequently affirm the necessity of self-denial and the abolition of selfishness, this is never equated with the abolition of our finite human nature. Rather, he consistently holds to a humanistic vision, in which Christian faith is a fulfillment of human nature, a cure for the deformations of that nature due to sin. In fact, Kierkegaard goes so far as to say that "the religious is eternity's transfigured rendition of the most beautiful dream of politics" (PV, 103), and he affirms explicitly that "the essentially religious is the true humanity" (PV, 104).

My conclusion is that the objectionable themes in the attack literature are not a logical outworking of central elements in Kierkegaard's thought that were there all along. Rather, they are an aberration, in which Kierkegaard turns away from his own form of Christian humanism. Why did he move in this direction? I do not think we will ever know the answer. My own guess is that in his late years, Kierkegaard's thought was distorted by years of loneliness and embitterment. In his younger days, Kierkegaard spent hours walking around Copenhagen and conversing. He himself described this as his therapy, a way of keeping his depression at bay. After the nasty controversy with the *Corsair*, a satirical newspaper that made fun of Kierkegaard's appearance, this simple pleasure was denied him, since he was

14. For a defense of these claims, see my *Kierkegaard's Ethic of Love*, 205–22.

literally jeered when he appeared on the streets. He was increasingly alone and anxious about his future, as his financial assets dwindled away. He really had no close friends or confidants. Furthermore, whatever illness (perhaps spinal tuberculosis) eventually led to his death was very likely already ravaging his body and causing him physical as well as psychological pain. All in all, I believe that Kierkegaard's writings from 1854–55, as well as the late journal entries, still come from a man of genius, but one who is no longer truly himself. I find it very sad that on his deathbed, Kierkegaard refused to allow his older brother, Peder Christian, to visit him. The two had never gotten along well, and Peder had wounded Søren deeply by something he had written. Still, Søren's act was an act of cruelty, not love. I do not think that this was the act of a man who had written so beautifully about loving the neighbor in *Works of Love*.

Some have tried to defend Kierkegaard's attack as a necessary "corrective" to the worldliness and "cheap grace" of contemporary Danish Christianity. It is true that Kierkegaard did think in these terms about the attack, and I agree that he realized that he was exaggerating to make sure people took notice of his protest. However, I believe that the anti-humanist elements I have described, rather than providing a useful corrective, actually provide the established form of Christianity with an excuse to ignore Kierkegaard's important work. Kierkegaard is quite right to insist that a gospel of grace is not a gospel that implies that works are unimportant, and he is quite right to remind us that a commitment to Christ means a willingness to sacrifice any earthly goods, to be willing to endure suffering and persecution when necessary. Linking these points to a repudiation of the goodness of God's creation tends to discredit them. I conclude that the attack literature, rather than being the culmination of Kierkegaard's authorship, should be viewed as an unfortunate aberration. It describes a form of spirituality that is really incompatible with the spirituality found in Kierkegaard's authorship up to that point.

Perhaps Kierkegaard himself was at least partly aware of this. In the middle of the firestorm, he chose to publish another Christian discourse that focuses on his favorite passage from James 1:17–21. This text, which was the first that Kierkegaard wrote on and which he returned to repeatedly, deals with "the unchangeableness of God." This discourse, dedicated to Kierkegaard's father, is one that Kierkegaard had actually delivered in the Citadel Church in Copenhagen in 1851. It is markedly different in tone and content from the attack literature and would have fit nicely into the earlier *Christian Discourses*. Perhaps Kierkegaard's decision to publish it was a signal that the attack literature was a departure from his authorship as a whole, and thus a clue that the attack writings should not be viewed as "the definitive Kierkegaard." I am also comforted by the fact that on his deathbed, Kierkegaard was willing to see his old friend, Emil Boesen, a pastor in the very state church that Kierkegaard was so bitterly attacking. In his conversations with Boesen, which Boesen recorded for posterity, Boesen asked Kierkegaard whether the hope for life after death Kierkegaard had expressed was "because you believe in Christ and take refuge in him in God's name." Kierkegaard's answer was "yes, of course, what else."[15] Even though Kierkegaard felt it necessary as a kind of "deed" to attack the state church, in the end he still affirmed his own faith in Christ.

15. For Boesen's account of his conversations with Kierkegaard, see Bruce Kirmmse, ed., *Encounters with Kierkegaard: A Life as Seen by His Contemporaries* (Princeton: Princeton University Press, 1996). This part of the conversation is on p. 125.

# CHAPTER 9

# Conclusions: Spirituality as Accountability

We have seen that Kierkegaard conceives of humans as inherently spiritual beings. Our spirituality is understood in terms of the freedom we have been given to define ourselves. That process of defining ourselves is always carried out in relation to some ideal that is outside the self. Every human self is a "relation that relates itself to itself by relating to another."

The character of an individual's spirituality is a function of both a "how" and a "what." The "how" refers to the quality or intensity of the relation to the ideal. The "what" is the ideal itself as understood by the self. Those who define themselves by such finite goods as money and fame do not achieve genuine spirituality because such ideals, even if passionately pursued, cannot be the foundation of genuine selfhood. Those who define themselves by some abstraction such as race, or nation, or social class, do no better. All such people define themselves comparatively. The racist thinks he has value because of his skin color or ethnicity; he is not like those "others" whom he sees as inferior. The nationalist thinks in a similar way about his nation and looks down on those from other nations. He thinks, "I am a genuine self because I am superior to others by virtue of being an American (or a Russian, or a German, or anything else)." This kind of person really fails to achieve genuine selfhood, and this spirituality is a kind of counterfeit of the real thing. Kierkegaard thinks of this kind of spirituality as pagan, whether in classical paganism or in Christendom, because the "gods" the person lives for are finite.

Genuine spirituality always involves a relation to an ideal that is truly divine; it is rooted in a reality that Kierkegaard describes as infinite or eternal or absolute, and thus requires no relative comparisons to other humans.

Rather, the higher ideal has an ethical character; the self understands that what is ultimately important is not whether one is rich or poor, white or black, male or female, but whether one strives for moral ideals such as honesty, justice, and compassion. On Kierkegaard's view, the call to live in this way is a call from God, though the call can be recognized without realizing that God is the source of the call, though recognizing the call as coming from God provides a clearer and more penetrating understanding of the task. In this book, I have termed this kind of spirituality (both the kind that involves belief in God and the kind that does not) Socratic spirituality because for Kierkegaard Socrates provides the ideal exemplar of it.

It is because one can have an encounter with God without realizing that it is an encounter with God that Socratic spirituality can be found in two forms. The first is the spirituality of the person who is spiritual but not religious. This kind of person recognizes the ideal and is drawn to it as something higher but conceives of the ideal as an abstraction. Such a person lives for what is "higher" but does not understand this higher ideal as a personal reality. This person lives in relation to God but does not consciously live "before God."

As I argued in chapter 3, all genuine human spirituality conceives of the self as a task. For Kierkegaard, it is the task that gives human life meaning. My life derives meaning from the fact that there is something I was meant to do, a unique purpose for me. When someone understands God to be the origin of the task, then the nature of the task changes. The meaning of the task deepens. The task a person has is now understood as a *gift*, and the person can recognize the debt of gratitude owed to God as the giver. This debt means that the task is now one that a person is *accountable* to fulfill. God has given me the task that defines my identity, and God holds me accountable for how I use this gift.

It is difficult today to think of accountability as a gift. In contemporary society, to hold someone accountable often just means to punish the person. We do not like to be evaluated by others, and most of us would prefer not to undergo annual reviews or have our performance at work rated. We embrace accountability only for others, particularly for others who have wronged us or wronged someone else.

However, there are good reasons to think more positively about accountability. When we work hard and achieve something noteworthy or remarkable, what we want most of all is for someone to recognize what we have done. It is demoralizing to discover that *no one cares* about us or our lives. We are particularly eager for the approval of those we love and admire.

Much of our aversion to accountability is surely explained by the fact that the human people we are accountable to are often *not* people we love and admire. We lack confidence that the people we must report to really care about us or our good. When that is the case, accountability becomes a burden. However, when we are accountable to someone who is wise and good and cares about our good, things are different. If we are wise, we will realize that we become better if we are accountable in this way, and we will welcome being held accountable.

Keeping these positives in mind allows us to understand why Kierkegaard thinks that living before God, as people who are accountable to God, is a gift. We can also understand why receiving and using the gift well constitute a virtue. On Kierkegaard's view, God is completely good: sheer love and unchangeably so. Even what we might call God's punishments are not motivated by any desire for retribution. God's "chastisements" are solely directed toward our good.

Since God loves us and wants only our good, to be accountable to God gives depth and meaning to our lives and does not threaten our autonomy. God himself has given us freedom, and thus God does not wish to take away our freedom. Rather, the relationship to God enhances the value of our freedom. Our choices matter, not only to us and to those humans who care about us, but to God, who is eternal. The task we have been given is one that means something. The stakes are very high, since the one whose approval we seek loves us, is completely good, and is eternal. The person who understands this and welcomes being accountable to God possesses an excellence, a virtue that I call accountability. The virtue must, of course, be distinguished from the state or condition of being held accountable. Accountability is not a virtue that one can exercise only in relation to God. Those who have this virtue in relation to God will also see that it is virtuous, when certain conditions are met, to welcome accountability to other humans as well.

I believe that Kierkegaard is here recovering an understanding of a biblical virtue that our culture has almost lost sight of: what the ancient Hebrews called "the fear of the Lord." In the Old Testament, the "fear of the Lord" is said to be "the beginning" or foundation of wisdom. Since wisdom is almost always seen as a fundamental virtue, if the fear of the Lord is the foundation of wisdom, it follows that this trait will also be an important virtue.

It is hard for us to understand what is meant by "the fear of the Lord." We think of fear as a negative emotion, something to be avoided. However, I do not think the biblical concept should be understood as actually being afraid of God. Why should one be afraid of a God who is completely good and loving? Rather, I think that "fear" here means something like a "holy reverence," in which one recognizes one's accountability to God but is grateful for this as a gift. We can see this by looking at the way the ancient Israelites viewed God's law. God's law was not seen as an imposition on freedom, but as a gracious gift that makes human life meaningful and contributes to human flourishing. Understanding one's life as lived before God is indeed a virtue, an excellence that makes many other excellences possible.

The person who has Socratic spirituality and thus lives before God gains this awareness of God through what Kierkegaard calls "immanence," whether that person thinks of the divine as a set of abstract principles or a personal God. His or her understanding of the task and of God is gained through conscience and ordinary human reflection. This kind of spirituality grasps the problems of guilt and suffering but has no real answer to those problems. Everything changes when the God to whom one is accountable becomes incarnate in history and gives his own life as an atonement for sin.

The task of becoming a self is transformed when a person encounters God as the incarnate Christ. Living before a God known through immanence is changed to living before a historical person, someone who makes clear demands on those who would be his followers. The task of human selfhood is itself given new meaning and value by the fact that God became a human self. The debt of gratitude is immensely greater, for Christ provides both an exemplar of how the task can be carried out and, through his atonement, grace and forgiveness to make it possible for humans who are willing to be accountable to Christ to make progress toward fulfilling the task.

Kierkegaard insists that the person who has received this grace and recognizes this debt will want to be a follower of Jesus, an imitator. Such a person will want to serve others, to extend love to those who are marginal, to seek to offer healing and forgiveness to others, just as Jesus did. The motivation for this is that the person has received healing and forgiveness from God. The task of selfhood the person has been given must now be understood as the person's calling to reflect Christ in the unique ways that individual can. As Kierkegaard affirms, the person who fully embraces this calling must be willing to sacrifice any and all finite goods for the sake of the kingdom of God that Christ brings. What this means for a particular individual must be determined by that individual, who must seek to discern his or her calling with God's help, though Kierkegaard clearly thinks that one means of communicating this will be through Scripture, when it is read as a "love letter" from God, and not simply viewed as an object for scholarly study.

I have tried to show that Kierkegaard's view of spirituality sees spirituality as something that is always grounded in what is "higher" than the self. That higher reality is in fact God, although it is possible for someone to encounter God's ideal for him or her without understanding the ideal as God's call to him or her. The spirituality that does recognize that God is the intended ground of the self offers a clearer and deeper self-understanding. The truth is that humans were created by God to have a relation to God. We are accountable to God, and genuine spirituality is thus tied to accountability.

Kierkegaard's relational understanding of spirituality contrasts sharply with the kind of individualist view of spirituality that has become popular in our culture. It is common to view spirituality as a kind of individual choice, something that the individual creates and develops on his or her own. There are many forms of such spirituality on offer, and indeed, on this view, spirituality becomes something like a consumer choice. On Kierkegaard's view, our spiritual character is something offered to us as a gift, not something to be created. It is true that spirituality is something that must be freely actualized by the individual, but it is not invented by the individual.

There are plenty of reasons to think that Kierkegaardian spirituality, which holds that the highest forms of spirituality require being accountable to God, will be unpopular. After all, Christian theology affirms the universality of sin among humans, a doctrine that Kierkegaard vigorously supports. From a biblical view, sin always has the character of a kind of rebellion against God. Even in the story of the garden of Eden, the serpent's temptation was to promise Adam and Eve that they would no longer be accountable to God but would themselves "be like God." There is plenty of experiential support for the view that humans still would like to achieve this status and that they find the idea that they must be accountable to God offensive. It is an affront to their "autonomy."

What kind of autonomy is really valuable, though? Kierkegaard believes that humans have a kind of relative autonomy, a freedom given them by God to choose whether and how to become the kind of selves God intends. When humans seek absolute autonomy, what they are really doing is using their spirituality, the freedom that God has granted them to participate in their self-actualization, to rebel against God. This kind of freedom may seem appealing, but ultimately it has no value. Relative autonomy has value because it exists within a context of values that are objective and make a claim on me. Absolute autonomy is a choice of what is to count as good and evil, but such choices in the end are arbitrary. I cannot appeal to what is good to justify my choice if I am the one who decides what is good.

As we have already seen in chapter 2, Kierkegaard sees this kind of autonomy as a form of despair:

The self is its own master, absolutely its own master, so-called; and precisely this is the despair, but what it regards as its pleasure and delight. On closer examination, however, it is easy to see that this absolute ruler is a king without a country, actually ruling over nothing; his position, his sovereignty, is subordinate to the dialectic that rebellion is legitimate at any moment. Ultimately, this is arbitrarily based upon the self itself. (SUD, 69)

Jean-Paul Sartre's account of selfhood is eerily similar to this, and Sartre himself describes the human project as the attempt to become God.[1] Kierkegaard believes that the moral confusion and demoralization of contemporary culture is the result of this kind of rebellion. The cure is freely to accept one's position as someone who exists before God, is accountable to God.

I have a recollection that somewhere Sartre says that God's existence would be intolerable, because if God existed, his gaze would be inescapable.[2] There would be no place to hide. Sartre's comment shows how important it is for us to have the right concept of God, if we believe we are accountable to God. I believe that one of the conditions for accountability to exhibit itself as a virtue is that the one to whom a person is accountable must be good and must care about the good of the one who is accountable. A God who is infinitely good obviously meets this condition. However, if someone has the wrong view of God, this may appear not to be the case. Popular versions of Christianity, and even some theologies, sometimes see God as someone who resembles Santa Claus, keeping a list of who is naughty and nice and adjusting his favor and love in light of the list. If we think that God's forgiveness and love are in some way conditional on human effort, then Sartre's view would not be completely wrongheaded.

---

1. Jean-Paul Sartre, *Being and Nothingness*, trans. Hazel E. Barnes (New York: Washington Square, 1992), 724.

2. I cannot find the passage any more. However, the claim follows logically from Sartre's thought. In *Being and Nothingness*, he argues that we are objectified by the "gaze of the other," using the gripping example of a man who is peering into a hotel room through a keyhole, who is suddenly "caught" by someone who comes around the corner (see pp. 347–49). However, God's gaze would be inescapable; all of us would be "caught" all the time. In fact, Sartre says that thinking of God's gaze on us gives us a kind of shame he calls "shame before God," since this gaze constitutes a "reification of my object-ness" and causes me to exist in an alienated form (p. 385).

However, I believe the biblical God's love is unconditional. As Paul says in 2 Corinthians 1:18, God's promises to us in Christ Jesus are not "yes and no" but always "yes." The gaze of a God whose grace and love are unconditional is a gaze that can be welcomed and not just endured. In *Works of Love*, Kierkegaard describes the gaze of a loving person who has "overcome" another person who has wronged the loving one, winning the wrongdoer for the good, and also seeking reconciliation: "Would that I could describe how the one who loves looks at the one overcome, how joy beams from his eyes, how this loving look rests so gently on him, how it seeks, alluring and inviting, to win him" (WL, 342). Kierkegaard is describing a loving human person here, but his description surely is an apt image of the way God looks at sinners. Perhaps if Sartre had been able to picture God's gaze in this way, he would not have found it unendurable.

Some might object to the idea that God's love is unconditional on the grounds that this amounts to condoning evil, failing to take sin seriously. Surely, the objector might say, a God who is just cannot accept and approve of those who do evil. Can God offer forgiveness and acceptance to those who are unrepentant?

I believe this objection stems from a misunderstanding of the nature of love. Genuine love includes a desire for the good of the beloved, but it is not in fact good for a person to do or to love evil. To the contrary, an alliance with evil destroys the unity of the self and blocks the self from its intended destiny as part of a loving community united to God. The objection thus fails to recognize that God's unconditional love is not a sentimental wish for a person to achieve whatever the person desires, even when that desire is for what will destroy the self. God's love is ultimately not opposed to God's justice, because genuine love cares about and values justice. If I see a friend who is acting unjustly to others, it is not loving of me to ignore my friend's actions. If I love the friend, I will hold my friend accountable. God's love is also a love that, out of desire for our good, holds us accountable.

God's love is a tough love that wishes the best for everyone, and that means God will unilaterally do what God can do to make the good of a loving relationship to God possible. Christ loved us "while we were still sinners" (Romans 5:8). What God cannot do is force such a relationship, because such force would amount to the destruction of the person as a person, making a loving relationship impossible. Love cannot be coerced. God can and does offer love and forgiveness unconditionally, but God cannot achieve a reconciliation with those who refuse God's love. However, it is precisely God's unconditional love and offer of forgiveness that may crack open the hardened self and make possible a transformation that leads to reconciliation.

As a contrast to Sartre's view of God's unendurable gaze, consider the parable of the prodigal son in Luke 15:14–31. In the story, a man has two sons, and the younger one demands his share of the inheritance early, then goes away and wastes it all. Destitute and in misery, the son finally decides to return to his father's house, asking only to work as a servant. However, when the son "was still a long way off, his father *saw* him." The father must have been looking, still longing for his son, always ready to welcome the prodigal home. We can imagine the father's gaze, as he, "filled with compassion" for his son, "ran to him, threw his arms around him and kissed him." If God is like this father, then his love is unconditional, and he is always willing to forgive and welcome us to our spiritual home.[3]

For Kierkegaard, Christian faith allows us to cease our futile quest to hide from ourselves and from God. The definition of faith offered in *The Sickness unto Death* is concise but profound: "Faith is: that the self in being itself and in willing to be itself rests transparently before God" (SUD, 82). When God is known through Christ, the self, however broken and sinful it may be, can will to be itself. It can accept itself because the self is accepted by God and, out of gratitude, can take on the task of becoming the self God finally wills it to be. No matter how strenuous such a life may be, the person who is spiritual in this sense can be at rest, with no need to hide or evade God's loving gaze. The prodigal can find rest and be at home.

---

3. Our imagination here can be aided by great art and literature. I recommend Henri J. M. Nouwen, *The Return of the Prodigal Son: A Story of Homecoming* (New York: Image/Doubleday, 1994). In this book, Nouwen looks at the story from the point of view of all the characters through an extended meditation on Rembrandt's great painting of the return of the prodigal.

# Index

Abraham and the sacrifice of Isaac, 67
Abramson, Lyn Y., 33n11
accountability, viii, 16, 17, 26, 38, 52, 61, 78,
    110, 113, 124, 165, 168, 176. *See also*
    freedom
  as absolute, 69–80, 110, 184
  and autonomy, 38, 200–203
  and Christ, 124, 184, 199
  and freedom, 54–56, 196–203
  as a gift, 56, 127, 196–203
  as grounded in gratitude, 113
  and individuality, 53, 168
  and the knowledge of God, 52, 78
  and living before God, 109–11, 176
  as a task, 16
  as a virtue, viii, 26, 198–203
Acts of the Apostles, 9, 123, 124, 173, 176,
    182
Adam and Eve, 54, 200
Adams, Robert M., 72n6, 102–3n12
Agamemnon, 67–68
Alston, William, 58n13
*Amadeus* (film), 106–7
Anti-Climacus (pseudonym), xi, xii, 5,
    6n6, 10, 18, 113n2, 141–59, 169
anti-Semitism, 138n23
Aquinas, Thomas, 24n7
Aristotle, 105
Armstrong, D. M., 58n13
atheism, 3, 48–49, 61–62
  and motivated reasoning, 51–56
"attack on Christendom," viii, 8n8, 96n8,
    162, 169
  as a "corrective," 144–45, 194
  and the "disappearance of Christianity,"
    186–88
  as embodying a strenuous doctrine of
    salvation, 142–45, 186–95

  as espousing a duty to seek out perse-
    cution, 155–58
  as hostile to human nature, 143–44, 153,
    179, 186–95
  as inconsistent with Kierkegaard's
    earlier vision, 116, 124, 140, 193–94
  and misogyny, 191–92
Augustine of Hippo, 72

Barnes, Hazel E., 11n12, 37n12, 201n1
Barnett, Christopher, 2–3, 14–15n16
Barth, Karl, 1
Bauckham, Richard, 96n8
Boesen, Emil, 145n3, 195
Bookbinder, Hilarius (pseudonym), 51
Buddhism, 75–76
Bukdahl, Jørgen, 93n6
Bultmann, Rudolf, 1
Butler, Bishop Joseph, 183

Calvin, John, and Calvinism, 44–45, 138
Camus, Albert, 1, 44, 49
Christendom. *See also* "attack on
    Christendom"
  and Christ as "Pattern," 135
  as conformist, 62, 75
  critique of, 115
  and enculturation as insufficient for
    spirituality, 129–30
  as foreshadowing the "attack literature,"
    141–42
  and the importance of "subjectivity,"
    170–71
  as impossible, 124, 159–60
  as lacking in guilt-consciousness, 86
  as lukewarm, 85
  and the need of works as an expression
    of faith, 112–13, 163–64

as transcendent, 106–7
and unconditional meaning, 28, 93–97, 132
and works, 112–15, 163–64
faithfulness of God, 138–39
fear of the Lord. *See* reverence/fear of the Lord
feminist critiques of Kierkegaard, 32–34
Feuerbach, Ludwig, 61
forgiveness
and the burden of guilt, 117
Kierkegaard's view of, during the "attack period," 143
and our debt of gratitude, 112–14, 199
and "sacred history," 146–47
and the seriousness of guilt, 101–2
as the solution to the problem of despair, 39
as unmerited, 143, 201–3
freedom. *See also* Sartre, Jean-Paul: and the self as godlike
as existing preeminently in God, 8–9, 12
formal vs. normative dimensions of, 9, 14
as a gift, 8–10, 198
as grounding the possibility of sin and despair, 2, 14, 20–21, 36–39, 43, 200
as limited in humans, 12
as perfected through accountability to God, 54–55, 198–99, 201
as a precondition of "spirit," 8–9, 14, 153, 196
from vice, 75, 127, 128–29
Freud, Sigmund, 29, 52, 174

Garff, Joakim, 144n2, 188n9
Genesis, book of, 37
German Idealism, 4
God, natural knowledge of. *See also* Paul, apostle
and atheism, 48–49, 51–52, 56–58
conscience and, 52–56, 66–68
*de dicto* and *de re*, 46–47, 68
faithfulness of, 138–39
and natural theology, 50–51
as not requiring argument, 49–50, 52, 56–58
as a precursor to Christian faith, 60–62, 63–66

and subjectivity, 45–47, 59–60
Goldman, Alvin, 58n13

happiness
as compatible with spirituality, 110, 179
the debt of gratitude for, 53
as elusive, 7
of eternity, 43–44, 69, 70–73, 82–83, 86–87, 117, 121, 122
as a false measure or spiritual development, 34
of fortune, 76, 109
impugned by Kierkegaard during the "attack period," 156, 190–91
and moral goodness, 54, 70–73
and the need for sacrifice, 178
as willed by God, 53, 110
Hare, John, 84n14
Harris, Sam, 51
Haufniensis, Vigilius (pseudonym), xi, 20
Hegel, G. W. F., 4
as a foil for Kierkegaard, 68, 93–94, 149–50, 176
influence on Kierkegaard, 5–6
*Phenomenology of Spirit*, 4
and the primacy of social duties, 15, 67, 149–50
and reality as dialectical, 5
and reality as "subject-like," 4
and spirit as the character of reality, 4
and spirit as socially embedded, 135n22
Heidegger, Martin 1
H. H. (pseudonym), 156n9
Hinduism, 91
Holy Spirit 4, 5, 135–36
and "becoming sober," 182–86
and death to selfishness, 177–79
the gifts of the, 180–82
as life-giving, 176–77
Hong, Howard V., and Edna H. Hong, ix, xi, xii, xiii, 18n2, 23, 36, 46n3, 63n1, 76n8, 83n13, 92nn4–5, 101, 102, 103n14, 104n15, 113n1, 125n14, 130, 133n18, 134n19, 141, 145n4, 187n8, 188n10, 191n13
Hume, David, 57, 105, 120
Hyde, Janet S., 33n11

idols/idolatry, 14, 43, 45–47, 65, 149
Islam, 47

James, Epistle of, 96–97, 104, 113, 163–64, 172, 194
James, William, 11, 115
Jesus of Nazareth/Jesus Christ. *See also* accountability: and Christ; faith; forgiveness; "Religiousness B"/ Christian spirituality; sin
the atonement of, 81, 101, 121–24, 135–40, 199–203
Kant's view of, 86–87
and the "leap of faith," 41
the life of, as a special revelation, 50, 62, 64, 93, 96, 102, 111, 112–16, 124, 125–30, 146–56, 161, 184
as a perfect exemplar of humanity, 19, 199
as Redeemer and "Pattern," 113–14, 129, 134–40, 143–45, 182, 185
as the second person of the Trinity, 47
as a teacher, viii–ix, 92, 98, 118, 123–24, 173–75, 185, 199–203
Johannes the Seducer (character), 51
John, Gospel of, 114–15, 137–39, 152, 155, 173
Judaism, 40, 138, 192
Judge William (character), 51

Kant, Immanuel, 84n14
and the derivation of the content of morality from its form, 102
and the hope that the guilt of "radical evil" can be resolved, 87–88
and morality as known through *a priori* reason, 55–56
and "ought implies can," 127
and the problem of morality and happiness, 70–71
as undermining the rational case for God, 57
Kierkegaard, Peder Christian (brother), 162, 194
Kierkegaard, Søren, works
*Christian Discourses* (CD), xi, 125–40
*The Concept of Anxiety* (CA), xi, 20, 125n14
*Concluding Unscientific Postscript* (CUP 1 and 2), xi, 6–7, 41n15, 43–46, 52–53, 62, 66, 68–70, 72, 75–89, 123
*Discourses at the Communion on Fridays* (DCF), xi, 2, 134–35, 140

*Eighteen Upbuilding Discourses* (EUD), xii, 90, 92–101, 109n20
*Either/Or* (EO 1 and 2), xi–xii, 51, 135
*Fear and Trembling* (FT), xii, 67–68
*For Self-Examination* (FSE), v, xii, 116, 134, 141–42, 145, 162–95
*Judge for Yourself!* (JY), xii, 182–89
*"The Moment" and Late Writings* (TM), xi–xii, 8n, 186–87, 189, 190–92
Newspaper Articles (NA), 187
*Philosophical Fragments* (PF), xii, 20, 48–49, 52, 60n15, 63–64, 94, 147–48
*The Point of View* (PV), xii, 44, 79, 193
*Practice in Christianity* (PC), xi, xii, 19, 113, 116, 135–37, 141–61, 169
*The Sickness unto Death* (SUD), xi, 5–6, 8, 10–16, 18–42, 52–55, 80, 110, 141–42, 158, 189, 193, 201, 203
*Two Ages* (TA), xi, 56
*Upbuilding Discourses in Various Spirits* (UDVS), xiii, 53, 68, 71–72, 90, 101–10, 113, 115–17, 122–23, 125, 130
*Works of Love* (WL), xiii, 53–55, 103, 116, 131–34, 160, 181, 187, 193–94, 202
King, Martin Luther, Jr., 160–61

Leon, Celine, 32n10
Lessing, Gotthold Ephraim, 41n15
Lewis, C. S., 59n14, 61–62, 181–82n6
Linden, Wolfgang, 33n11
Lippitt, John, 131n17, 181n4
Locke, John, 57
Lowrie, Walter, 113n1, 125n14, 187n8
Luke, Gospel of
and the "communion discourses," 136–40
and the difficulty of attaining the kingdom of God for a wealthy person, 77n10
and the offense of loftiness, 150
and the parable of the prodigal son, 203
and sacrifice, 178–79
and suffering as a teacher of obedience, 118–19
Luther, Martin, and Lutheranism, 2, 112–14, 138, 163–64

MacIntyre, Alasdair, 38
Martens, Paul, 48n4, 96n8
Martensen, Hans Lassen, 187

INDEX